Writing the History of the Global

Writing the History of the Global

Challenges for the 21st Century

Edited by
Maxine Berg

Published for THE BRITISH ACADEMY
by OXFORD UNIVERSITY PRESS

UNIVERSITY PRESS

Great Clarendon Street, Oxford OX2 6DP
United Kingdom

Oxford University Press is a department of the University of Oxford.
It furthers the University's objective of excellence in research, scholarship,
and education by publishing worldwide. Oxford is a registered trade mark of
Oxford University Press in the UK and in certain other countries

© The British Academy 2013

The moral rights of the authors have been asserted

Database right The British Academy (maker)

First published 2013
Reprinted 2015

All rights reserved. No part of this publication may be reproduced,
stored in a retrieval system, or transmitted, in any form or by any means,
without the prior permission in writing of Oxford University Press,
or as expressly permitted by law, or under terms agreed with the appropriate
reprographics rights organization. Enquiries concerning reproduction
outside the scope of the above should be sent to the Publications Department,
The British Academy, 10 Carlton House Terrace, London SW1Y 5AH

You must not circulate this book in any other form
and you must impose this same condition on any acquirer

British Library Cataloguing in Publication Data
Data available

Library of Congress Cataloging in Publication Data
Data available

ISBN 978-0-19-726532-1

Contents

List of figures and tables		vii
Preface		ix
Notes on contributors		xi
1	Global history: approaches and new directions MAXINE BERG	1

Part I Interpretations: Ideas and the Making of Global History — 19

2	Problems in global history DAVID WASHBROOK	21
3	Reflections on doing global history JAN DE VRIES	32
4	Notes on some discontents in the historical narrative JEAN-FRÉDÉRIC SCHAUB	48

Part II Approaches: Methods and Methodologies in Global History — 67

5	Comparison in global history PRASANNAN PARTHASARATHI	69
6	Regions and global history R. BIN WONG	83
7	Institutions for writing the economic history of the global JAN LUITEN VAN ZANDEN	106

Contents

Part III Shaping Global History   115

  8 Writing about divergences in global history: some
     implications for scale, methods, aims, and categories   117
     KENNETH POMERANZ

  9 The European miracle in global history: an East Asian
     perspective   129
     KAORU SUGIHARA

Part IV Knowledge and Global History   145

 10 Technology and innovation in global history and in the
     history of the global   147
     DAGMAR SCHÄFER

 11 The art of global comparisons   165
     CRAIG CLUNAS

 12 Global objects: contention and entanglement   177
     GLENN ADAMSON AND GIORGIO RIELLO

Part V Round Table   195

 13 Panel discussion: ways forward and major challenges   197

     Globe and empire   197
     JOHN DARWIN

     Africa and global history   200
     MEGAN VAUGHAN

     Writing the history of the global and the state   201
     PEER VRIES

     Identity in global history: a reflection   205
     SUFUMI SO AND BILLY KEE-LONG SO

     Index   209

Figures and tables

Figures

12.1	Japanese armour gifted by the Emperor of Japan to King James I of England and Scotland in 1613. (Royal Collection Trust / © HM Queen Elizabeth II 2012. Photograph: The Royal Armouries)	180
12.2	Bombay (Mumbai), early twentieth century. (By permission of the author)	184
12.3	St Pancras Station, London c.1900. (By permission of the author)	185
12.4	The Municipal Building by Stevens, Bombay (Mumbai), 2005. (By permission of the author)	187
12.5	Puma's 'Peace One Day' ball, designed by the Japanese consultancy Nendo, 2008. (© Nendo)	190

Table

12.1	Global objects: a matrix	193

Preface

Writing the History of the Global: Challenges for the 21st Century arises out of a conference of the same title held at the British Academy on 21–22 May 2009. The conference was led by the Global History and Culture Centre at the University of Warwick, and funded by the British Academy and the University of Warwick. It provided an opportunity for major historians of European, South Asian, East Asian, African, and Latin American history, as well as those from museums and subfields such as art history, economic history, and the history of science, to come together and discuss what a 'global' approach meant to their history writing. This broad historical perspective contributes now to wider public agendas in international policy and to major new themes in the arts and culture. The conference addressed the framing of key debates on 'divergence', and engaged with wider perspectives on 'comparison' and 'connectedness'. Global approaches to history raise aspirations of broadening our engagement with other historians; but there are major challenges of method, language, and expertise. The conference allowed a wide discussion of new ways of positioning our questions, and of ways of collaborating.

All those contributing chapters to this volume took part in the conference. Others who presented papers at the conference or took part in discussion panels included Sir Christopher Bayly, Tim Brook, Linda Colley, Diogo Ramada Curto, Jack Goldstone, J. D. Hill, Sevket Pamuk, Kapil Raj, Lissa Roberts, Simon Schaffer, and Sanjay Subrahmanyam. Panel chairs and discussants were David Arnold, William Gervase Clarence Smith, Anne Gerritsen, Luca Molà, Patrick O'Brien, and Nigel Thrift. We were delighted to have among the participants in general discussion Professor Sir John Elliott, Professor Eric Hobsbawm, Professor Li Bozhong, and Professor Felipe Fernandez Armesto.

A full recording of the conference is available on the Global History and Culture website, University of Warwick, as well as a series of interviews, 'Global Conversations' with a number of the historians who took part in the conference: this is available at <http://www2.warwick.ac.uk/fac/arts/history/ghcc/resources/>.

Preface

A conference of this type and the follow-up preparation for the book rely on collaboration and committed assistance. I am especially grateful to my colleagues Giorgio Riello and Anne Gerritsen at Warwick for helping me to shape the conference. Angela Pusey at the British Academy and Amy Evans and Anna Boneham at Warwick provided the crucial administrative assistance in launching both the conference and the book, and the European Research Council helped to fund the time given to editing the volume.

Notes on Contributors

Glenn Adamson is Head of Research, Victoria and Albert Museum. He is co-editor of the triannual *Journal of Modern Craft*, and the author of *Thinking Through Craft* (2007) and *The Craft Reader* (2010). His other publications include *Industrial Strength Design: How Brooks Stevens Shaped Your World* (2003), and *Gord Peteran: Furniture Meets Its Maker* (2006).

Maxine Berg is Professor of History and founding Director of the Global History and Culture Centre at the University of Warwick. A Fellow of the British Academy, she is now an ERC Advanced Research Fellow with her project 'Europe's Asian Centuries: Trading Eurasia 1600–1830'. Her publications include *Luxury and Pleasure in Eighteenth-Century Britain* (2005); and 'In Pursuit of Luxury: Global History and British Consumer Goods in the Eighteenth Century', *Past and Present*, 182 (2004).

Craig Clunas is Professor of History of Art, Oxford University and Fellow of the British Academy. His publications include *Empire of Great Brightness: Visual and Material Cultures of Ming China, 1368–1644* (2007); *Elegant Debts: The Social Art of Wen Zhengming (1470–1559)* (2004); *Superfluous Things: Material Culture and Social Status in Early Modern China* (1991); and 'Modernity Global and Local: Consumption and the Rise of the West', *American Historical Review*, 105 (1999).

John Darwin is Beit University Lecturer in the History of the British Commonwealth, University of Oxford, Fellow of Nuffield College and a Fellow of the British Academy. His publications include *After Tamerlane: The Global History of Empire* (2007) (Winner of the Wolfson Prize in History for 2008) and *The Empire Project: The Rise and Fall of the British World System 1830–1970* (2009) (Winner of the Trevor Reese Prize in Imperial and Commonwealth History 2010).

Prasannan Parthasarathi is Professor of History, Boston College. His publications include *Why Europe Grew Rich and Asia Did Not: Global Economic Divergence, 1600–1850* (2011); *The Transition to a Colonial Economy: Weavers,*

Merchants and Kings in South India, 1720–1800 (2001); and 'Rethinking Wages and Competitiveness in the Eighteenth Century: Britain and South India', *Past and Present*, 158 (1998).

Kenneth Pomeranz is Professor of History, University of Chicago, formerly Distinguished Professor of History, University of California, Irvine. He is the current President of the American Historical Association. His publications include *The Great Divergence: China, Europe, and the Making of the Modern World Economy* (2000); (with Steve Topik), *The World that Trade Created: Society, Culture and the World Economy, 1400 to the Present* (1999); and 'Beyond the East–West Binary: Resituating Development Paths in the Eighteenth-Century World', *Journal of Asian Studies*, 62 (2002). He is currently writing a book entitled *Why is China so Big*.

Giorgio Riello is Professor of History, University of Warwick, and Philip Leverhulme Fellow. His publications include *Global Cotton: How an Asian Fibre Changed the European Economy* (forthcoming 2012); (with Glenn Adamson and Sarah Teasley), *Global Design History* (2011); (edited with Prasannan Parthasarathi), *The Spinning World: A Global History of Cotton Textiles, 1200–1850* (2009); and (edited with Tirthankar Roy), *How India Clothed the World: The World of South Asian Textiles, 1500–1850* (2009).

Dagmar Schäfer is Professor for Chinese Studies, Manchester University. Her publications include *The Crafting of the 10,000 Things* (2011) and (with Dieter Kuhn), *Weaving an Economic Pattern in Ming Times (1368–1644)* (2002).

Jean-Frédéric Schaub is Professor of History, École des hautes études en sciences sociales, University of Paris. His publications include *L'Europe a-t-elle une histoire?* (2008); *Le Portugal au temps du comte-duc d'Olivares (1621–1640): Le conflit de juridiction comme exercice de la politique* (2001); (with Robert Gildea), 'Has History again Become a Branch of Literature?', in *Writing Contemporary History*, ed. Robert Gildea, Anne Simonin, and Stefan Berger (2008); and 'La Catégorie "études coloniales" est-elle indispensable?' *Annales HSS*, 3 (2008).

Sufumi So is Director of Japanese Language Teaching, Japanese Studies, George Mason University, Virginia. Her publications include *Process and Product: Singaporeans Write in Japanese* (1990).

Billy Kee-Long So is Professor and Chair of Humanities at the Hong Kong University of Science and Technology and Honorary Professor of the

Chinese University of Hong Kong. His publications include (with Ramon H. Myers), *The Treaty-Port Economy in Modern China: Empirical Studies of Institutional Change and Economic Performance* (2011); and *New Perspectives on Historical Chinese Market Economy: Eight Studies of Late Imperial Lower Yangzi Delta* (2011).

Kaoru Sugihara is Professor in the Graduate School of Economics, University of Tokyo, formerly Professor of Economic History CSEAS University of Kyoto and Director of the COE Programme In Search of a Sustainable Humanosphere in Asia and Africa. His publications include 'Southeast Asia in the History of the East Asian Miracle', *Newsletter*, Center for Southeast Asian Studies, Kyoto University, 63 (2011); 'The East Asian Path of Economic Development: A Long-term Perspective', in *The Resurgence of East Asia*, ed. G. Arrighi, T. Harmashita, and M. Selden (2003), 'The Resurgence of Intra-Asian Trade, 1800–1850, in *How India Clothed the World: The World of South Asian Textiles, 1500–1850*, ed. Giorgio Riello and Tirthankar Roy (with Om Prakash and Kaoru Sugihara) (2009); *Japan, China and the Growth of the Asian International Economy 1850–1949* (2005); and *Labour-Intensive Industrialization in Global History*, ed. with Gareth Austin (2013).

Megan Vaughan is Smuts Professor of Commonwealth History, Cambridge, and Fellow of Kings College. She is a Fellow of the British Academy. Her publications include *Creating the Creole Island: Slavery in Eighteenth Century Mauritius* (2004); *Curing Their Ills: Colonial Power and African Illness* (1991); and *The Story of an African Famine: Gender and Famine in Twentieth Century Malawi* (1987).

Peer Vries is Professor and Director of the Institute for Economic and Social History, University of Vienna. His publications include *Via Peking back to Manchester: Britain, the Industrial Revolution, and China* (2003); 'Governing Growth: A Comparative Analysis of the Role of the State in the Rise of the West', *Journal of World History*, 13 (2002); and 'The California School and Beyond: How to Study the Great Divergence', *History Compass*, 8 (2010).

Jan de Vries is Professor of History and Economics, University of California, Berkeley. His publications include *The Industrious Revolution: Consumer Demand and the Household Economy, 1650 to the Present* (2008); (with A. M. van der Woude), *The First Modern Economy: Success, Failure, and Perseverance of the Dutch Economy from 1500 to 1815* (1997); and 'The Limits of Globalization in the Early Modern World', *Economic History Review*, 63 (2010).

David Washbrook is Professorial Fellow, Trinity College, Cambridge. His publications include *The Emergence of Provincial Politics: The Madras Presidency 1870–1920* (1976); 'Economic Depression and the Making of "Traditional" Society in Colonial India', in *Transactions of the Royal Historical Society*, vol. 3 (1993); and 'India in the Early Modern World Economy: Modes of Production, Reproduction and Exchange', *Journal of Global History*, 2 (2007).

R. Bin Wong is Professor of History and Director of the Asia Institute, University of California, Los Angeles. His publications include (with Jean-Laurent Rosenthal), *Before and Beyond the Great Divergence: The Politics of Economic Change in China and Europe* (2011); *China Transformed: Historical Change and the Limits of European Experience* (1997); 'The Search for European Differences and Domination in the Early Modern World: A View from Asia', *American Historical Review*, 107 (2002).

Jan Luiten Van Zanden is Professor of Global Economic History, Utrecht University. His publications include *The Long Road to the Industrial Revolution: The European Economy in a Global Perspective, 1000–1800* (2009); (with Jan Lucassen and Tine de Moor), 'The Return of the Guilds: Towards a Global History of Guilds in Pre-industrial Times', *Special Issue International Review of Social History* (2009); and (with Bas Van Bavel and Tine de Moor), 'Factor Markets in Global Economic History', *Special Issue of Continuity and Change*, 24/1 (2009).

1
Global history: approaches and new directions

MAXINE BERG

'Global history' encompasses a new approach to historical writing which has emerged during the past fifteen years. Debates over 'globalization' and paradigms such as the 'great divergence' stimulated historians in many specialisms to think about the historical formation of these phenomena. Just how unique, how distinctive, is our current condition of an intense interlinking of economies and polities? We are now rethinking our histories in relation to those of others beyond Europe or beyond the nations and regions in which we specialize.

Global history first challenged the old national histories and area studies. It is now stimulating a recasting of imperial history, and of Atlantic world history. This volume brings together those who have written major books and articles shifting parts of the historical discipline in this direction, together with historians in fields including empire, area studies, the arts, and technology. It engages them in reflection and debate over what 'global' approaches to history mean, how it has changed the questions they ask, and the ways they do history. It raises the limitations and problems of this approach to history, but also opens out new perspectives.

First, where does global history come from? Many connect global history to debates over globalization. The new level of international flows and connections among economies and polities which social scientists addressed from the 1990s soon attracted historians, who pointed to the long history of global connections, some going back to the prehistoric period, but more significantly to the interlinking of land and sea routes from the first millennium AD. Thus they asked, 'does globalization have a history'?[1]

---

[1] See, for example, Antony G. Hopkins (ed.), *Globalization in World History* (London, 2002) and Jürgen Osterhammel and Niels P. Petersson, *Globalization: A Short History* (Princeton, 2005).

For many historians, however, an interest in the global did not stem from an attempt to join the globalization debate with its initial focuses on international politics, governance, and the economic order. Instead, during this past ten years they have been profoundly affected by the turning to the global in our history writing and teaching. The recent appearance of 'global history centres', 'world history groups', and 'transnational history centres', along with university appointments focused on 'wider world' and 'global' research agendas, provides a new institutionalization of this direction in historical writing. The titles of conferences, 'Global History of Science', 'Global Material Cultures', World and Global History Congresses, and a new range of MA programmes and undergraduate courses convey just how far this has reached. These perspectives have also become central in the museum and art historical world. We have seen high profile events such as the 'Encounters' exhibition at the Victoria and Albert Museum in 2003, the series of 'Empires' exhibitions at the British Museum, and exhibitions with a similar focus in New York, Paris, Hong Kong, Shanghai, and Tokyo. A total of 850,000 attended 'The First Emperor' exhibition at the British Museum in 2007–08; 54,000 bought the exhibition catalogue. The British Museum's venture in 2010 into an extended radio series, 'The History of the World in 100 Objects', led by its Director, Neil MacGregor, was combined with a presentation on its website, and later a CD series.[2]

A seminal volume, Kenneth Pomeranz's *The Great Divergence: China, Europe and the Making of the Modern World Economy*, published in 2000, brought new agendas to the large-scale comparative histories that had re-emerged in economic history, notably David Landes's *The Wealth and Poverty of Nations: Why Some are so Rich and Some so Poor* (1998). The great divergence demanded the research on China and India that would challenge histories of European exceptionalism, represented by texts such as that by Landes or Eric Jones's earlier work, *The European Miracle: Environments: Economies and Geopolitics in the History of Europe and Asia* (1981) or his *Growth Recurring: Economic Change in World History* (1988). For all the problematic hypotheses of these books, they did push us to think beyond Europe: there was a growing dissatisfaction with national histories and area studies. Those borders and boundaries needed to be crossed.[3]

---

[2] I am grateful to J. D. Hill, British Museum, for this information. See his presentation at the Challenging the History of the Globe conference, May 2009 <www2.warwick.ac.uk/fac/arts/history/ghcc/resources/>.

[3] Kenneth Pomeranz, *The Great Divergence: China, Europe and the Making of the Modern World Economy* (Princeton, 2000); David Landes, *The Wealth and Poverty of Nations: Why Some are so*

Economic history was not the only source of this shift. From sociopolitical history there have been Jack Goldstone's *Revolution and Rebellion in the Early Modern World* (1991) and Sanjay Subrahmanyam's 'Connected Histories: Notes towards a Reconfiguration of Early Modern Eurasia' (1997), and more recently Christopher Bayly's *The Birth of the Modern World* (2004), John Darwin's *After Tamerlane: A Global History of Empire Since 1405* (2007), and Linda Colley's *The Ordeal of Elizabeth Marsh* (2006).[4]

A dissatisfaction with national histories and area studies brought a foregrounding of themes long studied in world history: environmental histories, migration, slavery, trade, and travel. But above all, the 'global' in history writing emerged from postmodernist and postcolonial directions where 'crossing boundaries' and going 'beyond borders' joined aspirations to write a 'new imperial history' and to undertake comparative studies of the West and the East. Earlier historiographies of colonialism and imperialism provided histories of East India companies and of private trade, leading on to colonial and territorial dominion. Subsequent histories have focused on the struggles of subaltern peoples and the new national histories of regions earlier marginalized as colonies. Historians of Asia and of empire focused on Asia's domination by Europe and its subsequent escape, but they gave less attention to the ways in which Asia reconfigured the cultural and economic landscape of Europe. In recent generations an area studies agenda has dominated with regard to many of these former colonies, with less emphasis on comparative research across these regions, and connective research on Europe and Asia.

At the same time, many historians have pursued the wider concepts of 'connectedness' and 'cosmopolitanism' as these have developed in social theory. Many are now trying to move beyond unilateral comparisons between Europe and China, or Europe and India, and are investigating linkages and interactions between world areas.[5]

Rich and Some so Poor (New York, 1998); Eric Jones, *The European Miracle: Environments: Economies and Geopolitics in the History of Europe and Asia* (Cambridge, 1981); Eric Jones, *Growth Recurring: Economic Change in World History* (Oxford, 1988).

[4] Jack Goldstone, *Revolution and Rebellion in the Early Modern World* (Berkeley, 1991); Sanjay Subrahmanyam, 'Connected Histories: Notes towards a Reconfiguration of Early Modern Eurasia', *Modern Asian Studies*, 31/3 (1997), 735–62; Christopher Bayly, *The Birth of the Modern World* (Oxford, 2004); John Darwin, *After Tamerlane: A Global History of Empire Since 1405* (London, 2007), and Linda Colley, *The Ordeal of Elizabeth Marsh: A Woman in World History* (London, 2006).

[5] See, for instance, Victor Lieberman, *Strange Parallels: Southeast Asia in Global Context, c. 800–1830*, vol. 2: *Mainland Mirrors: Europe, Japan, China, South Asia, and the Islands*

Global history, of course, had other earlier manifestations. It has a long pedigree stretching back to the ancient world, to Han and Tang China, and to Arab, Persian, and Hindu traditions.[6] In the early years of the twentieth century there was a resurgence of interest in world history, coinciding with a new interest in China and Japan among Europeans, and with the peace movements of these periods. Global economic history courses at the London School of Economics (LSE) are now reviving (perhaps unknowingly) those comparative histories of trade and agrarian change between West and East taught there in the 1920s and 1930s.[7] Craig Clunas tells us how Chinese art was part of the curriculum of the Courtauld Institute from 1933 until the Second World War, only to disappear thereafter.[8]

Other global approaches arose out of Marxism and the world systems method from the 1970s which turned analysis of capitalist development outwards to consider reproductions of metropoles and peripheries. Large-scale comparative syntheses, from Perry Anderson's *Passages from Antiquity to Feudalism* (1974) and *Lineages of the Absolutist State* (1974) to Immanuel Wallerstein's *The Modern World System* (1974–89), challenged historians to make connective perspectives.[9]

These works, in turn, joined with histories of colonialism and imperialism, histories which continued to provide grand narratives of domination and resistance, and which have left us with enormous amounts of research on trade flows, migration, and slavery, all set within the trajectory of imperial dominion. Again, these have been mainly histories of individual European nations and of the nations arising out of former colonies. They have involved less comparative research across regions

---

(Cambridge, 2010). See the review article on this by Alan Strathern, 'Reflections on Victor Lieberman's *Strange Parallels*. Volume 2: Mainland Mirrors', *Journal of Global History*, 7/1 (2012), 129–42.

[6] P. K. O'Brien, 'Historiographical Traditions and Modern Imperatives for the Restoration of Global History', *Journal of Global History*, 1 (2006), 3–39.

[7] Maxine Berg, *A Woman in History: Eileen Power 1889–1940* (Cambridge, 1996); also see William H. McNeil, 'An Emerging Consensus about World History?', *World History Connected*, 1/1 (2003), 1–4. On American, German, and Chinese historiography see Dominic Sachsenmaier, *Global Perspectives on Global History: Theories and Approaches in a Connected World* (Cambridge, 2011).

[8] Craig Clunas, 'The Art of Global Comparisons', this volume, Chapter 11.

[9] Perry Anderson, *Passages from Antiquity to Feudalism* (London, 1974) and *Lineages of the Absolutist State* (London, 1979); Immanuel Wallerstein, *The Modern World System* (New York, 1974–89).

or the kinds of connective research on Asia or Eurasia advocated by Subrahmanyam as far back as 1997.[10]

This has had some perhaps unintended consequences. Some of these were the result of national and radical political shifts in Europe: the 1974 revolution in Portugal led to the disappearance of Asian languages from the Portuguese humanities curriculum because they were associated with imperialism. The social-democratic shifts in Denmark and Sweden also led to a loss of historical interest in the former territories of the Danish and Swedish East India companies. Africa's history was written as a history of the slave trade and coastal wider-world maritime connections, with a vast hinterland left under-investigated.[11]

New directions in the history of empire have sought a wider comparative perspective and a longer chronology, decentring Europe in the story of empire, and setting its study within the new historical writing on global history. Bayly's *The Birth of the Modern World* (2003), Darwin's *After Tamerlane: The Global History of Empire* (2007), and Jane Burbank's and Frederick Cooper's *Empires in World History* (2011) compare the wider political and economic dynamics of empire. Histories that compare the empires of Rome and China with those of Spain, the USA, and Russia, or chart a broad Eurasian story of empire from China and Japan across Russia, Iran, South Asia, and Europe, provide frameworks that are markedly different from those of an earlier generation of studies, represented for instance by *The Oxford History of the British Empire* (1998–99).[12]

Some see global history as an attempt to displace the exploitation narrative of colonialism; be that as it may, the global framework has recast Britain and Europe as the products of their colonial experience. Global historical agendas, set, as so many of them have been until very recently, within a framework of economics and politics, have adopted methodologies still dominated by comparisons of the West and the East. They carry with them new 'centrism' issues. In many comparisons Europe remains the metropolis. The challenge is to convert Europe from a knowing subject to an object of global history. We also need to ask whether we have moved from a Eurocentrism to a Eurasian centrism. The 'global' for former

---

[10] Subrahmanyam, 'Connected Histories', 735–62; Dominic Sachsenmaier, 'Global History as Ecumenical History', *Journal of World History*, 18 (2007), 465–90, at p. 466.
[11] These points were raised in discussion at the Writing the History of the Global Conference 21–22 May, 2009. See Conference videos at <http://www2.warwick.ac.uk/fac/arts/history/ghcc/events/workshops_events/writingthehistoryofglobal/>.
[12] Bayly, *Modern World*; Darwin, *After Tamerlane*; Jane Burbank and Frederick Cooper, *Empires*

historians of Northern and Western Europe means comparison and connection with South, South East, and East Asia. 'Atlantic world' history connected historians of north-west Europe and North America, but did not penetrate the north–south divide.[13] The Spanish American and Pacific Ocean worlds still remain, for many historians, part of separate historiographies.

Divergence and comparison

Historians responding to the global turn have raised questions of transitions to modernity, of divergence and convergence. They are engaging with sociologists in discussing concepts of modernity.[14] Comparative history is now under discussion. The debate on divergence has opened a new space for economic history. That economic history now pursues frameworks of enquiry extending beyond Europe or America, beyond national histories into global comparisons and connections, and beyond this into material culture analysis. The development of different historiographies, as well as recent global perspectives, has reshaped frameworks for analysing the roots of industrialization.

The 'great divergence', which has framed so much of our recent thinking in global history, has yielded large-scale comparative studies on differences in resource bases, capital inputs, population and wages, or institutional structures and state building among the major regions of the world. Investigating the sources of the 'great divergence' attracts us because it challenges us to turn our sights away from our own internal histories, to compare, for example, the resource base of the Yangzi Delta with that of north-western Europe, or to compare London wage rates with those of Beijing. Much data have been collected on such comparisons; the focus has moved out to include comparisons with India as well as China and Japan, and also the Ottoman and Spanish empires.[15]

---

in *World History: Power and the Politics of Difference* (Princeton, 2011); *The Oxford History of the British Empire*, 5 vols (Oxford, 1998–99).

[13] William O'Reilly, *The Atlantic World 1450–1700* (London, 2012).

[14] See AHR Roundtable, 'Historians and the Question of Modernity', *American Historical Review*, 116/3 (2011), 631–7; G. K. Bhambra, 'Historical Sociology, Modernity, and Postcolonial Critique', *American Historical Review*, 116/3 (2011), 653–62. Also see Joseph M. Bryant, 'The West and the Rest Revisited: Debating Capitalist Origins, European Colonialism, and the Advent of Modernity', *Canadian Journal of Sociology*, 31/4 (2006), 403–44.

[15] The 'divergence' debate generated many studies which first appeared in the conferences of the Global Economic History Network (GEHN), with a number published later in *Itinerario*, *The Journal of Global History*, *The Economic History Review*, and *The Journal of Economic History*.

The 'divergence' debate has revived an increasingly narrow and even moribund economic history: 'Economic historians previously locked away in the study of their particular country and period have been forced to confront the inter-connectedness of their specialisms.'[16] We have learned much, but there is a sense in which the divergence debate has reinforced a series of much older questions.

First, it focused on what Europe had and Asia did not, subsequently using this as an explanation. Geography, ecology, and environment provided early key indicators of comparison. Pomeranz argued that ecological imbalance in access to coal followed by the development of technologies using coal set the course for a divergence in growth between Europe and Asia from the later eighteenth century. The ensuing debate among a wide group of European, Asian, and world historians has only left entrenched a long-standing emphasis on the part played by Britain's superior coal reserves in her industrialization.[17]

Another major issue arising out of the divergence debate is that of wages and prices, which has coalesced into the old question of wages and the standard of living. Once again, intensive and now global effort is focused on demonstrating the higher wages and standard of living in Britain—indeed, not even Britain but England—than in the rest of Europe, and also the rest of the world, with the ensuing consequences for the development of labour-saving technologies.[18] The 'divergence' debate originally challenged historians to think outside their national boundaries, and to

---

[16] Stephen Broadberry and Steve Hindle, 'Editor's Introduction', special issue: 'Asia in the Great Divergence', *The Economic History Review*, 64/S1 (2011), 7.

[17] E. A. Wrigley, *Continuity, Chance and Change: The Character of the Industrial Revolution in England* (Cambridge, 1988) and Wrigley, *Energy and the English Industrial Revolution* (Cambridge, 2010). The case is reiterated in Paul Warde, *Energy Consumption in England and Wales 1560–2000* (Rome, 2007) and Robert C. Allen, *The British Industrial Revolution in Global Perspective* (Cambridge, 2010). Also see Prasannan Parthasarathi, *Why Europe Grew Rich and Asia Did Not. Global Economic Divergence 1600-1850* (Cambridge, 2011) which argues a case for lower energy constraints in India. Britain's technological initiative was driven by fuel shortages, and hence the need to innovate in industrial uses of coal. See pp. 165–8; 175–82.

[18] Robert C. Allen, 'The Great Divergence in European Wages and Prices from the Middle Ages to the First World War', *Explorations in Economic History*, 38/4 (2001), 411–47; also see S. N. Broadberry and B. Gupta, 'The Early Modern Great Divergence: Wages, Prices and Economic Development in Europe and Asia, 1500–1800', *Economic History Review*, 59/1 (2006), 2–31; Robert C. Allen, Jean-Paul Bassino, Debin Ma, Christine Moll-Murata, and Jan Luiten van Zanden, 'Wages, Prices and Living Standards in China, 1738–1925: In Comparison with Europe, Japan, and India', special issue: 'Asia in the Great Divergence', *Economic History Review*, 64/S1 (2011), 8–38; Robert C. Allen, 'Why the Industrial Revolution was British:

compare Europe with parts of Asia in the period before Europe's industrialization. But economic historians risk turning back to a series of old methodologies and debates.[19] A key issue in all these comparisons is the question of what is being measured and how. Historians making these global comparisons face the challenges of lack of data and of scholarly work creating comparable accounts from widely differing sources compiled under different assumptions and purposes.[20]

Where has the divergence debate left us? After more than a decade, the subject is no less attractive to historians. A panel at the American Historical Association Conference in 2011 entitled 'Assessing Kenneth Pomeranz's *The Great Divergence:* A Forum' brought together Peter Coclanis, Jan de Vries, R. Bin Wong, Philip Hoffman, and Kenneth Pomeranz. De Vries challenged Pomeranz's 'informal' methodology of comparison. We must ask what the theories, models, or assumptions are that underlie any comparison, otherwise we fall victim to comparing what might be two ways of achieving the same result, or just two different things. 'More thought needs to be given to the methodology of a comparative history suitable for a globalized history.'[21] De Vries's critique of a neo-Malthusian analysis where chronologies of difference were more suited to the nineteenth century than to the industrial revolution raises new questions for sources of difference in labour productivity, in technology, and in changing structures of consumption. Hoffman and Wong point to other new agendas on science and technology (useful knowledge), war, and political competition and fragmentation.[22]

Commerce, Induced Invention, and the Scientific Revolution', *Economic History Review*, 64/3 (2011), 357–84. See, by contrast, the case made for higher standards of living in India by Prasannan Parthasarathi, 'Rethinking Wages and Competitiveness in the Eighteenth Century: Britain and India', *Past and Present*, 158, (1998), 79–109.

[19] Compare Liliane Hilaire-Pérez, *L'invention Technique au Siècle des Lumières* (Paris, 2000); Margaret C. Jacob, *Scientific Culture and the Making of the Industrial West* (Oxford, 1997); Joel Mokyr, 'Intellectual Origins of Modern Economic Growth', *Journal of Economic History*, 65/2 (2005), 283–351; S. R. Epstein, 'Craft Guilds, Apprenticeship and Technological Change in Preindustrial Europe', *Journal of Economic History*, 58/3 (1998), 684–713; S. R. Epstein and Maarten Prak, *Guilds, Innovation and the European Economy, 1400–1800* (Cambridge, 2008); Christine MacLeod, 'The European Origins of British Technological Predominance', in *Exceptionalism and Industrialism: Britain and its European Rivals, 1688–1815*, ed. Leandro Prados de la Escosura (Cambridge, 2004), pp. 111–26.

[20] Morten Jerven, 'National Income Estimates in Global Economic History', *The Journal of Global History*, 7/1 (2012), 107–28, especially pp. 109 and 111.

[21] Jan de Vries, '*The Great Divergence* after Ten Years: Justly Celebrated yet Hard to Believe', *Historically Speaking*, 4 (2011), 13–15; 'Assessing Kenneth Pomeranz's *The Great Divergence*: A Forum', *Historically Speaking*, 4 (2011), 10–25.

[22] Philip T. Hoffman, 'Comment on Ken Pomeranz's *The Great Divergence*', *Historically Speaking*,

The 'divergence' debate has invited economic historians into the wider comparative axis of Europe and Asia. The analysis derived has not changed our picture of Europe's and even Britain's transition in the eighteenth century. Ironically, it has if anything revived an economic history narrowly focused on English exceptionalism. What those large-scale comparative studies of resources, capital, and wages did not do was to investigate the extent to which connections between these parts of the world affected their subsequent development.

It is time to move to some more open-ended questions concerning global connections: how did the transmission of material culture and useful knowledge across regions of the world affect the economic and cultural developments in any one of these regions? This leads us into narratives of interaction which could take us deeper into the analysis of imperial domination, but could equally lead us into the connections that contributed to economic development in Europe.

Comparison has also generated new challenges to methodology from historians of the wider world. Gareth Austin has proposed a method of 'reciprocal comparison' as a response to long traditions of approaching African history from the stylized facts of European historiography. He compares the differences in labour and land endowments of sub-Saharan Africa with those of East Asia and the West, discussing reasons why an abundance of cultivable land can generate technological and institutional factors that limit economic growth. He asks that Africa be compared, not with Europe, but with other relatively poor, formerly colonized regions, including India, South East Asia, the Caribbean, and Latin America. Furthermore, Americanists and European historians might find new perspectives from looking at their own continents 'in an African mirror'.[23]

Likewise, the focus on China and Europe in the divergence debate has diverted historians from another significant comparative perspective, and one with a long historiography. This is the comparison of labour-intensive paths of industrialization, as in the case of Japan, with developments of proto-industrialization in Europe. Kaoru Sugihara's concept of an 'East

---

4 (2011), 16–17; R. Bin Wong, 'Economic History in the Decade after *The Great Divergence*', *Historically Speaking*, 4 (2011), 17–19. Also see Jean-Laurent Rosenthal and R. Bin Wong, *Before and Beyond Divergence: The Politics of Economic Change in China and Europe* (Cambridge, MA., 2011).

[23] Gareth Austin, 'Reciprocal Comparisons and African History: Tackling Conceptual Eurocentrism in the Study of Africa's Economic Past', *African Studies Review*, 50 (2007), 1–28 (at pp. 11 and 13).

Asian development path' that was labour-intensive can lead us to investigate the legacies of proto-industrialization in wider regions of Europe, and not to focus singularly on the English alternative of a capital-intensive path.[24] And yet comparison from the standpoint of Africa, of Japan, or of China still leaves us grappling with essentialist frameworks. What we see is what Jean-Frédéric Schaub calls a paradigm of asymmetries. Cultural and colonial encounters between ruling or ascendant powers and 'other', foreign or 'alien' peoples reveal the capacities of such dominant groups to change other societies and to dominate cultural transfers.[25]

Comparison and connection

Running parallel to methods of comparative history and the histories of encounters and colonial domination there is a long lineage of histories of composite regions and of regions bordering oceans: Braudel's Mediterranean world, Bailyn's Atlantic world, Chaudhuri and Das Gupta's Indian Ocean world. But these transoceanic perspectives have also been comparative histories of the maritime world.[26]

Recent global agendas drawing on social theory focus on concepts of 'connectedness' or 'cosmopolitanism', of 'entanglement', and even 'ecumenae'.[27] In so doing historians now seek the connections that impacted on Europe's and Asia's cultures and development. These new agendas, however, also risk losing the vigour of those big questions previously raised in comparative studies. And yet, moving away from comparative histories brings us a whole new set of questions and subject areas: those of diasporas, of embassies and trading missions, of religious ideologies, of the connected histories of city life, of the transmission of material cultures, and of useful knowledge.

Global history's methodological agendas have also challenged another great divide between economic history, on the one hand, and cultural and social history, on the other. Economic histories of early modern Europe and its colonial empires are still separated off from social and cultural

---

[24] Kaoru Sugihara, 'The European Miracle in Global History: An East Asian Perspective', this volume, Chapter 9.
[25] J.-F. Schaub, 'Global History: Notes on Some Discontents in the Historical Narrative', this volume, Chapter 4.
[26] Markus Vink, 'Indian Ocean Studies', *Journal of Global History*, 2 (2007), 41–62.
[27] Sachsenmaier, 'World History as Ecumenical History'.

histories of consumption and material cultures. Jan de Vries set out to unite these histories in his concept of the 'industrious revolution'.[28] His pan-European study connected household behaviour with macroeconomic labour and capital markets. De Vries opened the gates of economic history to questions of consumer desire, taste, and sentiment that changed households and fostered incentives for large-scale productivity growth. He also linked consumer cultures in Europe to encounters with wider-world material cultures. It is now time to pursue the possibilities he opened up; to connect up those divided and comparative questions asked by economic historians.

Microhistories and global history

Global approaches challenge us to recast the method and scale of our research in much the same way that microhistory did in the early 1980s. Microhistorians wrote of episodes of everyday life or of individual experiences as 'strange'; they thus required for analysis the insights of different disciplines such as cultural anthropology or literary textual analysis. Such microanalysis, once achieved, would, they believed, also provide access to the real. Such history was seen to convey a spirit of human agency, of sharing and communality, of sympathy and closeness. The issues of a different scale and a different point of view confronted by the microhistorians have their parallels in those issues confronting global historians. The search for an access to closeness and familiarity allowed by different historical and disciplinary methodologies is not so different from what we now seek to understand from distance and strangeness. Microhistory allowed interrogation of identity and human agency; it brought a critique of determinist history. But it often focused on the exception, on deviations; the microhistorian's use of court records shaped the methodology. Such microhistories rejected the grand narratives, but their plots were shaped by those narratives. As John Brewer has argued, they still aspired to notions of 'histoire totale', of writing history from the ground up.[29]

---

[28] Jan de Vries, *The Industrious Revolution: Consumer Behavior and the Household Economy, 1650 to the Present* (Cambridge, 2008).
[29] For a recent discussion of microhistory see John Brewer, 'Microhistory and the History of Everyday Life', *Cultural and Social History*, 7 (2010), 87–109; Pat Hudson, 'Closeness and Distance', *Cultural and Social History*, 7 (2010), 375–85; Filippo De Vivo, 'Prospect or Refuge,

Focusing on one individual or family, however, allowed transcendence of boundaries of identity and culture. Now historians found histories of families or of individuals migrating from one continent or culture to another, as for example in Natalie Zemon Davis's study of Al-Wazzan in *Trickster Travels*.[30] What many global histories missed out on were the historical actors and issues of agency so central to the plots of micro-narratives. Linda Colley, in *The Ordeal of Elizabeth Marsh*, used biography, and looked to smallness as a way of connecting to the large. She could investigate the lives of the conventionally marginalized—in this case, a literate but uneducated woman, a wife, a middle-class person of no wealth—through a research tool that globalization has given us—the world wide web. Although her story was of a woman in empire, she also wrote of all the global forces impinging on the lives of Marsh's family, friends, and those she encountered. Elizabeth Marsh noticed, for example, that the Sultan of Morocco drank tea out of porcelain cups and the women in his court wore Indian muslins. A more recent treatment of family and individual histories across continents, Emma Rothschild's *The Inner Life of Empires*, sets a court case centred on slavery and infanticide within a Scottish landed family whose members spanned the Atlantic, Caribbean, and Indian empires.[31]

Methods

Beyond economic history the comparative histories have given way to investigations of connectedness, cosmopolitanism and entanglement, and now of ecumenae, concepts often referred to and just as often left undefined. We are rapidly moving, however, into a new stage where the global and the transnational have taken over from where empire left off. The global is rapidly becoming a brand, and one that is losing the edge and the clarity of focus, the frisson offered by those big comparative questions of divergence and convergence, of wealth and poverty, of the crisis of

---

Microhistory: History on the Large Scale', *Cultural and Social History*, 7 (2010), 387–97. Also see Giovanni Levi, 'On Microhistory', in *New Perspectives on Historical Writing*, ed. Peter Burke (Cambridge, 2001), pp. 97–119.
[30] Natalie Zemon Davis, *Trickster Travels: In Search of Leo Africanus, A Sixteenth-Century Muslim between Worlds* (New York and London, 2007).
[31] Colley, *Ordeal of Elizabeth Marsh*; Emma Rothschild, *The Inner Life of Empires: An Eighteenth-Century History* (Princeton, 2011). Also see other collective biographies of individuals in the

empires. We may not have liked those questions raised in the comparative histories of the 1980s and 1990s, such as 'why are we so rich and they so poor?'. But these were the questions that pushed us out of our introverted localism. Historians have moved the questions of 'divergence' that dominated global history after 2000 out to other areas of the world: they have looked at regions, for instance the Islamic world and China; they have looked at composite zones, or, like Kaoru Sugihara, marked out an East Asian development path.

We have the excitement as historians of moving out of our national borders and of connecting across our former area studies. This will require new methodologies of collaboration and interdisciplinarity as well as the rapidly disappearing tools of foreign languages. Languages become more, not less vital as historians move beyond the imperial and national archive. Area studies specialists who do have the languages central to their chosen regions are now also breaking into comparative and connective questions. These may require, for example, not just Korean and Japanese language skills, but also Russian. Linguistic constraints shape possible networks among historians. They also shape possibilities of engagement in debate, in meetings, and in collaborations. Just how we go forward will also depend on collaborations. Many of us are not archaeologists, geographers, geologists, or environmental scientists, nor are we curators, art historians, or historical sociologists. We have different questions, we research and write differently. But we now need to work with the theories, findings, and techniques of these groups, and indeed work with them in collaborations. We can move from traditional models of the lone researcher to alternative academic models, experimenting with teamwork, networks, and electronic forums; we can engage in joint publications based on transnational research networks.

In recent years we have had great comparative studies of different empires in one region, such as John Elliott's *Empires of the Atlantic World*, or of one empire in two different parts of the world, such as Peter Marshall's *The Making and Unmaking of Empires*.[32] Few of us can aspire to the mastery of printed and archival material at this level, and perhaps this is only possible among very senior historians. But historians who have grouped

---

British Empire, for example, Miles Ogborn, *Global Lives: Britain and the World 1550–1800* (Cambridge, 2008).

[32] J. H. Elliott, *Empires of the Atlantic World: Britain and Spain in America 1492–1830* (New Haven, CT, and London, 2006); P. J. Marshall, *The Making and Unmaking of Empires: Britain, India and America c. 1750–1783* (Oxford, 2005).

themselves as economic historians, as imperial, new imperial and postcolonial historians, as European historians, Indian or Chinese historians, can draw on the large amounts of valuable research in all these different historiographical traditions, and approach these with new questions.

Contributions

Writing the History of the Global raises new agendas in historical research and questions the concepts we have deployed hitherto. But we are also in a period of great uncertainty over where this is going. This volume captures historians at a key moment of shifting their subject areas and how they write about them. Part I, 'Interpretations: Ideas and the Making of Global History', addresses how historians of Europe, India, and the Spanish American world have resituated their questions. David Washbrook addresses how writing history in a global perspective has recast many of the problems previously taken as given. The long periodization of global history puts notions of the modern under scrutiny. Global history challenges us to convert our understanding of Europe from a 'knowing subject' into much more of an object of that history. If the global history of the 'British' Industrial Revolution takes us to China, on the one side, and the Americas, on the other, by what rights does it deserve, any longer, to be described as 'British'? Global history has risen in the wake of the retreat from post-structuralism. There is a need for some meta-narrative or theory of causation. These will differ from those of earlier historiographical traditions. How successful has global history been, thus far, at finding or erecting signposts to a new, and significantly different, historical understanding of the past?

Jan de Vries addresses the difference that global history has made to non-national historical agendas, and raises problems as to how to conduct professional academic history at this level. His early work focused on ecological zones, and even in his most recent on the 'industrious revolution', that concept was applied to a zone or region. There is no special route to global history from this regional approach, but the methods of regional history have many parallels with global history. Boundaries are not a given, but a historical contingency inviting questions of connection and comparison. The conceiving of a polycentric early modern world challenges us to cross mental boundaries.

Finally, Jean-Frédéric Schaub, writing from a context of French historiography and the colonized Spanish American world, develops a concept of 'asymmetries' to address European writings on encounters and cultural transfers. European historians who compare societies risk essentialist frameworks, but their analysis must be placed within a longer and broader framework of conquered and colonized peoples.

Part II, 'Approaches: Methods and Methodologies in Global History', addresses approaches of comparative histories, the spaces of global history, and new directions in collaborative research. Prasannan Parthasarathi poses the methods of comparative history as an analytic focus for global history. This entails a problem-centred approach to writing history. Comparison must analyse not just one or two, but multiple paths of economic and historical development in the early modern world. Different economic and ecological contexts in early modern Eurasia produced not a dynamic Europe and stagnant Asia, but strikingly different needs and imperatives leading towards different paths of economic and technological change.

Whereas Jan de Vries discussed the role of the 'ecological' region or zone in his approach, and Prasannan Parthasarathi that of comparison across multiple development paths across Eurasia, R. Bin Wong takes up the regional approach from the context of China. He examines the Chinese empire as a part of multiple regions, for example of north-east Asia, or of the eastern and south-eastern maritime regions. How can an analysis of different kinds of space take us beyond environmental history into wider issues of global history?

Finally Jan Luiten van Zanden considers new research methodologies of teamwork and collaboration. He sets out the ways historians and economic historians can work together to provide historical datasets covering the world. Key questions are: 'when did global divergence begin and why?' and 'why the reversal of fortune?'. Much of the literature written thus far on these issues is impressionistic. We lack global datasets on economic performance, and on the economic, social, and cultural causes of development. New evidence-gathering and analysis through teams of historians pooling expertise can create new public goods for global history. There is currently a gap in approaches between history and the natural sciences. There is scope for greater teamwork in history, as indicated in some current collaborative projects on national income, prices, real wages, and labour relations. The problems with this approach that historians must confront include agreements over who owns the data, the division of labour, and who is to lead the projects and publications.

Part III, 'Shaping Global History', takes us further into comparative methodologies. Kenneth Pomeranz, whose book *The Great Divergence* was one of the key starting points for global history, develops in Chapter 8 a methodological approach to the concept of 'divergence'. Investigation of a particular divergence raises the key point that historical divergences are provisional unless we specify the time frame. Divergence in growth between Europe and the Lower Yangzi Delta shows the results of delays in initiating economic growth in the Chinese region. Historical divergences raise many questions: those of perspective, issues of 'origins', points where differences become divergences, and those of multiple timescales. Pomeranz uses the examples of Alfred Crosby's military metaphors in his environmental approaches, and of Jack Goldstone's comparisons of unique divergences and the more common efflorescence.

Comparisons must also be reciprocal. Kaoru Sugihara contrasts an East Asian development path with the 'European miracle'. He identifies in East Asia efficient institutions fostering greater use of labour, an 'industrious revolution' path entailing extensive use of family labour, and technological paths encouraging double cropping. The result was a path to 'labour-intensive industrialization' such as occurred in Meiji Japan. That labour-intensive path now shapes the centres of most of the world's manufacturing employment, centres that have shifted in recent decades from the West to East, South East and South Asia. The search for resources has also been a major force behind recent global history. The challenge for Japan and other East Asian economies has been to develop resource- and energy-saving technologies.

Part IV, 'Knowledge and Global History', takes us from global comparison to global connections in chapters on technology, the arts, and material culture. Dagmar Schäfer's chapter addresses the approach of the Chinese of the Ming/Qing dynasty to technology and invention. In what ways did the knowledge of Chinese craftsmen contribute to the development of scientific thinking in the Chinese world? The Chinese assigned a place and function to technologies and their products in statecraft, public life, and scholarly achievement. Ming connoisseurs valued craftsmanship. Court advisors defined which technologies were emblematic to the imperial eye. Porcelain and silk were used to negotiate political control and economic interests, or to buy obedience from servants of empire. But free markets emerged for the products of craftsmanship. How were the products marketed, and how were original designs and techniques claimed and marked by their craftsmen?

Craig Clunas asks us to consider comparisons made hitherto between Western and Chinese art. He considers Mieke Bal's cultural critique that comparison becomes a ground for relative judgement; it establishes hierarchies and distracts from looking. He uses the example of different attitudes to Chinese art before and after the Second World War. Chinese art was part of the syllabus of the Courtauld Institute between 1933 and 1945; it was excluded thereafter. Bernard Berenson's high regard during the 1930s for Chinese painting gave way by 1950 to his new judgements that relegated Chinese art to the margins of the exotic arts. Craig Clunas returns to Mieke Bal to argue that comparison should not be an instrument of judgement, but a source of differentiation.

From art we move to material objects, conveying contention and entanglement. Glenn Adamson and Giorgio Riello consider objects as displayed in museums, as architecture, and as consumer goods. They unwrap the meanings of a Japanese suit of armour in the Tower of London, discuss the hybrid architecture and design of Chhatrapati Shivaji Terminus, known in the West as Victoria Terminus, in Mumbai, challenging its former status as a symbol of empire, and finally present the football and soccer as evoking debates on globalization and the global condition.

Part V, 'Round Table', brings together short statements on issues under-explored in current writings on global history. John Darwin considers recent themes of 'connectedness' in global history, and assesses the contributions offered by archives of imperial history. All empires had a vested interest in making connections with the territories they conquered, but also interpreted and controlled the impacts of such connections. Megan Vaughan discusses the marginal place of Africa in current global history writing. But global history should not be the only approach; she also warns against framing the history of the entire African continent in terms of its external relations. A major area left underexplored in our new global narratives is the state. While we seek to move beyond histories of individual nation states, the role of the state remains crucial in global formations. Peer Vries questions the recent focus of global historians on connections, networks, exchanges, and transfers. This history leaves out wars, violence, conflicts, and especially the state. The big challenge is to encompass the role of the state without turning to narrowly national histories. Finally, histories of global connections can be conveyed through more studies of individuals and families. Recent histories of families and individuals in the British Empire, such as those by Linda Colley and Emma Rothschild, raise questions of global identities conveyed through transnational biographies of individuals. Sufumi So and Billy Kee-Long So ask whether a global identity can be found in narratives of individuals across time and place. We can seek to trace more stories of individuals in Asia as well as Europe who perceived themselves within wider-world identities through oral histories, biography, and autobiography.

Conclusion

Global and transnational histories have now become a significant part of the historical disciplines. There are many volumes now treating subjects once presented in a European framework in the broad comparative frameworks of the global. Historians coming from many different specialisms, not just regional, but also economic, cultural, and intellectual history, have been stimulated to rethink and to debate with each other by the idea of the global. *Writing the History of the Global* captures a group of historians from different countries and different specialisms at a key point of uncertainty and transition; here we find them debating concepts, methods, and the future of historical writing.

Part I
Interpretations: Ideas and the Making of Global History

2
Problems in global history

DAVID WASHBROOK

Perhaps the first problem raised by global history concerns what, exactly, it is: what kind of perspective does it offer? As, no doubt, is the case with all 'new' or revisionist movements in historiography, global history has spent most of its time distinguishing itself from its antecedents and clarifying to itself what it is not. Most obviously, it is not 'national' history and, fundamentally, it seeks to break bounds with those traditions which take the frontiers of 'the nation' to supply the ultimate determinants of history, meaning, and identity.[1] Also, it is not international history: a history of the world written simply in terms of the relations between different 'national' or 'proto-national' entities. In extension of that logic, especially for the last five hundred years, it is also not imperial history or the world seen largely through the lens of the 'expansion of Europe'. In global history, erstwhile colonial 'peripheries' are viewed as agents in their own right, interacting with erstwhile metropolises and capable of effecting change in the latter as much as they change the former. By that logic, too, global history is also not modern history in the sense of history as modernization: the transfer of the West's unique modern culture to the rest of the world or, more mystically, the universal sprouting of cultural seeds that were first planted in the West.

Yet, if global history is emphatically not any of these things, what precisely is it in its own right? This may be much more difficult to say. A great deal of self-styled global history explores two different, though often complementary, features. On the one hand, there are connections and networks, frequently spanning vast geographical spaces and epochs, which hint at the extraordinary interdependence of life on this planet, and over a

---

[1] For a panoptic survey of the historiography of the global, see A. G. Hopkins (ed.), *Global History: Interactions between the Universal and the Local* (London, 2006).

very considerable period: the tea, porcelain, and textile trades of the seventeenth and eighteenth centuries, which linked artisans in China and India to markets in the Levant and Western Europe; the sugar, cotton, and tobacco trades, which connected labour from Africa to land in the Americas to manufacturers in Bristol and Lancashire to consumers back across the globe; the timber and beaver-pelt trades, which engaged producers on the wildest frontiers of 'civilization' with the latest fashions of society in London and Paris.[2] The resulting networks created the context in which were forged the commercial and industrial revolutions taking place in the Western European 'middle' at the beginning of what we like to call the 'modern' era.[3] The emergence of industrialization in Britain by the early nineteenth century, for example, would now seem to have been a global event with multiple points of causation; and, also, with an astonishingly long gestation period, challenging previously neat conventions of periodization and, especially, putting facile notions of the origins of 'modernity' under scrutiny.

Equally, and on the other hand, global history may offer a rather different orientation of comparison, which particularly seeks not only points of difference between one culture or society and another—as in older applications of the comparative method—but also, and crucially, points of similarity. Very striking now, across the vast swathe of humanity who inhabited a 'Eurasia' stretching from the Atlantic to the Pacific Oceans, would seem the similarities in the bureaucratic states, scribal societies, commercial economies, and literary cultures (including, even, separation of classical from vernacular traditions) that developed in them all at or about the same time—if not in exactly the same way nor, of course, with exactly the same outcome.[4] Global history has helped to promote a much stronger sense of the commonalities in human affairs against which to set a much more refined appreciation of what precisely was different about

---

[2] Classic works include: K. N. Chaudhuri, *The Trading World of Asia and the English East India Company* (Cambridge, 1978); Philip D. Curtin, *Cross-Cultural Trade in World History* (Cambridge, 1984); Joseph E. Inikori, *Africans and the Industrial Revolution in England* (Cambridge, 2002); Maxine Berg, *Luxury and Pleasure in Eighteenth-Century Britain* (Oxford, 2005).

[3] Neil McKendrick, John Brewer, and John Harold Plumb (eds), *The Birth of a Consumer Society* (Bloomington, 1982); C. A. Bayly, *The Birth of the Modern World 1780–1914* (Oxford, 2004).

[4] Jack Goldstone, *Revolution and Rebellion in the Early Modern World* (California, 1991); Sheldon Pollock, *The Language of the Gods in the World of Men* (California, 2006); John Darwin, *After Tamerlain: A Global History of Empire since 1405* (London, 2007).

some contexts, and may have given rise to further differences between them.

So, then, connections and comparisons are the stock-in-trade of global history, often giving a starkly novel appearance to phenomena, events, and chronologies that had seemed familiar. But a new appearance for what purposes and to what ends? How exactly does global history reshape our perceptions of the past and the world in which we live?

Tritely, perhaps, it redirects attention back to the significance of the universal—a concept that has taken a severe battering in recent years from the post-structuralist revolt against the Enlightenment's supposed tyranny.[5] However, that may be no bad thing in a Western intellectual context which, since at least the rise of scientific racism in the nineteenth century, has been inclined to give greater emphasis to the differences between, and 'incommensurability' of, races/ethnicities/nations/cultures.[6] In the world post-9/11, if we can find no bases for a universalist history, we may have very little with which to oppose strategies of 'communication' between races/ethnicities/nations/cultures articulated principally through violence. As Tony Hopkins has recently put it, global history informs—it can be hoped—the re-emergence of a 'global citizenry'.[7]

More prosaically, however, global history may also serve as a critical tool to advance further that questioning and destabilization of received wisdom, or certainty, associated with the original post-structuralism of Michel Foucault, but whose spirit has rather been lost in the structuralist inversions of latter day 'post-colonial' theory.[8] In its own way, global history also challenges ideas about authenticity, determinacy, and authority (or authorship). If the global history of the 'British' industrial revolution takes us to China, on the one side, and the Americas, on the other, by what rights any longer does it deserve to be described as 'British': whose, really, is it? Equally, if, in global history, so much appears to have depended on the contingencies of 'conjuncture'—on the often chance coming together of events and developments having multiple origins, often on different continents—what any longer can be said to determine what? Global history provokes and promotes forms of disaggregation and 'deconstruction' in relation to which most of the signposts to our

---

[5] Not least, in Edward Said, *Orientalism* (New York, 1978).
[6] Michael Banton, *The Idea of Race* (London, 1977).
[7] Hopkins, *Global History*.
[8] Robert Young, *White Mythologies* (London, 1990).

conventional classifications of the world, and understandings of its past, get turned around or upside down. In a world made by the supposed rise of the nation state, the driving force of European capitalism, the immanent urges of modernity become dissolved into fragments, coincidences, accidents which often appear serendipitous. Things fall apart . . .

Yet is it possible to be satisfied if matters are left only there: with global history as a species of critique, pulling historical meaning apart but never putting it back together again? The retreat over the last decade from post-structuralism—and, indeed, the latter's adoption of modes of 'strategic essentialism' designed to secure 'position'[9]—indicates the difficulty. To find meaning, it still may be necessary to construct meta-narratives, theories of determinacy and causation, 'knowing subjects' to whom moral responsibility can be imputed. We just don't want the same ones as before: stories of the conquests of Western Europeans, theories validating the 'genius' of their Reason, moralities exposing the barbarity of their 'others'. But how successful has global history been, thus far, at finding or erecting those signposts to a new, and significantly different, historical understanding of the meaning(s) of the past? It is here that a number of problems remain, which is hardly surprising given the novelty of the perspective. In particular, three out of, no doubt, very many sets of issues currently seem particularly significant.

First, for the history of the last five hundred years, there is the problem of what, actually, to do with Western Europe? Our older world historiography was extremely Eurocentric: David Landes's *The Wealth and Poverty of Nations* leaves no doubts as to who has wealth and who not; John Roberts has entitled his version of world history *The Triumph of the West*.[10] Understandably, there has been a desire to turn away from such positions now, a desire to 'put Europe in its place'. But how exactly is that to be done?

Some historians have suggested that we simply leave Europe out: in postmodernist terms, 'refuse' it and seek to write from alternative, often deemed peripheral or marginal perspectives.[11] But there is an awful lot to leave out: empirically, forces and agencies emanating from Europe

---

[9] The concept was defined by Gyatri Chakraborty Spivak; see Donna Landry and Gerald Maclean, *The Spivak Reader* (London, 2006).

[10] David Landes, *The Wealth and Poverty of Nations* (New York, 1998); John Roberts, *The Triumph of the West* (Boston, 1985).

[11] Gyan Prakash, 'Writing Post-Oriental Histories of the Third World', *Comparative Studies in Society and History*, 32/2 (1990), 383–408.

over the last half-millennium obviously did impact on multiple societies around the globe and come to play an important role in reshaping them. Doubtless, it would be possible to find some peoples and groups whose existence has been unaffected by Europe: just as Richard Cobb, in a famous protest against the centrality accorded in French history to the Revolution, once found a man who had lived through the entire experience of 1789–95 without apparently noticing that a revolution was taking place.[12] But he was insane and lived locked up in an attic ... and one suspects that many of those in Asia, Africa, and Latin America who did not notice the Europeans also must have been somewhat remote from everyday life.

Rather more promisingly, perhaps, we might concentrate more on 'South-to-South' contacts: interactions between non-European societies, which have become marginalized in our understanding by the central focus on Europe. Very often, these were extremely important and extensive, especially so far as the Chinese and Islamic worlds were concerned. Recent studies have revealed 'networks of trade and civilization', pre-modern 'world systems', and 'informal' economic and cultural empires stretching across large areas of the globe long before Western Europeans emerged from their harbours, or even from their caves.[13] They have also started to challenge the significance attached to the European historical experience with regard to some of the latter's own chosen themes: for example, *Islamic Roots of Capitalism*.[14] However, the problem again is that, post-1500, very often what was carried along South-to-South trade routes or knowledge networks appears to have involved, or to have been mediated by, the European presence itself. In the end, from the sixteenth century, Asia may have come 'to meet Africa to meet America', but it was through goods, commodities, and slave trades organized principally by Europeans.

An alternative approach has been suggested by Dipesh Chakrabarty in his celebrated attempt to provincialize Europe.[15] Here, emphasis is placed on the reactions, adaptations, and resistances to European culture taking place in particular localities across the world—in Chakrabarty's case, Calcutta and Bengal. Europe, in global history, becomes many different

---

[12] Richard Cobb, *The Police and the People* (Oxford, 1972).
[13] K. N. Chaudhuri, *Asia Before Europe* (Cambridge, 1986); Janet Abu-Lughod, *Before European Hegemony* (Oxford, 1991).
[14] Peter Gran, *Islamic Roots of Capitalism* (Syracuse, 1998).
[15] Dipesh Chakrabarty, *Provincializing Europe* (Princeton, 2000).

things, in very many different places: its meanings reinterpreted in the light of local cultures and 'provincialized' across the world. And, of course, such an approach does have much scope. However, if we pull back from Chakrabarty's specific province to take a panoptic view of the world, another problem becomes obvious. If the rest of the world is to be presented as a series of provincial experiences of Europe, then Europe continues to remain at the centre of the global project, to be its metropolis. We still come back to a Eurocentric perspective in which it is the advent of Europe, very explicitly in Chakrabarty's case, which is taken to be the starting point of 'history' in Bengal itself.

However, another way to 'provincialize Europe' might be to turn the latter into a province itself: convert it from the 'knowing subject', and active agent, of global history into much more an object determined by that history. Here, much has already been done by the history of commodities and consumption to show how the Western European economy was reshaped and restructured by its interactions with other parts of the world. How, for example, in Britain the first 'national' markets were constituted by the import of tropical crops and Asian goods; how Britain's first modern industries arose in competition with, and to imitate, Chinese porcelain and Indian textiles.[16] Britain itself was a product of the global economy and not simply its progenitor.

Also, the history of colonialism has begun to invert its previous orientation: to consider how Western European society was affected by and developed as an artefact of its imperial context rather than just vice versa. For example, the British domestic state—even the idea of 'the state' in Britain—seems to have been transformed in the nineteenth century by the experience of 'ruling the world', especially India which even gave the British the concept of 'civil service'.[17] The evolution of British social ideas, especially the rise of 'scientific racism', also appears hard to dissociate from the experience of conquering large numbers of 'inferior peoples' at the time, especially in Africa.[18] And no less important, as Simon Shaffer particularly has shown, 'science' in Britain, perhaps from as early as the seventeenth century, developed as the nodal point of an imperial network of ideas and information, which sharply marked the character of its knowledge and

---

[16] McKendrick, *Birth*; David Washbrook, 'From Comparative Sociology to Global History', *Journal of the Economic and Social History of the Orient*, 40/4 (1997), 410–43.
[17] C. A. Bayly, *Imperial Meridian* (London, 1988).
[18] Christine Bolt, *Victorian Attitudes to Race* (London, 1971).

understanding.[19] With Europe now seen much more as the meeting place of ideas and experiences taken from across the world, and as the construct of its global context, conceptions of Europe's unique and originary 'genius', and of its singular role in remaking culture and society across the world, come to be 'put in their place'. Europe is perceived as a province within a global society, not as the metropolis determining all other provinces.

A second and related problem in global history concerns relations of power and exploitation. Obviously, moving away from a Eurocentric position means no longer being able to lay not only 'the glory' but also 'the blame' for projects of 'world domination' onto Europe and Europeans alone (since the category itself begins to dissolve). But does this mean that relations of power and exploitation have no, or only a limited, place in global history? Some critics have certainly claimed so: they see global history as an attempt to displace imperial history and the need to acknowledge the many culpabilities of the European historical record *outremer*. 'Connections' and 'networks' now stand in for relations of force and coercion; conjunctures and coincidences obscure moral responsibilities; violence towards others becomes a near-universal phenomenon; the expansion of trade and 'culture-contact' is celebrated in its own right, ignoring what might have been its quite disastrous effects on local distributive systems and livelihoods. Nonetheless, it may be important to avoid making global history into a simple vehicle of historical legitimation for the contemporary triumph of globalized capitalism, which certain of its formulations have come close to doing.[20] Yet how might this be accomplished?

Many of the tools of the 'old' Left—and even of the self-styled New Left of the 1960s and 1970s—now appear particularly blunt. Appeals to class sentiment, and suppositions regarding the rise of transnational, global bourgeoisie, become entangled when stretched across continents and imbricated in multiple and different social, religious, and cultural consciousnesses.[21] Equally, lines of gender and racial domination become confused when encountering multiple and different ideologies of social

---

[19] Wiiliam Clark, Jan Golinski, and Simon Shaffer (eds), *The Sciences in Enlightened Europe* (Chicago, 1999).

[20] Most notably, Niall Ferguson, *Empire* (London 2004).

[21] For a sensitive discussion of the difficulties of applying 'class' in non-European (specifically Indian) contexts, see Rajnarain Chandavarkar, *The Origins of Industrial Capitalism* (Cambridge, 1994).

hierarchy. If it seems 'simpliste' now to lay all of the world's evils at the door of European colonizers, it is no less so to put the blame on global 'property-owners', men, or the 'white' races.

However, one concept drawn from the older toolkit might still prove to have a valuable cutting edge, even if its passing into desuetude was not without good reason. This is the concept of 'dependence' or, perhaps, 'structured difference'. Following the sociological discourse of contemporary 'globalization', global history also has become much concerned with issues of universality and particularity, of homogeneity and difference, which it handles largely in terms of interactions and adaptations between imported and indigenous or local cultures—which is fair enough, as far as it goes. But what this may miss are the ways in which some differences are structured into particular localities by coercive—if also quite subtle—means; and also how it is precisely the differences between one thing and another that are important in sustaining the individual character of each.

For example, an amazing feature of nineteenth-century Britain—amazing and puzzling, not least, to many contemporary continental Europeans—was its capacity to sustain a liberal democracy at home while, at the same time, running a despotic empire across two-fifths of the world. How did these two starkly different political profiles subsist together? The answer would seem to lie in Britain's possession of India, where it kept and built up its military forces and practised forms of authoritarian government which its rulers could only dream of at home. British rule structured India as a military barracks, a garrison state, as a complement to its own domestic liberal constitution. Similarly, Britain's ability to continue expanding its cotton textile industry, in particular in the later nineteenth century, reflected its enforced access to the Indian market. Britain and India came to have very different histories in the nineteenth century, but this was a result of the very closeness of their relationship, not their distance—social, cultural—from each other. They existed as two sides of the same coin, but each with a very different face.[22]

Now 'dependency theory' of the older kind had its problems, especially from its insistence that structures could never change, and were fixed permanently.[23] With the BRICs (Brazil, Russia, India, and China) occupying pride of place on the floors of global stock-exchanges today, that theory is

---

[22] Washbrook, 'Comparative Sociology'.
[23] Andre Gunder Frank, *The Development of Underdevelopment* (New York, 1966).

obviously mistaken. But 'dependency theory' was at least capable of appreciating relations of 'structured difference' and 'unequal exchange', which are at risk of disappearing in other approaches to global history. In the last five hundred years, much of the world may have been made 'together' out of common historical processes, but it was not made the same nor with equal life opportunities for everybody.

A third set of issues or problems for global history concerns how to appreciate and evaluate those 'life opportunities'. One of the major benefits of global history has been the way that it has rescued economic history, which was in danger of falling prey to the enormous condescension of contemporaneity and disappearing from the curriculum: a valid response, perhaps, to the suicidal efforts of econometric historians from the 1960s onwards to professionalize their discipline (i.e. make it respectable to economists) and thus render it either trivial or incomprehensible to everybody else. However, global history has helped to rescue economic history from its darkest hour and to make it relevant once again, not least in informing the present context of capitalism's greatest crisis for seventy years. It may be no exaggeration to say that through attempts to re-explore 'the Great Divergence', reassess the origins of industrialization, and re-date the history of a global economy itself, global history has made its greatest contributions so far.[24]

But must its perspective only remain confined to the economic—or even more broadly 'materialist'—dimensions of the past? What of the world of the mind, of culture, ideas, and aesthetics, which informs how various peoples came to perceive and evaluate their own lives? To some extent these issues can be approached from materialistic groundings in consumption, fashion, and taste, and global explorations in these areas have been particularly fruitful. However, we may also need a global history of the mind: necessarily an 'intellectual' rather than a 'cultural' history since the concept of 'culture', with its links back to 'structuralism' and the relativism of late nineteenth-century racism, is necessarily suspicious. But how to write a global intellectual history?

Recently, we have been offered some significant attempts. Andrew Sartori's essay on 'global concept history' seeks to examine how major intellectual debates of the nineteenth and twentieth centuries—such as that around 'the problem of culture' in the Arnoldian sense—have been

[24] Kenneth Pomeranz, *The Great Divergence* (Princeton, 2000); R. Bin Wong, *China Transformed* (Cornell, 2000).

handled across the world, in his case specifically in Bengal.[25] Equally, Chris Bayly is currently engaged in exploring the global history of 'Liberalism'.[26] Such works are enormously valuable. At the same time, however, it may be necessary to be very careful about the nature of the concepts or ideas whose global histories are being examined, if we are to avoid sliding back towards Eurocentrism. After all, in both of these cases, not only did the ideas and the debates around them originate in Europe, but so did most of the more generally recognized contributions to their elaboration. Europe, here, would also become 'provincialized' only in Chakrabarty's quite limited sense. Perhaps it would be different if the focus instead were on 'Marxism' to whose theory, at least in the twentieth century, the greatest contributions have come from non-Europeans.[27] But these days doubt has arisen regarding the significance of Marxism—and, even then, the ghost of Eurocentricity would continue to haunt the proceedings.

An alternative might be to move to a higher level of abstraction and to consider conceptual themes which were common in many different settings: to look at how they were handled in each context, how ideas crossflowed between the settings, and how dialogues became interactive. Examples might include concepts of authority and obedience, of representation and equality and, not least, of rights and obligations—where, contrary to certain views, the idea of rights was not simply the provenance of 'freeborn Englishmen'. Of course, we already have a number of comparative studies of these phenomena in particular contexts, but usually under the aegis of structuralist conceptions of culture, designed to elicit only 'difference', and with the direction of historical change presumed to flow exclusively from West to East.[28] However, in my own field of India, recent research has suggested much wider possibilities. The works of Perlin, Guha, and O'Hanlon, for example, have drawn attention to the strong 'rights-based' political culture of pre-colonial western India.[29] Here,

---

[25] Andrew Sartori, *Bengal in Global Concept History* (Chicago, 2008).
[26] C. A. Bayly and E. F. Biagini (eds), *Guiseppe Mazzini and the Globalization of Democratic Nationalism 1830–1920* (Oxford, 2008).
[27] E.g., Mao Tse-Tung, Ho Chi Min.
[28] For example, Louis Dumont, *Homo Hierarchicus* (London, 1970).
[29] Frank Perlin, 'State Formation Reconsidered', *Modern Asian Studies*, 19/3 (1985), 415–80; Sumit Guha, 'Wrongs and Rights in the Maratha Country', in *Changing Conceptions of Law and Justice in South Asia*, ed. Michael Anderson and Sumit Guha (Delhi, 1997); Rosalind O'Hanlon, 'Cultural Pluralism, the State and Empire in Early Modern South Asia', *Indian Economic and Social History Review*, 44/3 (2007), 363–81.

individual rights were partially seen to derive from membership of specific (caste, religious, and ethnic) communities which collectively held statuses, identities, and real properties. Such a conception of rights came to inform the evolution of colonial—Anglo-Hindu—law, which by no means consisted only of the imposition of 'alien', Western nostrums. Indeed, it may even have affected the development of law in Western metropolises themselves.

In Britain, the law was very slow to move beyond a context of universal sovereignty and atomized, individualized rights to recognize the claims of a cultural pluralism in which different communities of subjects might be seen to have legitimately different prerogatives and needs—for all that medieval law had operated precisely on these principles in the distant past.[30] Arguably, it was not until the 1960s that British domestic law considered issues of 'positive discrimination' and differential religious obligation.[31] However, when it did, it is striking that the context should coincide with a major influx of migrants from the former colonial world, bringing with them their own ideas of right and re-creating in Britain something of the 'multiculturalism' that marked most colonial contexts. It is tempting to consider how far the discourse of rights in contemporary Britain draws on concepts taken from members of the 'other cultures' now inhabiting its space, and also on the experience of handling 'multi-culturalism' in the societies that Britain once attempted to rule. The Empire finally strikes back... Conventional forms of intellectual history have told us what Europe has given to the rest of the world. Maybe it is now time for a global intellectual history to tell us what the rest of the world is giving to Europe and, albeit at a remove, giving back to itself as well.

---

[30] Alfred P. Smyth (ed.), *Medieval Europeans* (New York, 1998).
[31] James Hand, 'A Decade of Change in British Discrimination Law', *Commonwealth Law Review*, 43/3 (2008), 595–605.

3
Reflections on doing global history

JAN DE VRIES

My path to global history

Global history is, it appears, a house of many mansions. At one level, up in the penthouse, it manifests itself as the history of globalization, and of mega-processes of global integration. At another—perhaps the ground floor—it focuses on transnational interactions, often of rather modest scale and scope. In between, one finds room for the study of little 'worlds' whose borders often cut through the familiar political borders. It offers accommodation for quite a bit of history, but not—it seems—for the established concept of world history.[1] If world history is a study of civilizations and state comparisons in a spirit of inclusion—a project of pedagogical reform more than of historical research—then global history is, at its various levels, the study of process at work in, or latent in, a sphere beyond, or even beneath, the state.

The study of the global directs our attention to a history that operates at levels not confined by the boundaries of the national state and that is

---

[1] Most historians who have been drawn to a world history—world, and not global history—have been most interested in it as a project of curriculum and pedagogical reform. In the United States its advocates present it as a history better suited to the contemporary world and to the objectives of progressive politics than the 'Western Civilization' courses that emerged some fifty years ago to arm young Americans with the knowledge needed to cope with the post-war world.

Still, in my experience at Berkeley, this has not been sufficient to persuade even the most politically correct of my colleagues to overcome their misgivings as professional historians about the amateur foundations of world history. World History is taught at Berkeley, but the courses are not run by the History department, which offers instead introductory courses on the history of nearly every continent/civilization on the planet. But perhaps global history offers a remedy to this problem. It aspires to be not a pedagogical project but a platform for historical research.

potentially global in reach. According to globalization's deep thinkers this *consciousness of globality*—'the idea that human beings inhabit a unitary and finite space, move along the same temporal scale of world-historical time, and constitute one single collective entity'— is as necessary as any specific facts of large-scale history in order to speak of a global history.[2]

Whether I have the requisite consciousness or not, I have always been intrigued by non-national units of historical analysis; chronicling the 'rise of the state' has never been my interest. As an undergraduate I wrote a senior thesis on the political economy of the spring wheat district, a vast region in the heart of North America divided in two roughly equal parts by the US–Canadian border. A single and peculiar political movement spread across this region, establishing political organizations in states and provinces alike. The forty-ninth parallel did not confine it, yet it had no purchase beyond the boundaries of the spring wheat zone itself. Even now, I think this an interesting subject; the United States has more than one 'borderland'. My first book, *The Dutch Rural Economy in the Golden Age*, was actually about the rural economy of an ecological zone extending through a part of the Netherlands and into neighbouring countries. Later, my study of *European Urbanization* traced the development of an international network of cities in which national boundaries were of only secondary importance. Indeed, it was among my intentions to show that the networks formed by cities commonly spilled over national borders and, in fact, could constrain state sovereignties.

Still, I never thought these works—were they transnational studies *avant la lettre?*—were related to a global history. And, as I think back on the many volumes of Annales School history I digested in earlier decades, they seem to fall into two categories: studies of regions, or towns and their regions (Languedoc, Burgundy, Beauvaisis, Amiens, Caen), and studies of Braudelian 'worlds' (the Mediterranean, the Spanish Atlantic). They were all units of analysis either bigger or smaller than the state. But these studies did not really speak to each other. 'They were presented as histories that are disconnected, with their backs to each other', not as intertwined histories.[3]

---

[2] David Armitage, 'Is There a Pre-history of Globalization', in *Comparison and History: Europe in Cross-National Perspective*, ed. Deborah Cohen and Maura O'Connor (London, 2004), p. 169. For other pronouncements on global consciousness, see Bruce Mazlish and Ralph Buultjens (eds), *Conceptualizing Global History* (Boulder, CO, 1993).

[3] Bartolomé Yun Casalilla, 'Localism, Global History and Transnational History: A Reflection from the Historian of Early Modern Europe', *Historisk Tidskrift*, 127 (2007), 665.

These non-national scales of historical study, valuable as they no doubt are, offer, in my view, no royal road to global history. The most that can be said for histories of regions and 'worlds' is that their boundaries are not a given or a starting point; rather, they are themselves an object of curiosity, a contingent historical fact that invites questions that lead potentially to the study of the connections and subtle interrelationships that appear to be the stuff of global history.

If the non-state boundary-line drawing that has fascinated me also diverted me from the contemplation of the global in history, an interest in early modern international trade certainly did lead towards the conceptual framework of globalization as a means of analysing the achievements and the failures of European long-distance trade, especially with Asia.[4] I will return to the concept of globalization later, but will pause here to consider briefly our options in approaching the history of trade from a global perspective. Contagion (or contact), convergence, and system (or network) are three organizing concepts that are commonly applied to the study of global trade; each has its strengths and weaknesses.[5]

Contagion refers to the consequences of contact on previously isolated social entities. The 'Columbian Exchange' (the introduction of Old World crops, livestock, etc. to the New World and vice versa) is perhaps the best-known example of contagion in the realm of trade.[6] Shocks of this sort give rise to disruption and destabilization of the affected societies, but also to syncretism, adaptation, and creativity. This concept is obviously of great importance in global history, but it affords only a partial view of trade, which is inherently an ongoing relationship, while contagion refers to either the initiation of trade, or to notable innovations that diffuse through existing trading systems—that is, to contacts and shocks.[7]

Convergence is central to economists' definitions of globalization, and is of obvious relevance to global history, which is premised, at least implicitly, on the vision of a long-term intensification of relations among

---

[4] Jan de Vries, 'Connecting Europe and Asia: A Quantitative Analysis of the Cape-Route Trade, 1497–1795', in *Global Connections and Monetary History, 1470–1800*, ed. Dennis Flynn, Arturo Giraldez, and Richard Von Glahn (Aldershot, 2003), pp. 35–106; 'The Limits of Globalization in the Early Modern World', *Economic History Review*, 63 (2010), 710–33.
[5] For more on these categories of global analysis, see: Pamela K. Crossley, *What is Global History?* (Cambridge, 2008).
[6] Alfred Crosby, *The Columbian Exchange: Biological and Cultural Consequences of 1492* (Westport, CT, 1972); *Ecological Imperialism: The Biological Expansion of Europe, 900–1900* (Cambridge, 1986).
[7] William H. McNeill, *Plagues and Peoples* (Garden City, NY, 1976).

peoples. It is similarly central to the notion that the growth of trade is directly related to the reduction of the cost of distance, whether through technological, organizational, institutional, or political means. It is therefore tempting to base global history within a framework of a growth of intercontinental trade.[8] The thirteenth-century establishment of a *Pax Mongolica* over the Eurasian silk route and, even more, the sixteenth-century construction of a globe-girdling seaborne trade by the Iberian powers speak to the imagination of the global historian. But, as Daniel Cohen cautions, 'Reducing the costs of distance does not [necessarily] bring either people or wealth any closer. It tends, moreover, to heighten the polarity between the center and the periphery.'[9] That is, convergence differentiates as well as homogenizes, but it is heavily implicated in teleological visions of long-term historical change. In theory, convergence is a neutral concept; any part of the world can converge with any other part through trade. In practice, convergence is far from a random phenomenon; with whom one is converging can make all the difference. This brings us to the third approach to a trade-based history.

Trade of any complexity is organized in networks, circuits, or systems, and these networks are coordinated from some point: seasonal gathering places, fortified strongholds, religious institutions, or cities. Trading networks may be rudimentary and rather isolated, but as they grow and connect with other such networks, one can imagine them forming extensive organized complexities, leading, at the limit, to a world-embracing system. In this sense global history reveals the extent and the limits of networks of regularly recurring contact and interaction. An extensive historiography approaches large-scale history in this way. Henri Pirenne's famous thesis about the emergence of Western Europe under Charlemagne was founded on a decisive disruption of long-standing Mediterranean trade networks; Janet Abu-Lughod described the Eurasian articulation of multiple overlapping regional trading systems before the 'age of discoveries'; Fernand Braudel described the European *economie-monde* as an expanding trading world organized around dominant cities, with infrequent, turbulent crises (decentrings and recentrings) as one city succeeded another as the centre

---

[8] This is the premise of Jeffrey G. Williamson and Kevin O'Rourke, 'After Columbus: Explaining Europe's Overseas Trade Boom, 1500–1800', *Journal of Economic History*, 62 (2002), 417–56; 'When Did Globalization Begin?', *European Review of Economic History*, 6 (2002), 23–50.

[9] Daniel Cohen, *Globalization and its Enemies* (Cambridge, MA, 2007), p. 77.

of international trade and finance.[10] Finally, Immanuel Wallerstein established 'world-systems' as a body of theory about how the globe came to be organized in core and peripheral regions and multiple 'world' economies.[11]

While this appears to lead us confidently towards the global, few of the scholars who study trade networks actually took their work in this direction. Trade networks reveal patterns of exchange and interaction, but they also reveal patterns of power.[12] Braudel and Wallerstein may have exaggerated the coercive aspects of trade, but it is difficult to avoid the fact that international trade was not a domain in which everyone had equal agency. While this may be a reasonable working hypothesis in studies focused on contagion or convergence, the study of trade networks, certainly after the fifteenth century, inevitably leads us to power centres, usually European centres. Indeed, international trade is one of a triad of features repeatedly invoked as the foundation of European exceptionalism. The autonomous merchant-controlled city, the fragmented sovereignty of feudal polities, and the escape of trade from the suffocating embrace of the state form, in work stretching from Max Weber via Henri Pirenne to Charles Tilly, a persuasive historical narrative that long has stood in the path of globalist accounts of the international economy.

In sum, the study of trade history certainly leads us to the world, and arguably towards an understanding of globalization, but not necessarily to a global history that creates an alternative to the overly familiar Eurocentric meta-narratives. Thus, while my work as a historian has almost always eschewed national themes, and has been drawn repeatedly to border crossing historical phenomena, it would not be correct to state that this has led me towards 'histories of the global'. It appears to me that important problems, both practical and conceptual, still adhere to a warranted practice of global history. I turn now to several of them.

---

[10] Henri Pirenne, *Mohammed and Charlemagne* (New Haven, CT, 1959); Janet Abu-Lughod, *Before European Hegemony: The World System AD 1250–1350* (Oxford, 1989); Fernand Braudel, *Civilization and Capitalism*, trans. Sian Reynolds, 3 vols (New York, 1984–92).

[11] Immanuel Wallerstein, *The Modern World System: Capitalist Agriculture and the Origins of the European World Economy in the Sixteenth Century* (New York, 1974).

[12] A recent comprehensive history of international trade, written by economists (Kevin O'Rourke and Ronald Findlay) with no attachment to either Braudelian or Wallersteinian traditions, was given the title: *Power and Plenty: Trade, War and the World Economy in the Second Millennium* (Princeton, 2007).

What is so great about global history?

Is global history possible as an academic enterprise?

This question has a narrower focus than it appears. I do not mean to suggest that scholars should not or cannot speculate fruitfully about historical processes at the highest, or global, level. The question is whether academic historical research is possible at this level. It is by now a cliché to observe that large-scale world histories had been common enough from the time of the Enlightenment to the early twentieth century. This, of course, was mostly the work of amateurs.[13] Professional history is grounded in archival, documentary evidence. It is firmly anchored in nation states and other, subsidiary, institutions that maintain archives. To be sure, historians succeeded long ago in breaking loose from the national and institutional focus of the Rankean project, but this has led most of them towards microhistory and cultural histories. The archives remain foundational; however, the documents they contain are now read differently. If this leads in any direction, it is away from histories of the global.[14]

It would go too far to say that global historical research is altogether without archival resources. Multinational organizations may appear to be phenomena of recent date, but the great trading companies of early modern Europe and many religious institutions offer possibilities that, to the uninitiated, are hidden by easy assumptions of economic and cultural imperialism. The extensive archives of the Dutch East India Company, with its trading establishments stretching from Cape Town to Nagasaki, have supported research that strays far from the commercial mission of the company.[15] Similarly, the records of Protestant missionaries, now being

---

[13] Gilbert Allardyce, 'Toward World History: American Historians and the Coming of the World History Course', *Journal of World History*, 1 (1990), 23–76. 'As the practice of history became professional, the practice of world history became identified with amateurism' (p. 5). Pamela K. Crossley states matter-of-factly: 'Global history is not history in the normal sense of the word, it is historiography—the study of the writing of history' in *What is Global History?*, p. 103. See also: Patrick O'Brien, 'Historiographical Traditions and Modern Imperatives for the Restoration of Global History', *Journal of Global History*, 1 (2006), 3–39.

[14] For a discussion of how 'normalized', professional world history research might be conducted, see: Patrick Manning, 'Methods and Materials', in *Palgrave Advances in World Histories*, ed. Marnie Hughes-Warrington (Basingstoke, 2005), pp. 44–63.

[15] While the Dutch company, the VOC, was the largest of them in the seventeenth and eighteenth centuries, valuable archives also have survived for the English, French, Danish, and Swedish companies.

exploited in the promising field of missiology, are capable of addressing secular as well as religious themes.[16]

The paths towards larger-scale history are, it seems to me, three in number:

(1) comparative history
(2) the study of connections and other diachronic interactions
(3) synthetic interpretive histories establishing meta-narratives.

The first and third are largely the domains of non-historians—sociologists, political scientists, anthropologists, economists—and senior historians who can permit themselves indulgences of this sort.[17] Comparative history, while useful, if not essential, to many historical questions (Marc Bloch famously asserted that 'all history is comparative history'), is commonly used to emphasize the special features of a nation's history, leading to its further essentialization.[18] This might be indispensable to world history, but I doubt that comparative history offers a road to true global history. My negative assessment would need amendment if a comparative method could be developed that did not 'privilege' one nation, culture, or civilization as a standard for comparison. It was Kenneth Pomeranz's goal, in *The Great Divergence*, to do just this by deploying what he called 'reciprocal comparisons'. He dispensed with the Eurocentric comparisons with which we are all familiar, a notable achievement, but did he locate a firm foundation from which to establish what was comparable and what was not in his study of the far ends of

---

[16] See the new journal, *Global Missiology*. David Hollinger, 'After Cloven Tongues of Fire: Ecumenical Protestantism and the Modern American Encounter with Diversity', *Journal of American History* 98 (2011), 21–48.

[17] Diego Olstein, 'Defining the History of Globalization: Defining World and Global History', Global History Globally conference, Harvard University, 8–9 February 2008; Georg G. Iggers and Q. Edward Wang, *A Global History of Modern Historiography* (London, 2008).

[18] Perhaps the most influential comparative-historical study in economic history is Alexander Gerschenkron's *Economic Backwardness in Historical Perspective* (Cambridge, MA, 1962). By comparing the patterns of economic development in nineteenth-century Britain, Germany, and Russia, Gerschenkron created a dynamic model of the development process (arguably, a contribution to global understanding), but this was based on a hierarchical order determined by the unique and essential characteristics of each nation.

Eurasia?[19] Pending further refinement of the methodology of comparative history, it appears that the second path—the study of connections and diachronic interactions—is that by which historians are most likely to move towards global themes. These works can be illuminating and certainly evocative, but this is an approach with distinct limitations, to which I will return.[20]

A final reflection on global history as an academic enterprise. We would, I believe, not be entertaining the notion of global history were it not for the special role of English as a global language. This lingua franca unites the 'global' community of scholars and reaches the 'global' audience. A particular historical conjuncture now gives those with confident access to the 'global language' the capacity to develop global history—or perhaps one should say a globalist discourse.[21]

Global history is flat

Global history is flat in the same way the journalist Tom Friedman claims that globalization causes the world to be flat. He argues that the combined influence of the internet (and modern information technologies more generally) and the end of the Cold War (and socialist ideologies more generally) introduced a new historical era, the era of globalization.[22]

---

[19] Kenneth Pomeranz, *The Great Divergence: China, Europe, and the Making of the Modern World Economy* (Princeton, 2000), pp. 3–27. For a critique of 'reciprocal comparison' see: Jan de Vries, '*The Great Divergence* after Ten Years: Justly Celebrated Yet Hard to Believe', *Historically Speaking*, 12 (2011), 13–15. For a more theoretically grounded comparative analysis of the institutions of Western Europe and China see: Jean-Laurent Rosenthal and R. Bin Wong, *Before and Beyond Divergence: The Politics of Economic Change in China and Europe* (Cambridge, MA, 2011).

[20] Examples: John E. Wills, Jr., *1688: A Global History* (New York, 2001); John and William McNeill, *The Human Web: A Bird's-Eye View of World History* (New York, 2003); Timothy Brook, *Vermeer's Hat: The Seventeenth Century and the Dawn of the Global World* (New York, 2008); Sanjay Subrahmanyam, *Explorations in Connected History: From the Tagus to the Ganges* (Oxford, 2005).

[21] I owe this observation about the special place of the English language to Bartolomé Yun Casalilla, 'Localism, Global History and Transnational History', 657–78. It leads to the further, epistemologically more difficult, problem of how this intellectual enterprise, thus far primarily a product of Western scholars, can overcome the 'paradox of self-reference'.

[22] Tom Friedman, *The Lexus and the Olive Tree: Understanding Globalization* (New York, 2000), pp. xi–xxii; *The World is Flat: A Brief History of the Twenty-First Century* (New York, 2005). Friedman's dating is based on the premise that the simultaneous coming of the internet and the end of the Cold War established the new era of globalization.

Not only is the world flat, it 'is ten years old' (that is, Friedman believed it emerged in 1990). His view is only a dramatic popularization of the most influential academic statement on the concept of globalization. David Held et al., in *Global Transformations*, are gracious enough to concede that globalization has a history, but they regard its contemporary manifestations as displaying 'unparalleled qualitative differences ... The contemporary epoch is historically unique.'[23] If globalization specifically defines the contemporary condition of human society, then global history properly addresses the study of contemporary history as a singular temporal unit. We *can* study it now, because of our new consciousness of 'spaceship earth', a perspective that could only emerge once astronauts could take the first pictures of the earth in its entirety—and in its round globality.[24] We *must* study it now, following Held et al., because its characteristic state-constraining forces are eroding the internal/external distinctions that were the foundation of the social sciences predicated on the 'Westphalian Model'.[25] In short, global history is flat because it is brief; it is the history of the current moment.

Such a truncated definition of global history is, of course, not designed to appeal to historians. But there is a second way in which global history is flat, and this is not the contribution of ahistorical journalists, sociologists, and political scientists, but of historians themselves. An approach—perhaps the dominant approach—to global history regards it as constituted by connections. That is, the global is not simply a level of analysis, a means to study the past on the largest scale. The global is the object of study and it is constituted through interactions; 'its specificity inheres in its relational quality ... It involves exploring interstices, overlappings, interpenetrations, interdependencies and circulations—of

---

[23] David Held, Anthony G. McGrew, David Goldblatt, and Jonathan Perraton, *Global Transformations: Politics, Economics and Culture* (Stanford, CA, 1999), p. 425. This explicit emphasis on globalization as the hallmark of the contemporary era goes back further still in cultural studies. See: Arjun Appadurai, *Modernity at Large: Cultural Dimensions of Globalization* (Minneapolis, 1996).
[24] Mazlish and Buultjens (eds), *Conceptualizing Global History*.
[25] Held et al., *Global Transformations*; see also Jan Aart Scholte, *Globalization: A Critical Introduction* (New York, 2000). For critiques of this linkage of globalization with 'extraterritoriality', see Paul Hirst and Grahame Thompson, *Globalization in Question* (Malden, MA, 1999), and Michael Lang, 'Globalization and its History', *Journal of Modern History*, 78 (2006), 98–105.

persons, objects, practices, bodies of knowledge, etc., among different scenes.'[26]

A global history that consists of a focus on the horizontal—on *transfergeschichte, métissage, histoire croisée* [entangled histories], reciprocity, and circulation—feeds a very modern, or rather, postmodern impulse. This is the impulse to eschew grand narrative as something that is simultaneously beyond belief and morally dubious, and to concentrate instead 'upon microhistories of difference, diversity, locality, biography . . .' that offer what Dipesh Chakrabarty calls 'a loving grasp of detail in search of the diversity of human life worlds'.[27] It also feeds an idealistic impulse that is very strong in the contemporary West (I doubt that it is a global impulse). Timothy Brook articulates this impulse in his recent study of 'the dawn of the global world' as a need to persuade humankind of its mutual interconnectedness. Among the aims of his book, *Vermeer's Hat*, was: 'Knowing that we as a species need to figure out how to narrate the past in a way that enables us to acknowledge and come to terms with the global nature of our experience.'[28]

Histories of connection—of interactions and the intensification of interactions—give agency to all parties, to everyone in the world. Such an approach eases the task of decentring established narratives, incorporating suppressed voices, and uncovering unsuspected influences. But they do so in a narrow, horizontal temporal plane. The resulting insights may have utterly charming hermeneutic possibilities, but they are otherwise incapacitated by their rich and loving flatness. I doubt that they can really enable us to escape the chaos of the present moment, which many still regard to be history's task.

To some, this incapacity is nothing to deplore. It promises a liberation; a liberation from the burden of history, perhaps, but certainly a liberation

---

[26] Bénédicte Zimmermann, '*Histoire Croisée* and the Fabric of Global History', paper presented at Global History> Globally conference, Harvard University, 8–9 February 2008, p. 1; Michael Werner and Bénédicte Zimmermann, 'Beyond Comparisons: *Histoire Croisée* and the Challenge of Reflexivity', *History and Theory*, 45 (2006), 30–50; Serge Gruzinski, *Les quartre parties du monde: Histoire d'une mondialisation* (Paris, 2004). Patrick Manning, a pioneering and influential figure in the World History movement, defines World History as 'The study of connections between communities and between communities and their environments' in *Navigating World History: Historians Create a Global Past* (Basingstoke, 2003), p. 15.

[27] Patrick O'Brien, 'Historiographical Traditions', p. 35. Dipesh Chakrabarty, *Provincializing Europe: Postcolonial Thought and Historical Difference* (Princeton, 2000), p. 18.

[28] Brook, *Vermeer's Hat*, p. 221.

from uncongenial historical narratives. If the future cannot be what we had hoped for and expected, then the past might still be what we would like it to have been. But does global history really offer fresh perspectives, or does it simply hide, underneath its fashionable coat of many colours, the same old, oppressive master narrative? A history based on the agency of everyone leads to a consciousness of commonalities. But what if the agency of some is really more potent than that of others, and what if human actions, channelled through myriad institutions, ideologies, and interests, are not in fact guided by a quest for commonalities? If the task of the history of the global is to prepare us for a toleration of difference—or cosmopolitanism—rather than a consciousness of connectedness—or universalism—it will, in my view, need something more than 'flat history'.[29]

This 'something more' involves establishing a basis on which the local can be connected to, or integrated into, the global. An 'entangled history', no matter how thick the description, does not achieve this by itself.[30]

Does global history banish Eurocentrism and modernization theory to the dustbin of history?

If world and global histories do not challenge Eurocentric historical narratives they do nothing. But many of these critiques, however illuminating and persuasive, replace Eurocentrism with what we might call Eurasia-centrism, and, often enough with Sinocentrism. Eurasia has long been home to a substantial majority of the world's people, and it is here we find the ancient agrarian civilizations. One need not apologize for studying its history: a big step in the right direction, one might say. But what we now have falls well short of displacing the old narratives. It dresses them in more attractive outer garments.

Consider two influential exercises in Eurasian history: *The Great Divergence* and *After Tamerlane*.

The 'California School' focuses on a bipolar Eurasia oriented around (portions of) China and Western Europe. Its basic premise is the long-term equivalence of material culture, institutional effectiveness, and economic performance in the two zones. On this foundation all arguments based on

---

[29] On cosmopolitanism and universalism, see the introduction to A. G. Hopkins (ed.), *Global History: Interactions Between the Universal and the Local* (Basingstoke, 2006), pp. 1–38

[30] Clifford Geertz, 'Thick Description and Interpretive Theory in Culture', in *The Interpretation of Culture: Selected Essays* (New York, 1973), pp. 3–31.

European exceptionalism are swept aside, since they propose making distinctions of kind where only distinctions of degree—variants on a common theme—are permitted.

In *The Great Divergence*, Kenneth Pomeranz argues along these lines until his narrative approaches 1800, when the long-enduring global balance is suddenly and dramatically lost. The resulting 'great divergence' is, he argues, unrelated to any of the preceding equivalent, or commensurate, events and processes—since their possible pregnancy with long-run consequences has been ruled out already. It is explained by invoking, in the manner of a deus ex machina, England's unique access to coal and to the resources of the New World—as though these were new phenomena—which suddenly released it from the Malthusian/environmental pressures then facing China and the rest of Eurasia. Surely, a truly global history would endogenize this phenomenon rather than leave it as a coincident, albeit world-changing, event?[31]

John Darwin's *After Tamerlane* also has a Eurasian scope of analysis, but its task remains, when all is said and done, to account for the 'rise of the West'. Darwin's point of orientation is central Asia rather than Pomeranz's perspective from the lower Yangzi Delta, but the overall vision is similar: an equilibrium among expansive states, equivalent if not equal, is swept away between the 1750s and the 1830s by a 'Eurasian Revolution' that 'opened the road for an imperial order in which European control was riveted on the rest of the globe'.[32] But, of course, this 'revolution' was not Eurasian—and this made all the difference. In global histories of this sort, ample and complementary recognition is given to the resilience of the various Eurasian states and cultures, but the story ends as it had before, and with explanations drawn from the same bag of tricks that had long stood at the side of more Eurocentric or, more correctly, Anglocentric historians.

The general problem that continues to adhere to the postmodern impulse in global history is how to make good the commitment to banish the centrisms and hierarchies that exclude and marginalize. No historical project can escape the necessity of selectivity. Simply rejecting the selection

---

[31] Pomeranz, *Great Divergence*, Part 3. For discussion and critique of the exogeneity of Pomeranz's explanatory device, see Peter Coclanis, Jan de Vries, Philip Hoffman, R. Bin Wong, and Kenneth Pomeranz, 'Assessing Kenneth Pomeranz's *The Great Divergence*: A Forum', *Historically Speaking*, 12 (2011), 10–25.

[32] John Darwin, *After Tamerlane: The Global History of Empire since 1405* (New York, 2008), p. 160.

criteria suggested by the existing grand narratives of modern Western history is not sufficient as a basis for going forward. Put differently, if as Roland Barthes and Jacques Derrida argue, there is no past 'out there' waiting to be discovered, but only an empty space waiting to be filled, then global history has the same obligation as any other type of history to state and defend the basis on which it furnishes its empty rooms.[33]

Modernization and globalization

We would be less interested in writing the 'history of the global' if we did not believe that the world is experiencing 'globalization'. Likewise, our preferences about how global history should be approached, and to what end, are shaped by our understanding of globalization as a historical phenomenon. [34] Consider the following definitions of this ubiquitous yet elusive term:

(1) Globalization 'is about shifting forms of human contact' leading towards greater interdependence and integration, such that the time and space aspects of social relations become compressed. It is characterized by the stretching of social connections between the local and the distant resulting in 'the intensification of the world as a whole'. This, in turn, relativizes the territorial borders of the nation state, creating 'superterritoriality'.[35]
(2) Globalization proceeds once 'all major zones of the world are connected by permanent trade links' and 'exchange products continuously ... and on a scale that generated deep and lasting impacts on all trading partners'.[36]

---

[33] See the discussion of Barthes and Derrida, among others, in Richard J. Evans, *In Defense of History* (New York, 1999), p. 81. Patrick O'Brien's essay launching the *Journal of Global History* recognized the importance of this problem, and suggested that global history's great task was to construct 'negotiable meta-narratives'. It remains to be seen what this can be in practice. Patrick O'Brien, 'Historiographical Traditions', p. 3.

[34] I cannot go into the definitions of globalization in any detail here. See my discussion in: Jan de Vries, 'The Limits of Globalization in the Early Modern World', pp. 710–33.

[35] This statement is a synthesis of comparable definitions offered by Manfred Steger, *Globalization: A Very Short Introduction* (Oxford, 2003), p. 8; Jan Aart Scholte, *Globalization: A Critical Introduction* (New York, 2000); Anthony Giddens, *The Consequences of Modernity* (Stanford, CA, 1990), p. 64.

[36] D. O. Flynn and A. Giraldez, 'Path Dependence, Time Lags, and the Birth of Globalization: A Critique of O'Rourke and Williamson', *European Review of Economic History*, 8 (2004), 83.

The second, Flynn and Giraldez's definition, is focused on economic connections leading to internal transformations of the entities connected—that are 'on the grid', so to speak. The first, the Steger-Giddens-Scholte definition, encompasses a fuller range of connections; it looks towards a 'deterritorialization' of social interactions at levels ranging from the individual to the state. The trade-based definition invokes a process that has long had a central place in all narratives of European economic and political hegemony, that traces its origins to the sixteenth-century 'age of discovery', and that had, arguably, a prehistory or protohistory of even greater antiquity. The definition that focuses on space–time compression has a more restricted historical reach. At the extreme, it collapses to Friedman's breathless proclamation that the world is 'ten years old'. But, if we move from consciousness to action—to the 'globalizing entities' of Chris Bayly, the economic policies and practices that reduce transaction costs, the institutions that distribute information and knowledge, etc.—do we not encounter that disreputable relic of Western social theory, modernization theory?[37] Put slightly differently: is there not, behind the flat window of the global, an operating system? And does this operating system not guide and shape the connections and interactions visible on the windows screen with—to change metaphors in midstream—what we recognize as the grand narrative of social betterment, the Western project asserting the possibility of progress in human affairs?

Whether the global can only be approached by contemplating the modern, whether globalization is simply today's manifestation of modernization, depends on our basic model of globalization. The available models point to different historical antecedents, different revolutions setting mankind on a globalizing path. The *promise* of a global history—as opposed to histories of civilizations, empires, etc.—is an escape from teleology. 'Globality has no goal, and it entails no normative implications for governance.'[38] But the *reality*, I believe, falls well short of this.

---

[37] C. A. Bayly, *The Birth of the Modern World, 1780–1914* (Oxford, 2004); A. G. Hopkins (ed.), *Globalization in World History* (London, 2002). Both authors describe the world's early modern empires as 'globalizing entities'—managers of large, expansive social systems that propel globalization. Lang observes that, for both Bayly and Hopkins, 'in the nineteenth century this empire form of globalization was reconfigured into a new global system of states'. Lang, 'Globalization and its History', p. 921.

[38] Lang, 'Globalization and its History', p. 929.

Periodization and narratives of global history

Let me turn, finally, to periodizations appropriate to global history. This is really simply another way to address global narrative—for what counts as a fundamental turning point in history, depends on the master narrative.

To begin, I must note that the numerous revolutions that populate national histories tend to fade from view when our focus is fixed upon the global. What sorts of historical phenomena remain important—or, perhaps, reveal an importance invisible to non-global forms of historical analyses?

It stands to reason that the revolutions of global history are those great events that advance globalization. Since this term enjoys no globally accepted definition, no consensus list of such events can now be proposed. But, simplifying greatly, it is possible to identify two broad tendencies, each with significant implications for the identification of origins, turning points, and hence periodization.

Globalization is an 'organized complexity'

For the economist who looks to market forces that lead to price convergence across space, and for the historian celebrating universal agency and the resulting emergence of webs of connection, interaction, and hybridity, globalization is a product of multiple forces, none of which acted with the intention of securing the ultimate outcome. A Smithian invisible hand guides this history. Diego Olstein labels this deus ex machina globalization, and notes that 'power has no say in it. Or, rather, when power appears globalization is banished.'[39]

At its extreme limits, globalization as organized complexity can have no unique origin or catalysing events. In a more historicized version, it *does* have specific origins: 'globalizing entities' (states, religions) act to penetrate, organize, connect, and control global space. They *aim* to advance an agenda through the assertion of power, but in their interactions with each other they *achieve* something unintended and unforeseen. Here power and hierarchy are critical to the launch of the project—especially the power of European empires—but they do not ultimately define what they set in motion. In short, imperial history is the path that merges into global history.

[39] Diego Olstein, 'Defining the History of Globalization: Defining World and Global History', paper presented at Global History > Globally conference, Harvard University, 8–9 February 2008.

Such a history can be congenial to the reformed, recycled historian of colonialism and imperialism. Thus, nineteenth-century globalization was a project of European empires, collapsing after 1914. Modern globalization began after the Second World War as an effort to reconstitute and update that regime, which then morphed willy-nilly—a la Friedman—into a flat world: the unique, unprecedented contemporary moment.[40]

Globalization is a path-dependent process

For the historian or social scientist who remains under the influence of Western social theory, contemporary globality is largely a product of European trade, empire, and settlement. These processes, launched by events unfolding between 1492 and 1571, established the patterns, institutions, knowledge, etc. that conditioned *all subsequent forms* taken by globalization.[41] Global connections are not sustained by themselves. They depend on power, especially hegemonic power, which, by definition, is a power capable of providing the 'public goods' needed for the operation of the international system as a whole.[42]

A globalization launched and presided over by the West does not imply that it will always remain so dominated. It can develop and change. But it cannot change in any old way: it is path-dependent upon the European intellectual, scientific, and institutional traditions that are at the base—that furnish the DNA—of the historiography of globalization. This should not be interpreted to mean that only one future path is possible, but that new developments build on the paths already taken.

Here the task of global history may be to provide a kind of solace—inclusion of others into the story of the path they are on whether they like it or not.

---

[40] A cynic might argue that an appreciation of the unity of humankind and its interdependence gained in appeal when it became clear that a Europe-centred world history could no longer be sustained. After the eclipse of the European empires, one could embrace a world in which 'nothing of importance can avoid affecting everyone, everywhere' or admit that a bipolar power system held the world in its cold embrace. After 1989–91 the choices became even more constrained and less appealing. The claims of globalism gained in appeal.

[41] A classic example: I. Wallerstein's 'world systems' approach.

[42] Patrick O'Brien, 'The Pax Britannica and the International Order, 1688–1914', in *Looking Back at the 20th Century: The Role of Hegemonic States and the Transformation of the Modern World-System*, ed. Shigeru Akita and Takeshi Matsuda (Osaka, 2000), 44–5. According to O'Brien, the public goods provided by the British Empire included 'peace, safe access to international waterways, international law for the protection of property rights, an open regime for foreign trade, and an international monetary system'.

4
Notes on some discontents in the historical narrative

JEAN-FRÉDÉRIC SCHAUB

European historians and ethnocentric narratives

To what extent are European researchers still able to think about the postcolonial paradigm and the new frontier of world history? Such a question may seem to be pointless or even impertinent. Nonetheless, what are now seen as classic statements by Dipesh Chakrabarty and Ranajit Guha, and, more recently, Jack Goody's exposition of the theft of history, have been indicting European scholars in global terms.[1] Old World scholars appear to be intellectually disabled, if not morally so, due to their political, cultural, and scientific situation. The political and moral legacies of the former European colonial empires are indeed indelible. Does this mean that European scholars cannot participate in the critique of scientific Eurocentrism, as a consequence of colonization and as a source of it at the same time? Does the colonial heritage disqualify analytic ambition?

The author's point of view begins with his experience as a French scholar. It provides the reader with a large, if partial and, of course, not exclusive, array of references of French research. The aim of the chapter is to propose a series of tentative answers to these questions, raised more than twenty years ago. Part of the charge of Eurocentrism originally came from literary criticism, but it derived much more significantly from anthropology. Situating the case of literary criticism requires an account of its abandonment of structural analysis, and its refusal to come back to a

---

[1] Dipesh Chakrabarty, *Provincializing Europe: Postcolonial Thought and Historical Difference* (Princeton, 2000); Ranajit Guha, *History at the Limit of World-History* (New York, 2002); Jack Goody, *The Theft of History* (Cambridge and New York, 2006).

traditional history of literature. With anthropology, the case is different. The discipline, at its core, was invented for challenging historical narrative in its classical form. In this sense, the history of the critique of historical Euro- and state-centred narratives is an old story. In France, for example, Marcel Mauss's and the young Lévi-Strauss's work, in the 1920s and the 1930s, deconstructed the illusions of mainstream republican and nationalist historiography. Eighty years ago, anthropology demonstrated how much the evolutionist schema, that is, the conception of a universal path to modernity among human societies, had been the main sanctuary of ethnocentrism. The critique of the evolutionist paradigm had weakened the historical narrative of a unique process of civilization led by the Europeans.[2] Closely tied to the anthropologists' discussion, historians joined the movement.[3] *Nihil novi sub sole* (is nothing new), in this very field? Perhaps the tools once reserved for anthropology are no longer so specific, while historians may still fuel the social theory.[4] They do so when their research challenges the European narrative from another point of view, for example from Chinese studies (Kenneth Pomeranz), from South East and South Asia studies (Denys Lombard, Jean Aubin, Sanjay Subrahmanyam),[5] from Russia (Jane Burbank), or from Africa (Frederick Cooper). But they also proved to be able to deconstruct the Eurocentric narrative from Western European studies: from Italian city states (Patrick Boucheron),[6] and from the expansion of the English and French feudal nobility (Robert Bartlett).[7]

In spite of the length of these debates, many questions remain open. One may note four major objections to the characteristics of European historians:

---

[2] François Hartog, *Anciens, modernes, sauvages* (Paris, 2008).
[3] Lucien Febvre, Marcel Mauss, Émile Tonnelat, Alfredo Niceforo, and Louis Weber, *Civilisation: Le mot et l'idée* (Paris, 1930); Jean Starobinski, 'Le mot civilisation', in *Le remède dans le mal: Critique de l'artifice à l'âge des Lumières* (Paris, 1989), pp. 11–59.
[4] Gérard Lenclud, 'L'anthropologie et sa discipline', in *Qu'est-de ce qu'une discipline?*, ed. Jean-Claude Passeron, Jean Boutier, and Jacques Revel (Paris, 2006), 69–93.
[5] Denys Lombard, *Le carrefour javanais: essai d'histoire globale*, 3 vols (Paris, 1990); Jean Aubin, *Le latin et l'astrolabe: recherches sur le Portugal de la Renaissance, son expansion en Asie et les relations internationales*, 3 vols (Lisbon and Paris, 1996 and 2006); Sanjay Subrahmanyam, *Explorations in Connected History: From the Tagus to the Ganges* (Delhi, 2004); *Explorations in Connected History: Mughals and Franks* (Delhi, 2004).
[6] Patrick Boucheron (ed.), *Histoire du monde au XVe siècle* (Paris, 2009).
[7] Robert Bartlett, *The Making of Europe: Conquest, Colonization, and Cultural Change* (Princeton, 1993), 950–1350.

(1) provincial overspecialization, as an obstacle for thinking about the world as a totality;
(2) conscious or, even worse, unconscious refusal to situate Europe in a broader scope;
(3) theoretical incapacity in facing the plurality of experience of time;
(4) deep dependence on the winner's paradigms and evidence—sources and narratives—to the detriment of dominated historical experiences.

A long time ago, and long before the invention of the postcolonial critical apparatus, historians had begun to break the linearity of this historical view of modernity. Amongst them, many assumed that connections and the reciprocal openness were reversible.[8] Collective and territorial experiences of splitting up and isolation took place after instances of incorporation and dilation. On the other hand, trends of aggregation and contamination had followed periods of cultural and political closure.[9] All these processes were discontinuous in time, and not always connected in space. Consider the Roman Empire, the Islamic, the Mongol, the Ottoman, the Iberian, the British empires, and the first phase of financial capitalism.[10] Each of these macroprocesses widened the connections between societies and territories, but, subsequently, trends of retraction took place. Who knows whether so-called globalization will not be followed by the constitution of mutually hostile macro-regional ensembles? The unforeseeable future of Eastern Asia and the fuzzy construction of Europe give us examples of these uncertainties.

There are meeting points between history and anthropology, based on a common rejection of evolutionist ideology. But not all historians assume the existence of discontinuous and diverse paths to 'modernity', to the politicization of societies, to the development of economies, or to cultural improvement. The paradigm of modernization—probably too vague—and that of rationalization—probably too specific—still seem to be pillars of historical thinking in fields such as: (a) the genesis or birth of the modern state, (b) the worldwide triumph of commercial, industrial, and financial

---

[8] Michael Werner and Bénédicte Zimmermann, 'Penser l'histoire croisée: Entre empirie et réflexivité', *Annales HSS*, 1 (2003), 7–36.
[9] Dejanirah Couto and François Lachaud (eds), *Empires éloignés, l'Europe et le Japon (XVIe—XIXe siècle)* (Paris, 2010).
[10] Frederick Cooper and Jane Burbank, *Empires in World History* (Princeton, 2009); Suzanne Berger, *Notre Première Mondialisation: Leçons d'un échec oublié* (Paris, 2003).

necessary to abandon these kinds of frameworks. Historians do not have to reward or condemn sociocultural or socio-political experiences of the past such as, for example, the Enlightenment. Those ideas and forms that became accepted, imposed, enforced, and spread abroad from the locations where they were born cannot be considered better than the ideas and shapes that had a more restricted record or diffusion. The asymmetry framework has to be rigorously descriptive. The proposal consists of measuring, without any political courtesy, the capacity of some societies to change alien societies, and to dominate those processes of cultural, social, and political transfers. It admits, a priori, that in the history of interactions between societies, this capacity has not been equally effective in all human societies. If we compare, for example, the evolution of the two Iberian empires, the processes are by no means similar. The destruction of native societies in the Americas after European conquest has nothing in common with the arrangements of the tiny Portuguese authorities along the coast of India that faced local populations and political structures.[12]

Before turning to the main use of the framework of asymmetries, we must first discuss a paradigm that proved to be very popular among scholars involved in the international debate about world history, namely, that of *mestizo* societies. Its contribution is to strengthen the criticism against discrete forms of essentialism that re-emerge in the framework of comparative studies.[13] On the one hand, scholars are more and more committed to comparative studies; that is certainly excellent. Nonetheless, in many cases, at least in France, comparison strengthens essentialist definitions of each entity being compared. For example, a series of books published in the early 2000s that tried to compare France and Spain in early modern times share the same defect. Presumably, the model of the *mestizo* could prove helpful for understanding the interactions that took place between actors on both sides of the history of expansion. It is also helpful for describing processes in which social actors are constantly moving in time and space. In this respect, the *mestizo* paradigm is a good tool for spotting the risk of comparing artificially fixed realities.[14]

Nonetheless, this model harbours a naturalistic metaphor, if not a genetic one. The begetting of the *mestizo* child refers to the basic symmetry of the progenitors, a woman and a man. Any serious approach of gendered

---

[12] Sanjay Subrahmanyam, *The Career and Legend of Vasco da Gama* (Cambridge, 1997).
[13] Serge Gruzinski, *La pensée métisse* (Paris, 1999).
[14] Serge Gruzinski, *Les quatre parties du monde: Histoire d'une mondialisation* (Paris, 2004).

capitalism, (c) the domestic processes of civilization, and (d) the enlargement of literacy networks, among others. At the same time, historians, even when they recognize that every source is constructed by the scholarly endeavour, still insist on the mandatory separation between traces produced by the social processes themselves, and any discourse written as theoretical fiction or as merely discursive. It has been known since the nineteenth century that the nineteenth-century positivist methods historically have been the best tools for producing teleological narratives of human progress, when the narratives are not epics of local nation states. Nonetheless, these two professional signs of identity among historians—the modernization paradigm and the positivist method—cannot explain the brutality of past and even current criticism against the mainstream way of envisioning world history.

A tentative model for the history of contacts: asymmetries

The lowest common denominator of any reflexive position is to reject the dissociation between the phenomena historians describe and the production of the categories required to produce scholarly descriptions. Starting from this point, historians have to take account of the processes of the spread of models (political, social, religious, technical, economic, scientific) and paradigms of intelligibility on several scales of observation.[11] Such scientific endeavour develops its programmes from a critical point of view. If so, it cannot postulate the existence of a modernization, one that is mandatory, and for this reason common if not altogether singular. But historical research should not stop here, in replacing unified narratives with a collection of fragmented masterpieces of thick descriptions. Historians have to face the asymmetrical morphology of the experiences of spreading models.

Asymmetry could be defined as the differential between diverse societies in their capacity to be influential upon one another. It is certainly not a case of comparing value systems. To propose asymmetry is not to say that ideological or cultural contents and objects should be ranked according to their supposed intrinsic pertinence. For methodological purposes, it

---

[11] Jacques Revel (ed.), *Jeux d'échelles: La micro-analyse à l'expérience* (Paris, 1996).

capitalism, (c) the domestic processes of civilization, and (d) the enlargement of literacy networks, among others. At the same time, historians, even when they recognize that every source is constructed by the scholarly endeavour, still insist on the mandatory separation between traces produced by the social processes themselves, and any discourse written as theoretical fiction or as merely discursive. It has been known since the nineteenth century that the nineteenth-century positivist methods historically have been the best tools for producing teleological narratives of human progress, when the narratives are not epics of local nation states. Nonetheless, these two professional signs of identity among historians—the modernization paradigm and the positivist method—cannot explain the brutality of past and even current criticism against the mainstream way of envisioning world history.

A tentative model for the history of contacts: asymmetries

The lowest common denominator of any reflexive position is to reject the dissociation between the phenomena historians describe and the production of the categories required to produce scholarly descriptions. Starting from this point, historians have to take account of the processes of the spread of models (political, social, religious, technical, economic, scientific) and paradigms of intelligibility on several scales of observation.[11] Such scientific endeavour develops its programmes from a critical point of view. If so, it cannot postulate the existence of a modernization, one that is mandatory, and for this reason common if not altogether singular. But historical research should not stop here, in replacing unified narratives with a collection of fragmented masterpieces of thick descriptions. Historians have to face the asymmetrical morphology of the experiences of spreading models.

Asymmetry could be defined as the differential between diverse societies in their capacity to be influential upon one another. It is certainly not a case of comparing value systems. To propose asymmetry is not to say that ideological or cultural contents and objects should be ranked according to their supposed intrinsic pertinence. For methodological purposes, it is

[11] Jacques Revel (ed.), *Jeux d'échelles: La micro-analyse à l'expérience* (Paris, 1996).

necessary to abandon these kinds of frameworks. Historians do not have to reward or condemn sociocultural or socio-political experiences of the past such as, for example, the Enlightenment. Those ideas and forms that became accepted, imposed, enforced, and spread abroad from the locations where they were born cannot be considered better than the ideas and shapes that had a more restricted record or diffusion. The asymmetry framework has to be rigorously descriptive. The proposal consists of measuring, without any political courtesy, the capacity of some societies to change alien societies, and to dominate those processes of cultural, social, and political transfers. It admits, a priori, that in the history of interactions between societies, this capacity has not been equally effective in all human societies. If we compare, for example, the evolution of the two Iberian empires, the processes are by no means similar. The destruction of native societies in the Americas after European conquest has nothing in common with the arrangements of the tiny Portuguese authorities along the coast of India that faced local populations and political structures.[12]

Before turning to the main use of the framework of asymmetries, we must first discuss a paradigm that proved to be very popular among scholars involved in the international debate about world history, namely, that of *mestizo* societies. Its contribution is to strengthen the criticism against discrete forms of essentialism that re-emerge in the framework of comparative studies.[13] On the one hand, scholars are more and more committed to comparative studies; that is certainly excellent. Nonetheless, in many cases, at least in France, comparison strengthens essentialist definitions of each entity being compared. For example, a series of books published in the early 2000s that tried to compare France and Spain in early modern times share the same defect. Presumably, the model of the *mestizo* could prove helpful for understanding the interactions that took place between actors on both sides of the history of expansion. It is also helpful for describing processes in which social actors are constantly moving in time and space. In this respect, the *mestizo* paradigm is a good tool for spotting the risk of comparing artificially fixed realities.[14]

Nonetheless, this model harbours a naturalistic metaphor, if not a genetic one. The begetting of the *mestizo* child refers to the basic symmetry of the progenitors, a woman and a man. Any serious approach of gendered

---

[12] Sanjay Subrahmanyam, *The Career and Legend of Vasco da Gama* (Cambridge, 1997).
[13] Serge Gruzinski, *La pensée métisse* (Paris, 1999).
[14] Serge Gruzinski, *Les quatre parties du monde: Histoire d'une mondialisation* (Paris, 2004).

reality of the relationships would deny that in the reproduction (social as well as biological), the actors, female and male, stay in an equivalent position. But the *mestizo* model, in its metaphorical dimension, pictures contact as symmetry, as a reciprocal fertilization. That is precisely why it cannot help to describe those experiences in which the will to meet the other has plainly been a unilateral movement. No doubt the experience of colonization changed the invaders. Many experiences of this kind have been described: the return to 'savagery' by Europeans in the colonial context—as the mirrored inverse of the imposed spreading of the colonizers' cultural model—and the incorporation by invaders of the culture of sophisticated colonized societies. Nevertheless, these processes, however important, are marginal in the broader context of global and large-scale transfers of population and culture. It seems more realistic to stress the fact that curiosity and desire towards the other went on within the context of brutal domination, rather than to imagine a reciprocal contamination as the result of a smooth trade, whether carnal, literate, or commercial.

Adolf Eichmann, with horrific candour, during his trial in Jerusalem, explained that, in spite of Heydrich's prohibition, he continued to study Hebrew with a rabbi because he was fascinated by the history of the Jewish people. His knowledge of Jewish culture was of significant help when he planned the destruction of European Jewry.[15] This extraordinary case may be a useful reminder to all scholars. No one acquired a more deep-rooted knowledge of the Aztec Empire system than did Hernán Cortés, who destroyed its capital city Tenochtitlan. In the last thirty years, hundreds of papers and monographs have shed light on the implicit or explicit links between scientific research, particularly regarding natural history, archaeology, physical anthropology, and social ethnology, and the implementation of colonial regimes abroad.

Contact is also the desire to know the alien in order to change it, the art of valuing men in order to sell and buy them. In this precise sense, when ships left the ports of Western Europe in the early fifteenth century and began to draw the world as a world, the experiences of contact were not symmetrical, and the search for knowledge about others was certainly not reciprocal. Nonetheless, from the very beginning of this unilaterally driven series of experiences, some discoverers and settlers began to invent

---

[15] Harry Mulisch, *Criminal Case 40/61, the Trial of Adolf Eichmann: An Eyewitness Account* (Philadelphia, 2005); Joseph Kessel, *Jugements derniers: Les procès Pétain, de Nuremberg et Eichmann* (Paris, 2007), pp. 171–2.

alternative narratives of European expansion. They discovered not only the New World but also their own brutality and arbitrary behaviour, if not the fragility of their supposed superiority.[16] Among dozens of important examples, let us recall the tribute Claude Lévi-Strauss paid to Jean de Léry, Calvinist settler in the Bahia de Guanabara (Brazil) in the middle of the sixteenth century. Léry's description of the customs of the natives of the present-day Rio de Janeiro area proves that, from the beginning, the Western machine that was created to reduce otherness to inferiority and identity was at the same time cracked.[17] This very point is probably the most unacceptable and most unsettling for the ideological endeavour to rebalance what happened from the start of European expansion. The restoration of a tentative equilibrium depends on the restitution of voice to those who were never considered legitimate interlocutors. It depends, no less, on our skills in neutralizing the twists of the narratives written by those dominant people who recorded the voices of the weak. And here, the *mestizo* model may be more of an obstacle than an appropriate tool, as it refuses to consider the prior purity of any society before a massive contact from outside, as the object of an essentialist approach. Anthropologists and archaeologists work very hard to give tentative answers to such dramatic questions as, for example, what were the figures for the native population of America prior to the contact.[18] The magisterial work of Nathan Wachtel has demonstrated that it is possible to reconstitute elements of genuine native culture and social systems of Amerindian societies starting from fields overwhelmed by the realities of social *métissage*. And the research of the most accurate description of these societies takes into account, at each step, the fact that they were historical, that is, in motion and internally composite.[19]

This methodological agenda does not subvert the chronicle of reciprocal borrowing from any society to an alien society. Is it fair to substitute one for one the 'dark side of the Renaissance' for its sparkling side?[20] There is

---

[16] Jean-Frédéric Schaub, '"Nous, les barbares": Expansion européenne et découverte de la fragilité intérieure', in *Histoire du monde au XVe siècle*, ed. Patrick Boucheron (Paris, 2009), pp. 813–29.
[17] Frank Lestringant, Une sainte horreur ou le voyage en Eucharistie, *XVIe–XVIIIe siècle* (Paris, 1996); Michel de Certeau, *L'Ecriture de l'histoire* (Paris, 1975), pp. 215–48.
[18] Manuela Carneiro da Cunha (ed.), *História dos Índios no Brasil* (São Paulo, 1992).
[19] Nathan Wachtel, *La vision des vaincus: Les Indiens du Pérou devant la conquête espagnole, 1530–1570*, new edn (Paris, 1992).
[20] Walter D. Mignolo, *The Darker Side of the Renaissance: Literacy, Territoriality, and Colonization* (Ann Arbor, 1995).

no doubt that the 'colonization of imagination' is a major issue, and that it makes so crucial the efforts at reconstructing the 'visions of the vanquished'.[21] One of the central issues of this chronicle is the invention of theories of reflexivity by the winners, such reflexivity that they first implemented in relation to themselves. Here, historical analysis must bring together the study of the forms of resistance that were opposed to colonial systems everywhere, with the vision the conquerors had of their own experience. Those social, political, and cultural movements must be considered also as major sources of the development of reflexive thinking in Europe. Michel de Montaigne's Brazil could be seen as a spectacular example of the genre.[22]

Europeans have historically produced, printed, and disseminated several theories of their own supremacy, which contradicted one another. Among those contradictions was the criticism of the brutality of colonizers and settlers, which has been a major source of the critique of triumphant universalism.[23] Scepticism has been equally important in the forging of European culture, as is evidenced by the scientific revolutions.[24] Sources of sceptical early modern thinking are not to be found exclusively in the reshaping of Greco-Roman wisdom. When major contemporary thinkers and writers interpreted the sixteenth century as an Iron Age, or a tragic period, the colonial experience helped them to envision their discontent.[25] Although it has not always been popular to recognize the fact, Europe, early on, has been a source for the theoretical deconstruction of the ideological foundations of European worldwide domination. Think of the celebrated last chapter of *Lemuel Gulliver's Travels*. The late conception of Hegel's *Phenomenology of Spirit*, and *Lectures on the Philosophy of World History*, cannot seriously be considered as the correct source for describing the relationship between Europeans and the others.[26]

---

[21] Serge Gruzinski, *La colonisation de l'imaginaire: Sociétés indigènes et occidentalisation dans le Mexique espagnol: XVIe–XVIIIe siècle* (Paris, 1988); Inga Clendinnen, *Ambivalent Conquests: Maya and Spaniard in Yucatan, 1517–1570* (Cambridge, 1987); Stuart B. Schwartz (ed.), *Victors and Vanquished: Spanish and Nahua Views of the Conquest of Mexico* (Boston, 2000).
[22] Frank Lestringant (ed.), *Le Brésil de Montaigne: Le Nouveau Monde des Essais (1580–1592)* (Paris, 2005).
[23] Marcel Bataillon and André Saint-Lu (eds), *Las Casas et la défense des Indiens* (Paris, 1973).
[24] Richard H. Popkin, *The History of Scepticism: From Savonarola to Bayle* (Oxford, 2003).
[25] Paul Hazard, *La crise de la conscience européenne: 1680–1715* (1935; 3rd edn Paris, 1961).
[26] Sankar Muthu, *Enlightenment against Empire* (Princeton, 2003).

Historical research and the dynamic of compensation

The narrative of asymmetrical experiences may produce inconsolable pain to those who share the legacy of having been dominated. Even so, history cannot decide to offer alternative stories, grounded on the basis of political compensation. One cannot give an answer to legitimate moral suffering, or pay a historical debt, through a scholarly methodological twist. Though there might be a powerful temptation to do so, one could instead perhaps offer to those people who have been wronged the resources for the (re)building of their own identities. But once more, the process would depend on the mediation of scientific and political institutions producing something like ready-made identities. As a consequence, through this path, there is no chance to avoid a spiral of perpetual suspicion, with no perspective from which to establish any common ground for discussion.

Two main options seem available. Authors who do not belong to the milieu of the masters of Western academic narrative, have given better answers in scholarly fields about the history of interactions, or the lack of interactions, between Western and non-Western societies. In this case, their success is established according to Western academic criteria. On the other hand, authors may decide to abandon the Western academic criteria, arguing that they made impossible the production of truly alternative narratives. The very notion of history as a cumulative narrative producing a specific philosophy of time and change may be discarded in this case. If so, there is no longer a challenge from inside historical research that nevertheless harbours several narratives.

Currently, scholars are considering both options. One can express doubts about their real capacity to act as vehicles of compensation. Moreover, one can be sceptical about their capacity to restore to the missing actors of history the place they deserve. Historians may prefer to follow a more modest path. The first step is to study the historical understanding of the processes by which some actors crushed others. From the beginning of European contact in the Caribbean, Bartholomew de Las Casas wrote a pledge against extreme violence committed by Christian conquerors. He also denounced the hypocritical use of legal rules by the settlers and deputies of the royal authorities. At the end of the colonial period, in the context of disruption of the last European overseas empires, E. P. Thompson, after Antonio Gramsci, and after the Russian populists, wanted historical narratives to reconstitute the voice of silent people.

Even after agreement to avoid the political issues surrounding these questions—which are at the same time ethical ones—and to stress the methodological issues, the phenomena of asymmetry still seem central. The history of failed transmissions, rejected influences, and broken processes of Westernization deserves as much attention as the classical narrative of global Westernization. In fields as important as the economy of exchanges, the secularization of political institutions, the relationship of men and nature, the balance of gender, and many others, the contemporary world is far from being homogeneous and reduced to a European standard. But if one field has reached a very large diffusion from Europe to the rest of the world, it is precisely that of the order of scientific rationalization built by Western scholars. Western academic knowledge and scientific research, more so than other human activities, may be accused of abusing this dominating position. The intellectual, administrative, and material architecture of many non-European universities, even of postcolonial and post-imperial foundation, reproduces a style invented in Western Europe, from Renaissance Bologna to the London School of Economics.

Among the most astonishing cultural achievements of Westerners is the Promethean ambition of producing a global or universal encyclopaedia of human experiences, considered from the point of view of their diversity. In Europe and in the Europeanized Americas, writers and scholars gave birth to several projects devoted to describing all known 'others' on earth. The mid-eighteenth-century invention of the concept of civilization is extremely illuminating.[27] It bypasses the long debate about monogenetic or polygenetic origins of human societies.[28] Starting from the legacy of sixteenth- and seventeenth-century colonial experiences, the Enlightenment rationalized a sort of three-step ladder: savagery, barbarism, and civility.[29] Precisely at the same time, the scientific debate on nature produced the theory of a unique natural order with a hierarchy from the less organized beings to the more complex, but also the theory of dynamic, if not separate, transformation. The belief that nature is composed of several simultaneous orders, with no continuity between them, helped

---

[27] Jean Starobinski, 'Le mot civilisation'.
[28] Giuliano Gliozzi, *Adamo e il Nuovo Mondo: La nascità dell' antropologia corne ideologia coloniale* (Florence, 1976); Michèle Duchet, *Anthropologie et histoire au siècle des Lumières* (1971; 2nd edn, Paris, 1995).
[29] Fermín Pino Diaz, 'La Renaissance et le Nouveau Monde: José d'Acosta, jésuite anthropologue (1540–1600)', *L'Homme*, 122–4 (1992), 309–26.

to create the conception of a plurality of civilizations. So there were scientific, cultural, and social arguments against a unified theory of civilization from the very beginning of the spread of the notion of civilization itself. Nonetheless, such a brilliant intellectual as François Guizot, in his lectures on European Civilization at the Sorbonne in 1828–29, defended the unitary interpretation of the same concept.[30] As a result, the notion seems to have been simultaneously a monistic and a pluralistic one.

The encyclopaedic impulse is to be understood here as a historical object and as the central piece of the intellectual genealogy of the current debate as well.[31] Its initial pluralistic and monistic framework is still current, for example, in legal history and constitutional discussions, particularly after the Second World War, after decolonization, and in an epoch dominated by worldwide migrations. Starting from this scientific framework, the notion of asymmetrical connections seems particularly helpful, since scholarly discussion today is fortunately a worldwide one. To assert that several major phenomena in the history of alien-to-alien contacts have been asymmetric is the most respectful and, at the same time, the least paternalistic way of organizing a discussion with those who present themselves as heirs of the victims of European domination. By contrast, there is something odd in the moral and political will to reach a consensus grounded in soft formulas. We may refuse the unitary concept of civilization in favour of the pluralistic one, if this dichotomy seems still useful. But the recognition of pluralism does not need to be grounded in a narrative that ignores the empirical capacity of Westerners to overwhelm others de facto from the fifteenth to the twentieth centuries.

The *mestizo* model, as we have suggested, gives back to the victims of expansion a status of actors of their own history, that is, people with their own agency. Those individuals and those collective subjects controlled and took over, at least partially, the processes Western conquerors imposed on them. But the restitution of their dignity as historical actors should not have a softer narrative as a consequence. One may pay attention to subtle processes of interaction, but it seems unfair if this becomes an attempt to erase the brutality of asymmetries, of the infliction of violence and domination.

---

[30] François Guizot, *Histoire de la civilisation en Europe: Depuis la chute de l'Empire romain jusqu'à la Révolution française; Philosophie politique de la souveraineté*, ed. Pierre Rosanvallon (Paris, 1985).
[31] Silvia Sebastiani, *Razza e genere nell'Illuminismo scozzese* (Bologna, 2008).

There is also a much more radical answer. It consists of attributing to all partners of connections and interactions the same 'level' in respect of values or performances. That is exactly the case of repairing and restoring statements. The problem is that this path mixes the scales up, and avoids the central problem. To say that each culture has humanized men as completely as every other culture is precisely the principal discovery of anthropology. This notion has fortunately acquired an axiomatic strength in all the social sciences and humanities. Nevertheless, it does not help us to understand why some societies and cultures have been more capable of overwhelming others.

A plea for a general model of asymmetries

Invasion, occupation, and absorption, inflicted by societies upon other societies, are the frames of human history. These phenomena may take place at a local, regional, or at a much broader level. In such a framework, European expansion against other regions seems to be often the final assault, after an unconnected series of processes of domination and incorporation. Romanization of the Mediterranean, the takeover of the Central Andes by the Inca civilization, Mexicanization, Sinicization, Mughalization, Islamization: all these processes, among many others, were not necessarily less brutal in their procedures than modern practices of colonialism, and no more legitimate, if we think anachronistically and retroactively, in terms of sovereignty. The chronological distance favours a colder point of view on previous processes of invasion and absorption. The events that occurred prior to Western expansion, often extremely violent, have been naturalized by collective memories and by historiographies. And even these have been described as beneficial for the societies that were dominated. Non-Western previous invasions are not ethically evaluated, whereas European expansion seemingly deserves to be indicted by the tribunal of political values. The worldwide distribution of power created by European expansion and its reflux, has been one among diverse historical experiences of invasion and one among a large scope of relationships of domination. The history of men can be described as one of interlocked experiences of submission. In these series or chains of connected and asymmetrical relations, many societies had to receive cultural models from abroad, and continue at the same time to impose their own models on weaker societies they dominated.

Thus, Sinicization of Eastern Asia and Westernization can be put on the same level in terms of performances, as a way to abolish any kind of hierarchy. Nevertheless, the second deserves a moral conviction, from which the first is spared. Such a difference is not innocent. Many societies and cultures had been victorious and conquerors of their own expansion area, before Western colonization made them dominated societies and cultures. Today, sixty years after the beginning of decolonization, those societies and cultures find their interest in organizing collective memories, if not national (communion), around their status as victims. That is certainly acceptable, but with two conditions. First, that the new sovereign states do not select the victimization narrative when facing Westerners, and the glorious, even imperial, one when considering internal nation building, which is often done in order to reduce social and cultural diversity within. Second, that they do not ask the societies and cultures dominated locally by their strong neighbours before European expansion, to forget previous, local antagonisms.[32] In other words, the victims of the victims of Western colonization should not be forced to feel something like an essential solidarity with their local or regional dominators because Europeans had been their common oppressors.

In a historical series of dominations, the European step is grounded in its worldwide scale. The last conqueror has also been the only global one. Within the context of enormous diversity, it functions like a common experience for all non-Western societies. From the Americas to the former Ottoman Empire, from Africa's former kingdoms to Imperial and Republican China, from Central Asian societies to Japan, in all these scenes Westernization has been or still is an issue. However, to dull or flatten different strata of local, regional, and imperial domination would be dangerous. The final Western domination cannot erase all previous experiences of domination and abuse. But if scholars follow such a path, they impoverish scientific approaches to the subject at hand. Polarizing the discourse in terms of non-Western versus Western domination puts aside the narratives of internal conflicts, which provide an essential knowledge to be used in opposition to political mythologies, beginning with 'imagined communities' and nationalistic epics. These narratives of internal conflicts offer alternative narratives vis-à-vis the origins of society that link human communities with supernatural powers and forces. They are powerful

---

[32] Nathan Wachtel, *Le Retour des ancêtres: Les indiens Urus de Bolivie, XXe–XVIe siècle: Essai d'histoire régressive* (Paris, 1990).

obstacles in the face of modern nationalisms based and nurtured on the anti-colonial impulse.

If one reduces all struggles for identity to face-to-face struggles between native peoples and their European abusers, it becomes impossible to offer any critical analysis, in anthropology and in history, about current tensions within formerly colonized societies. If the coming of Westerners is understood as the most radical cut ever inflicted upon pre-colonial spaces, or understood as a 'meta-event', one may expect quite perverse effects. Thus, if scholars, politicians, and activists do so, what they do is to produce an ahistorical and essentialist narrative of their own society and polity, at least concerning the period before European interruption. They give scientific arguments to the promoters of unification, of the eradication of remaining plurality, and ethnicization in the framework of sovereign nation states—exactly what happened to Europe itself. The postcolonial population is then asked to sacrifice the remains and the memories of its diversity. It is asked to support the defence of global or national identities, being victims of processes of unification that began before the colonial experience, and which continue now in its aftermath.

Brutality and violence from Europe and in Europe

Since scholarship and scientific activities are among the fields in which asymmetries have been so radical, their discontent seems to be particularly high. Major intellectual projects for mapping the plurality of domination and contact experiences, at different scales and in different environments, were promoted until the end of the twentieth century mostly by Western academic institutions. One may consider that, in these conditions, the narratives, even if convincing, are suspected of reproducing always the same Western *logos*. The situation could be tempered when a programme of political compensation fuels ideologies based on suspicion. How can we, and here I specifically mean Europeans, answer those who would argue that a chapter like this is the latest twist invented by former dominators, still so arrogant?

The rejection of rewriting history according to the ethical necessity of promoting symmetries is not, by any means, an obstacle to the critique of European brutality, and techniques of domination, among which I include modern ideologies of universalism. The refusal of soft symmetries and the description of European proclivity to extreme violence are particularly compatible since the Second World War. For the last seventy years, Europeans have seen their continent as the area where the most radical experience of mass murder took place.[33] This side of the question is central. After Auschwitz and Treblinka, the problem of the specific importance of Europe in world history can no longer be understood in terms of values. 'European consciousness' cannot in future lecture anyone. That is exactly why the legal construction of the European Union is based on a dynamic reshaping of lost values. We are, then, very far from any neo-Straussian temptation! Consider the general consensus among European historians against two popular essays from the USA, those by the optimistic Francis Fukuyama, and the pessimistic Samuel Huntington. That is also why our defence against the accusation of being still ethnocentric scholars is perfectly compatible with a scrupulous attention towards the terrible violence inflicted by Europeans on conquered and colonized societies. Historians have proved themselves capable of describing genocides committed in the context of Western expansion. They develop large programmes about slavery, white supremacy, imposed migrations, and ethnic cleansing. With their colleagues in anthropology, they are concerned with the political processes of dehumanization. Nothing is done any more to erase the intensity of violence. Euphemisms no longer seem acceptable in historical narratives. In other words, the asymmetries proposal has nothing to do with an ideology tending to restore a clean conscience to Europe. Its goal is exclusively to offer a more accurate framework for global history.

If, once more, we reject the production of a narrative for compensation, other paths are open for scientific discussion. The core of European myopia and of its rejection is the same: the fiction of an essentialized Europe, considered a coherent historical reality, with its own values, specific or supposedly universal.[34] The answer, of course, could not be something like a defence of a 'Western canon'; that is the most ideological and the least effective one. The orders of moral, political, and aesthetical values are not useful for this debate. At the same time, these orders cannot be mobilized either by those scholars committed to the critique of methodological ethnocentrism. At this point, we probably need a tentative theoretical pause.

---

[33] David El Kenz (ed.), *Le massacre, objet d'histoire* (Paris, 2005); José Emilio Burucúa, *Eadem Utraque Europa*, 10/11 (Buenos Aires, 2011).
[34] Jean-Frédéric Schaub, *L'Europe a-t-elle une histoire?* (Paris, 2008).

Let us try to present a hypothesis. People in medieval Europe, with some non-continuous legacy from Greek and Roman antiquities, developed very high and sophisticated skills in such fields as rhetoric and argumentation, legal technique, conceptual analysis, grammar, and encyclopaedic ambition. Such a series of performances can be compared with cultures of literacy no less sophisticated, for example in the Islamic world, in China, in India. The Western debt to Arabic literacy and algebra was pivotal for understanding medieval Europe, but became marginal from the beginning of European expansion.[35] What has developed in Europe since then is much more than rapacity, mysticism, and analytical skills. The new feature has been the birth of reflexive thinking about processes in progress. In other words, the roots of the very successful spread, if ever partial, of Western models have not only been due to the military force of Western settlers, or even due to a technological superiority that was challenged at least until the late eighteenth century. Rather, the roots are to be found in the play of the simultaneously dogmatic and critical approaches spread by the colonists themselves and their counterparts in the metropolis. Here, the history of sociocultural experiences and the history of scientific proposals cannot be dissociated. Maybe the best product Europe has ever spread abroad is a complex cultural system, in which dogma and the critique of dogma were two sides of the same coin, in which inflicting collective violence gave birth to both sceptical and individualistic horizons.

This hypothesis is not a way to reaffirm the centrality of Europe. On the contrary, it suggests that the expansion, and the connections and interactions it implied, are major sources of the blooming of reflexive thinking in Europe. When the dynamic of expansion sent back puzzling doubts, Europeans began to ask new questions about their own polity and civility. In a sense, we are still recording the effects of such an earthquake. Who can ignore how the 'Great Discoveries' challenged the very narrative of Genesis? What was at stake was the open play of interpretations about the Fall, about Babel and the question of human linguistic diversity, about migrations, about climate and collective tempers, and finally about races.[36] The new narratives about the history of human societies were negotiated

---

[35] Philippe Büttgen, Alain de Libera, Marwan Rashed, and Irène Rosier-Catach (eds), *Les Grecs, les Arabes et nous: Enquête sur l'islamophobie savante* (Paris, 2009).
[36] Anthony Pagden, *The Fall of Natural Man: The American Indian and the Origins of Comparative Ethnology* (Cambridge, 1982); Maurice Olender, *Les langues du paradis. Aryens et Sémites: Un couple providentiel* (Paris, 1994).

between the medieval legacy and the shock created by overseas conquests. But, from the beginning, the chronicle of European power and triumph has also been thought of as a moral disaster, and later as an economic failure. What happened to the ideal of the *'caballero cristiano'* from the spread of the hideous image of the rapacious conquistadores committing genocide?[37] The young blood of American conquest immediately made Europe older, and covered it with such ugliness, comparable to Wilde's portrait of Dorian Gray. From the early sixteenth century the worldwide success of Westerners produced alarm in the order of values. On the one hand, we have maps, printing, and missions, on the other Las Casas, Swift, and Mably.

Conclusion: Europe, colonial and colonized

Are we suggesting then, as a conclusion, that the domination of Western *logos* is inevitable? That the world is to be conceived according to European thinking, as a result of colonial expansion, and of European skills in criticizing its own colonialism? Is a dogmatic Europe offering to others its method for deconstructing dogmatic thinking? Are we left without an agenda for restitution? These questions seem too large, if we expect sincere scientific answers. The proposal is much more modest. Empirically, we must begin by accepting that the asymmetries model has to be applied to the history of Europe itself. Historians, ethnologists, and philosophers have stressed the importance of research about women, witches, heretics, the poor, lepers, nomadic people, slaves, dialect-speakers, sodomites, fools, the disabled, gypsies, Jews, Moriscos, Cagots, Highlanders, Irishmen, and many other internal others, who were simply the huge majority of the European population! Those scholars, in thinking about the experience of politicization in Europe from bellow, from this (heteronymous) majority, rewrote the history of European societies as a series of processes of colonial domestication, or dynamics of discipline. When researchers produce knowledge in the field of the historical sociology of economic domination, when they try to define the mechanisms of the 'politics of truth' (Michel Foucault), what are they doing if not illuminating asymmetries?

---

[37] See Alain Milhou's historical introduction to Bartolomé de Las Casas, *La destruction des Indes*, trans. Jacques de Migrodde (1579).

In giving back voice to the subalterns, this majority of the population, historians must abandon the project of aggregating heteronymous social actors and fragmented territories in a fictional European unity. Why should we admit this fantasy at a global scale, if such a frame could illuminate none of our research fields? Think about the world settlers and colonists left behind as a unified society and culture: that is probably the most dramatic misinterpretation. It seems ironic to notice that essentialist conceptions of the West—positive as well as negative—are still popular in European and American campuses. From the 'Western canon', to the 'clash of civilizations', from a Europe to-be-provincialized to the Asian alternative, historians will not face their discontents and new horizons efficiently if they refuse to consider some of the issues we have tried to discuss here. If so, Europe will continue to be understood in abusive terms of 'Occidentalism', according to the same arbitrary methods that gave birth to 'Orientalism'. And it seems, for the same reason, unacceptable to consider societies and territories once conquered by Westerners as united and essential realities. The narrative of asymmetry proposes that the experiences of domination have to be considered as delocalized phenomena. Recognizing the ubiquity of domination, of asymmetry, offers a richer scientific agenda. But it may also deepen our anxiety.

Part II
Approaches: Methods and Methodologies in Global History

5
Comparison in global history

PRASANNAN PARTHASARATHI

Comparison is, in many respects, the poor stepchild of global history. Of course, global historians know that comparisons are a critical part of their arsenal of techniques, but it is wielded too little and it is often deployed without sufficient attention given to goals and methods. The purpose of this chapter is to elaborate upon these issues. It begins with a discussion of comparison in history, with a focus on Marc Bloch's methodological observations. It then moves to consider the use of comparison in the writing of global history. The global historical problem in which comparison has figured the most prominently is the divergence between Europe and Asia in paths of economic development. The chapter argues for a new comparative approach in the study of divergence, which is not deterministic and does not assume an endpoint for economic development. A non-deterministic method of comparison is presented, which draws upon my book *Why Europe Grew Rich and Asia Did Not*. The major conclusions of the chapter are that the method of comparison can lend greater rigour and analytic sophistication to the writing of global history and that global history has a great deal to contribute to the development of the comparative method itself.

Marc Bloch's 'A Contribution towards a Comparative History of European Societies', first published in 1928, is a systematic discussion of the comparative method. In the essay Bloch identifies two methods of comparison. The first compares across space and time such as 'an examination of Mediterranean civilisations—Hellenic or Roman—alongside contemporary "primitive" societies'.[1] For Bloch the pre-eminent work in this vein

---

[1] Marc Bloch, 'A Contribution Towards a Comparative History of European Societies', trans. J. E. Anderson, in *French Studies in History*, vol. 1: *The Inheritance*, ed. Maurice Aymard and Harbans Mukhia (New Delhi, 1988), p. 37.

was Frazer's *The Golden Bough*.[2] Most historians today, global or otherwise, reject the universalism and determinism that underlie this method of comparison. But they are more sympathetic to Bloch's second mode of comparison, which consists of making 'a parallel study of societies that are at once neighbouring and contemporary, exercising a constant mutual influence' and 'exposed throughout their development to the action of the same broad causes'.[3]

In the essay Bloch then proceeds to discuss enclosures in England and France as an illustration of this use of the comparative method and makes the now familiar point that the greater part of England experienced a large movement of enclosure while historians were only beginning to note this shift in France. While for Bloch the state of knowledge was far too primitive to explore the significance of the contrasts in these two movements, the comparative method was leading to the discovery of facts. The first fruits of the comparative method for Bloch, therefore, were insights into the right questions to ask of our sources. As Bloch put it, 'A document is like a witness; and like most witnesses, it does not say much except under cross-examination. The real difficulty lies in putting the right questions. That is where comparisons can be of such valuable help to the historian.'[4]

With the facts discovered the historian can then move on to their interpretation. And here Bloch says that comparisons can provide two kinds of assistance. First, comparisons can yield insights into the 'mutual influences' between 'different and neighbouring societies'. For Bloch the contribution of mutual influences to historical understanding is less exciting than the second insight that comparisons can provide, which is the discovery of real causes. (Although we shall see shortly that mutual influences have a great deal to contribute to the writing of global history.) 'This is where the comparative method seems capable of rendering the most conspicuous service to historians by setting them on the road that may lead to the discovery of real causes', Bloch writes.[5] Through a rigorous analysis of similarities and differences, the comparative method allows a deeper interpretation of causation in history, and to reach the holy grail of at least some history writing, a deeper understanding of change over time.

Marc Bloch, then, opens up an array of possibilities for the historian armed with the comparative method. His essay has been cited widely in

---

[2] James George Frazer, *The Golden Bough: A Study in Magic and Religion* (London, 1900).
[3] Bloch, 'Contribution', p. 38. See Frazer, *The Golden Bough*.
[4] Bloch, 'Contribution', p. 39.
[5] Bloch, 'Contribution', p. 44.

discussions of comparisons and has informed a large body of writing. William Sewell has drawn upon it to set forth the 'logic of comparative history'.[6] Sewell reads Bloch in more positivist than interpretive terms (the comparative method becomes one of hypothesis testing), an observation that Sewell himself makes in a later essay.[7] Bloch was the object of critical analysis in a forum on historical comparisons in the *American Historical Review* in 1980.[8] Surprisingly, Charles Tilly did not draw upon Bloch in his sociological statement on comparison, *Big Structures, Large Processes, Huge Comparisons*, even though many of his conclusions are compatible.[9]

And what of global history? One measure of Bloch's impact, admittedly partial and incomplete, is how often his insights on comparison appear in the *Journal of Global History*. Surprisingly, they were mentioned only three times in the first four years of the journal. Bloch and his approach to comparison, filtered through William Sewell, are discussed in Patrick O'Brien's prolegomenon for the journal. The other two mentions of Bloch on comparison are both in review essays, one by Anthony Hopkins on comparing British and American empires, and the other by Michael Adas in a review of John Darwin's *After Tamerlane*. (Incidentally, Bloch has merited only two other mentions in the *Journal of Global History*. One is a mention of his work on serfdom and the other is a discussion of his *Strange Defeat* in a review of a work on the international history of the 1940s.) Bloch fared better than his intellectual partner Lucien Febvre, however, who did not merit a single citation in the journal in the same period.

I should note that the lack of attention to Bloch does not reflect a lack of interest in comparison in the journal. In the opening editorial, the editors declared a wish to make the journal a part of the process of 'proposing innovative comparisons'.[10] And comparisons do loom large in its pages, although often more implicitly than explicitly. Global history more broadly does contain major works of comparison. The macrohistories of Eric Jones and David Landes come to mind, and more recently the writings of

---

[6] William H. Sewell, Jr., 'Marc Bloch and the Logic of Comparative History', *History and Theory*, 6 (1967), 208–18.
[7] William H. Sewell, Jr., *Logics of History: Social Theory and Social Transformation* (Chicago, 2005), pp. 23–4.
[8] Alette Olin Hill and Boyd H. Hill, Jr., 'Marc Bloch and Comparative History', *American Historical Review*, 85 (1980), 828–46. Also see the comments by William H. Sewell, Jr. and Sylvia L. Thrupp and the reply from the Hills in the same issue.
[9] Charles Tilly, *Big Structures, Large Processes, Huge Comparisons* (New York, 1984).
[10] 'Editorial', *Journal of Global History*, 1 (2006), 2.

Bin Wong and Kenneth Pomeranz.[11] All of the above rest upon explicit comparisons. Bin Wong and Pomeranz also contain some important reflections on the method of comparison. With the above writings as a point of departure, the remainder of this chapter is devoted to exploring how Marc Bloch's insights on the method of comparison may be more rigorously applied to global questions so that comparison may be used more fruitfully in the writing of global history.

To recapitulate, Bloch identified three ways in which comparison can aid in historical enquiry. The first was to help in the construction of questions. The other two had to do with interpretation and they were the elucidation of mutual influences and a more rigorous approach to understanding causation in history. I will now take up each of these.

Let me begin with asking the right questions. In his essay on the method of comparison Bloch discussed this in relation to asking the right questions of documents, which was only one element in his larger problem-centred approach to the writing of history. Bernard Bailyn has put the importance of the historical problem in admirable terms in a review of Fernand Braudel's *Mediterranean*, published in the *Journal of Economic History* in 1951: 'The formulation of a valid problem is as much the necessary ingredient for superior work in history as the sympathetic identification of scholar and subject. Such problems must first be concerned with movements through time in the affairs of men living in organized groups.' Bailyn then proceeds to cite with approval Bloch's *Feudal Society* which is 'organized around the clear historical problems that follow from the question, What was the nature of feudal society?'[12]

The method of comparison, therefore, forces the historian to formulate problems and to ask questions that need answering, which lends the writing of global history an analytic rigour. For one cannot do comparisons without a larger purpose in mind. For this reason, the mutual influences that emerge from comparison are more rigorous forms of connections. They emerge from an attempt to answer a specific question or solve a specified

---

[11] Eric Jones, *The European Miracle: Environments, Economies and Geopolitics in the History of Europe and Asia*, 3rd edn (Cambridge, 2003); David Landes, *The Wealth and Poverty of Nations: Why Some Are So Rich and Some So Poor* (New York, 1998); R. Bin Wong, *China Transformed: Historical Change and the Limits of European Experience* (Ithaca, NY, 1997); and Kenneth Pomeranz, *The Great Divergence: China, Europe and the Making of the Modern World Economy* (Princeton, 2000).
[12] Bernard Bailyn, 'Braudel's Geohistory: A Consideration', *Journal of Economic History*, 11 (1951), 280.

historical problem. Therefore, the method of comparison pushes global historians beyond the descriptive mode into the analytic and lends global history sophistication and rigour.

The second way in which comparisons can aid in historical enquiry, according to Bloch, was with the identification of mutual influences. For Bloch this was a more obvious and less interesting use of the comparative method than that of identifying causes. (He wrote that the discernment of mutual influences was the 'most obvious service we can hope for from a careful comparison', while comparison for the elucidation of causes is the 'most conspicuous service'.[13]) From the perspective of writing global history, however, the identification of mutual influences may be an equally significant contribution of comparison. And here it is worth recalling that Bloch's essay was a contribution to a comparative history of European societies. The discovery of mutual influences on a European canvas may appear trivial in comparison with the identification of real historical causes. On a global canvas, however, the identification and interpretation of mutual influences has more profound implications.

Let me illustrate this claim with some examples drawn from *The Spinning World: A Global History of Cotton Textiles, 1200–1850*, which I edited with Giorgio Riello. The volume was a product of the Global Economic History Network and cotton textiles were selected for their potential to shed light on the problem of divergence between Europe and Asia, but the study of cottons evolved into something larger, as we wrote in the introduction to the volume:

> The project matured into a global history with a far broader agenda, however, as it identified a number of striking parallels in the production and consumption of cotton textiles around the world between 1200 and 1700. The identification of this global cotton revolution, which preceded the European cotton revolution of the eighteenth century, emerged from putting a number of regions of the world next to each other, so to speak, which revealed striking similarities in patterns of change. In other words, it was an exercise in comparison which revealed a striking global pattern.

Central to this global pattern were a set of mutual influences—which may also be seen as connections—that linked together different regions of the world. In the volume the most important form of connection was trade, but the simple act of exchange spurred new connections on the basis of

---

[13] Bloch, 'Contribution', pp. 42, 44.

knowledge, the movement of people, and the transmission of notions of fashionability and forms of consumption. The Indian subcontinent was critical in these links as it was the nodal point from which many of these connections emanated in the period between 1200 and 1800.

I am now using mutual influences interchangeably with connections, but these mutual influences or connections were derived from the starting point of comparison. And this starting point lent them great analytical rigour. I will say more shortly on why these mutual influences were invested with great rigour, but first I examine how the identification of mutual influences makes a second and even more important contribution to global history.

From the study of mutual influences, comparison must, in a kind of dialectic fashion, produce a new synthesis of the objects of comparison into a single framework of analysis. Again, please allow me to quote from my introduction with Giorgio Riello to the *Spinning World* in order to elaborate upon this:

> In this volume, a consideration of mutual influences and the integration of the cases of comparison into a single framework lead logically to the global economy. For the Indian subcontinent had a truly global reach and putting together its areas of influence in the centuries from 1200 to 1800 leads to the global trading system. And it was this global economic order, in which the cotton manufacturers of the Indian subcontinent were dominant, that provided the context and an impetus for cotton consumption and production in many regions around the world. A focus on the global economy, and therefore a history written at the global level, emerges organically from the study of cottons in disparate locations itself. It is only within a global framework that the many connections and mutual influences can be contained and made sense of. The need to confront the global, in other words, emerges from the study of cotton textiles themselves and is not imposed from the outside. Or to put it another way, this volume requires a global history not because it is interesting or fashionable but because the comparative interpretation of the material and evidence demands it.

The use of comparison to identify and interpret mutual influences provides a powerful logic and argument for the writing of global history, which is why the study of mutual influences is equal in importance to the search for causes when using the method of comparison.

Let us now turn to the question of causation. In the study of causes in history, the most fruitful and dynamic work of comparison within global history addresses the problem of the 'Great Divergence', as it has come to be known since the publication of Kenneth Pomeranz's groundbreaking book of that title. The method of comparison can certainly be applied to broader sets of problems as sociologists have demonstrated for decades in works such as Barrington Moore's study of dictatorship and democracy, which appeared in 1966, and Theda Skocpol's study of revolutions, published in 1979, but global historians have not developed it very far outside the divergence problem.[14]

For the question of divergence, however, comparison has been critical since at least the late nineteenth century when Max Weber relied upon that method in his studies of the rationalization potentials of world religions. Eric Jones in his *European Miracle* undertook a broad-ranging set of comparisons that extended from Western Europe, the Ottoman Empire, and Mughal India to China. David Landes's *Wealth and Poverty of Nations* also operated with a broad comparative framework.

The problem with Weber, Jones, and Landes, as well as much other comparative work on the problem of divergence, is that they operate with a deterministic world view. The European path of development is taken as the norm and those followed by other regions of the world as deviations from the normal or ideal path due to blockages or the lack of the proper preconditions. Such determinism is not inherent in the method of comparison. In his *French Rural History* Bloch himself uses comparison to reach some non-deterministic conclusions. There he attributes the different agrarian paths of late medieval Europe to contrasts in political and social conditions: 'The depreciation of rents was a European phenomenon. So was the effort of the ... seigneurial class at re-establishing its fortunes ... But the differing social and political conditions of the various countries imposed different lines of action.'[15] It was of course this insight that Robert Brenner developed further, giving rise to a famous debate on the transition from feudalism to capitalism.[16]

The problem then is not with the method of comparison but with historical determinism. One way out of this dilemma is the method of 'reciprocal comparison', which Bin Wong developed and Kenneth

---

[14] Barrington Moore, *Social Origins of Dictatorship and Democracy: Lord and Peasant in the Making of the Modern World* (Boston, 1966); Theda Skocpol, *States and Social Revolutions: A Comparative Analysis of France, Russia, and China* (Cambridge, 1979).

[15] Marc Bloch, *French Rural History: An Essay on its Basic Characteristics*, trans. Janet Sondheimer (Berkeley and Los Angeles, 1966), p. 126.

[16] Robert Brenner, 'Agrarian Class Structure and Economic Development in Pre-Industrial Europe', in *The Brenner Debate: Agrarian Class Structure and Economic Development in Pre-Industrial Europe*, ed. T. H. Aston and C. H. E. Philpin (Cambridge, 1985), pp. 10–63.

Pomeranz then deployed to great effect. According to Pomeranz, this method allows the historian to view 'both sides of the comparison as "deviations" when seen through the expectations of the other, rather than leaving one as always the norm'. The task then, is 'to look for absences, accidents, and obstacles that diverted England from a path that might have made it more like the Yangzi Delta or Gujarat, along with the more usual exercise of looking for blockages that kept non-European areas from reproducing implicitly normalized European paths'.[17] This procedure denaturalizes the European path of development. However, it continues to operate within the framework of presences and absences, of things that Europe possessed but Asia did not. It therefore conceives of economic development as following one of two paths, the European and the non-European or the industrial or the non-industrial, rather than opening up to the plural possibilities for change that existed in the eighteenth century. This is the familiar determinist problematic of industrialization as the universal path of development, unless it is prevented from emerging.

An alternative approach broadens the canvas to not just two, but to the multiple paths of economic development that existed in the early modern world. The path that was taken, to borrow the words of Rajnarayan Chandavarkar, was 'the interaction of a whole constellation of social forces ... that determined the sometimes wayward direction of change'.[18] The method of comparison is then broadened beyond an enumeration of similarities and differences to a far more rigorous and careful consideration of context. And historical outcomes and paths are related to these contexts.

To elaborate a little, as related to the divergence problem, in the seventeenth and eighteenth centuries states and economic actors across the great Eurasian landmass were seeking to improve their economic conditions. The form that this economic improvement took, however, varied widely. Unlike the nineteenth century, when industrialization became the universal yardstick for economic improvement and progress, in the seventeenth and eighteenth centuries the advanced regions of Europe and Asia were following different paths of economic change as they each responded to their own economic, ecological, political, and social pressures and needs. Therefore, in the centuries before 1800, the paths of economic change were diverse, plural, and multiple. Given different economic and

---

[17] Pomeranz, *Great Divergence*, p. 8.
[18] Rajnarayan Chandavarkar, 'Industrialization in India before 1947: Conventional Approaches and Alternative Perspectives', *Modern Asian Studies*, 19 (1985), 637.

ecological contexts, it is not surprising that the advanced regions of eighteenth-century Eurasia followed strikingly different trajectories of change. It is not a contrast between a dynamic Europe and a stagnant Asia. Rather, it is a contrast between different needs and imperatives which led to different paths of economic and technological change. One of them, that of Western Europe, proved to be more revolutionary. But that is not because of stagnation or a failure to change in Asia.

For, as Marx wrote in *The Eighteenth Brumaire*, 'Men make their own history, but they do not make it as they please; they do not make it under self-selected circumstances, but under circumstances existing already, given and transmitted from the past.' If historical change is conceived as an interaction between agency and structures, economic, political, social, and ecological structures define the range of choices within which individuals operate and act. And these structures varied systematically—most critically because of different positions within the global economy and different ecological contexts—across the economically advanced and prosperous regions of Europe, India, and China. It is, therefore, not surprising that individuals focused on different issues and made different choices across these regions.

These insights on comparison are developed in my *Why Europe Grew Rich and Asia Did Not*, which examines the problem of divergence in the eighteenth and early nineteenth centuries, with a focus on the advanced areas of India and Great Britain, the latter being the most economically prosperous part of Europe.[19] Although the advanced areas of India and Britain serve as the two poles of the book, comparisons of these two regions comprise a small part of the total work, much of it confined to one chapter in which economic, political, and demographic institutions are shown to be roughly similar in the seventeenth and eighteenth centuries. For example, the chapter shows that interest rates, insurance premiums, family and household size, and standards of living were more similar in Britain and the advanced regions of India than has long been believed.

The above comparisons are used to refute existing explanations for divergence and to establish the timing of divergence. On the former, differences in demographic, political, and economic institutions are not compelling factors in the divergence between Britain and India. On the latter, there were more similarities than differences in British and Indian

[19] Prasannan Parthasarathi, *Why Europe Grew Rich and Asia Did Not: Global Economic Divergence, 1600–1850* (Cambridge, 2011).

economic life till the late eighteenth century, pointing to this late date as the moment when divergence commenced.

The Indian–British comparisons in *Why Europe Grew Rich and Asia Did Not* are not used to explain why the path of economic development in Britain diverged from that of Bengal or South India, however. The book contends that an explanation for divergence cannot be found in such comparisons because of differences in economic context. Therefore, a comparison of Britain with advanced regions of the Indian subcontinent would not be comparing like with like. In order to compare places that are alike, we must identify regions that were in the same economic situation or context.

In *Why Europe Grew Rich and Asia Did Not* the two crucial elements of the economic context for Britain in the eighteenth century were global economic competition, most critically in cotton textiles, and ecological shortages, most importantly in wood. With respect to cotton textiles, British manufacturers faced the competitive pressure of Indian cotton textiles, both at home and abroad, and these cloths were increasingly preferred to traditional British textile wares. These competitive pressures and the desire to match Indian cloth fuelled innovation in eighteenth-century textile manufacturing and gave rise to the spinning machinery that would revolutionize the world, including the jenny, the water frame, and the mule. With respect to wood, for several centuries Britain had faced growing shortages of wood, which propelled experimentation with coal as an alterative fuel. This experimentation led to advances in the steam engine and the use of coal in a number of industrial processes, perhaps the most important being the substitution of coal for charcoal in the smelting of iron.

The advanced regions of India faced neither of these challenges. They were the source of the cotton textiles that British manufacturers were seeking to surpass. And most of the subcontinent, including the economically advanced areas, were heavily forested until the nineteenth and even twentieth centuries and did not face an energy crisis of the kind that was impinging on Britain from a much earlier date. A comparison of the advanced regions of India with Britain cannot help us understand the factors that led to the revolutionary British path because the Indian regions were not responding to the same economic situation. To reveal the factors that went into the British path, we must compare Britain with regions of the world that were in analogous positions. This is precisely what the bulk of the comparisons in *Why Europe Grew Rich and Asia Did Not* set out to do.

To begin with cotton, in order to identify the reasons for the exceptional British path, Britain is compared with the Ottoman Empire and France, both places that also came under the competitive pressure from Indian cottons and where local cotton manufacturing arose in imitation of Indian goods. The Britain–Ottoman Empire comparison shows the importance of state policies for the development of cotton industries. While Britain, along with much of Europe, closed its borders to Indian cloth, the Ottoman Empire welcomed Indian imports. European political authorities operated in a mercantile world in which they aimed to minimize imports and maximize production at home. Ottoman authorities approached the economy from the vantage point of consumption and sought to make available abundant supplies of goods at low prices so as to provision the population. From this perspective, imports of Indian goods were welcome as they expanded the supply of cloth in the markets of the empire.

Ottoman manufacturers who attempted to emulate the cottons of India faced unrelenting and continued competition from the Indian originals, which limited their success and confined their efforts to lower quality cloths, for which the costs of transport from India were a larger proportion of the final price. In Britain, by contrast, cotton manufacturers were insulated from Indian competition and the development of British cotton manufacturing closely corresponded to the policies of protection. In 1700 imports of Indian printed and painted cloth were banned and a local British printing industry grew rapidly to fill the void. In 1720 imports of Indian white cloth, which had been the raw material for the printers of Britain, were banned, which gave rise to British efforts to produce a locally made substitute. These efforts first produced in the 1730s a light cotton–linen mixture, which, however, was an imperfect substitute for all-cotton Indian goods, and culminated in the spinning inventions of the 1760s and 1770s, the jenny, water frame, and mule, which allowed British manufacturers to make an all-cotton cloth that matched Indian standards.

Protection alone cannot explain the British path, however, for Britain was not alone in Europe in closing its borders to Indian cottons. A comparison with France shows the importance of the form of protection. While Britain blocked Indian imports, it allowed the continued consumption of cotton goods, which were now of British manufacture; France, however, banned the use and wear of cottons altogether, which led to a thriving trade in smuggled cotton goods and restricted the development of local cotton manufacturing. France was also less involved in the commercial world of the Atlantic, especially the slave trade which, for much of the eighteenth century, was the major source of demand for British cotton cloth. This meant that there was less pressure on France to manufacture cotton goods for export. What distinguished France from Britain with respect to cottons, therefore, was a combination of state policy and market opportunity.

Why Europe Grew Rich and Asia Did Not argues that the mechanization of cotton manufacturing in late eighteenth-century Britain produced a dramatic transformation in the British economy and shifted the source of the world's cotton cloth exports from the Indian subcontinent to northwestern Europe. However, cotton alone cannot explain the revolutionary remaking of European economic life in the nineteenth century. Coal, and the new energy economy to which it gave rise, lay at the centre of that economic change. Why did this energy complex emerge in Europe and not Asia? To answer this question, the book compares the economy of coal in Britain and the lower Yangzi Delta, the most prosperous region of eighteenth-century China. Both of these places came under pressures of deforestation and shortages of wood, unlike the advanced regions of India, which, as mentioned, had plentiful supplies of this material.

Kenneth Pomeranz has argued that the adoption of mineral fuel was easier in Britain than in the lower Yangzi because of the more favourable location of coal deposits. In Britain coal was located near centres of demand and proximate to water, which eased transport, but in the lower Yangzi coal was less accessible as it was located at some distance in North China. This explanation underplays the innovations in transport that made possible the growing coal consumption in Britain and ignores the extensive evidence for coal consumption in the lower Yangzi. These indicate that more than just location is needed to explain the differing patterns of coal use. A major difference between Britain and China was in their respective state policies towards coal. While British political authorities supported and promoted the consumption of coal—especially via the coastal trade from Newcastle to London—their Chinese counterparts were at best indifferent, and at worst hostile, to the expanding use of coal.

Chinese opposition reflected a more general fear of miners and the potential threat that they posed to the stability of the state. Since a major miners' revolt in the fifteenth century, Chinese political authorities had tried to restrict the activity. The British state, on the other hand, encouraged the coal trade because the taxes collected from coastal shipping became an easy and reliable source of revenues and coal was essential for the wellbeing of Londoners. Provisioning London with fuel became a political priority as it maintained the peace of the realm. With this in mind, the British state regulated the coal trade and protected shipping convoys with the Royal Navy. The Chinese state was not uninterested in provisioning its population, but Chinese provisioning focused on grain. The eighteenth-century Qing granary system moved grain from surplus to deficit areas and guaranteed the food security of millions. The granaries, however, absorbed the administrative energies of what was a limited central state apparatus and did not have the economic and technological ramifications that coal had in Britain.

With coal, as with cottons, *Why Europe Grew Rich and Asia Did Not* compares nations or regions of the world in similar situations in order to unravel the reasons for different paths of economic development. The advanced regions of India do not figure in these comparisons because their situations were different. They do feature in the final chapter of the book, however, which examines the question of why these regions, which ranked amongst the leading centres of the eighteenth-century global economy, were unable to emulate British industrial development in the decades after 1800.

The core of this chapter consists of comparisons between the advanced regions of India and the nations of Europe, which all faced the same dilemma of cheap British exports of cotton textiles and iron. While Belgium, France, and the German areas of central Europe successfully developed their own industrial base, the advanced areas of India failed to do so and entered into a long-term decline. Although the comparison shows broad similarities in the availability of capital, entrepreneurial ability, and worker skills and knowledge, there was a striking difference in the contribution of the state to economic development. States in Europe, in order to amass their own power, promoted industrial forms of production, the expansion of knowledge, and technological capability. A variety of policies were used, including protection for new industries, state enterprises, state purchasing policies, and funding for education, study tours abroad, and recruitment of knowledgeable individuals from abroad for the transfer of know-how. In India, which had come under British rule, colonial officials did none of these things. They were opposed to protection for Indian enterprises because the market had to be kept open for British exports. Similarly, purchasing policies for things like armaments and later railways favoured British-made goods. Colonial authorities undertook little investment in enterprises, education, or knowledge production because that would have reduced the gains from colonial rule. As a consequence, colonialism produced not only economic decline but also a decline in knowledge in nineteenth-century India.

To conclude, the method of comparison has a great deal to contribute to the writing of global history. It pushes global historians to be more analytic as it forces a problem-centred approach to the writing of history. It also provides a profound justification for the writing of history at a global level when comparison leads to mutual influences. This, in turn, demands a global context for the interpretation of these mutual influences. At the same time, global history enriches the method of comparison itself. The non-deterministic histories that global historians are now developing require a more sophisticated approach to the act of comparison. The use of comparison in global history, therefore, can lead to innovations in method, and produces more subtle, more sophisticated, and more contextual forms of history writing.

6
Regions and global history

R. BIN WONG

The movements and spaces of world history

Some of the great successes in world history have come from reconstructing the movements of people, ideas, crops, manufactured goods and production processes, social organizations, and political institutions across vast distances. World history research has also responded to the contemporary concerns about environment and ecology for the past generation. Increasingly, scholars pursue world history by expanding the subjects and techniques used to study the past, including biology and genetics, geology, and climatology, among others.[1] These have all been additions to what history as a discipline previously did. They augment the arsenal of techniques and the battery of queries that historians consider part of their discipline, but they do not always tell us much about how to change the ways we do our more conventional work. While much is being gained through research at mega-spatial scales and by working in interdisciplinary groups that take on thematic challenges defined in historical terms, the practice of history more generally remains less changed than we might wish or imagine.

By crossing large stretches of space world history undermines one of the basic pillars of disciplinary organization for the profession. In a taxonomy of specialties defined by a combination of spatial and temporal markers, world history observes explicitly only the temporal distinctions among periods of history. In practice, world history projects each have spatial

---

[1] William McNeill, *Plagues and People* (New York, 1976); Alfred Crosby, *Ecological Imperialism: The Biological Expansion of Europe, 900–1900* (Cambridge, 1986); John Richards, *The Unending Frontier: An Environmental History of the Early Modern World* (Berkeley, 2003); David Christian, *Maps of Time: An Introduction to Big History* (Berkeley, 2005).

dimensions far less grand than the world entire. What defines those spaces is less clear than what does not confine them. Proponents of modern and contemporary world history often criticize the practice of national histories for failing to cross political borders. Those working on earlier periods reject, at least implicitly, a focus on civilizations for the kinds of simplifications that make foreign cultures historically homogenous internally and different from others. But the failure to conceive research and teaching of world history within smaller spatial frames means that the conventional structuring of the discipline by time (ancient, medieval, modern) and space (continents, nations) is not actively engaged. Can world history more directly encourage changes in the ways we organize research and teaching?

Much historical work continues to be done at a local level in order for the scholar to achieve control over sources relevant to a particular topic. But rather than think of the local study as representing features of the country or part of a country in which the locale is situated, historians are more likely to suggest global connections. This is especially true for more contemporary topics; to some extent this situation simply reflects the increasing amount of contact that many places have with people, goods, ideas, and practices that have come long distances. The notion of the 'glocal' aptly captures the repositioning of local studies to move outside older spatial containers, while remaining anchored in a particular place as historical studies have customarily been. Yet a juxtaposition of local and global doesn't give much guidance to navigating the space in between and implicitly reduces the relevance of spatial contexts between local and global to irrelevance. The intellectual costs of such a move are high. For one, they make it difficult to know how to organize and interpret 'local' studies. This already was a problem when the 'local' was only within the national. But the problem threatens to become intractable when we leap to the global level.

One strategy to acknowledge the world beyond the local is to invoke the global to define the shared traits and the local as the distinctive or particular and stop there. This allows us to recognize the presence of large processes affecting local situations—migrations of people or capital, the movements of political and economic power—and find a space for local agency to react. But on its own this does not help us identify what is similar and different about our local studies. Can we interpret or explain variations among cases of the same or similar phenomena in different places? Surely, much of what we observe in world history is common patterns of connection and change that establish similarities among places or define differences between them.

It may be that the kinds of connections and mixtures of similarities and differences found within regions are distinct from those that occur between them. For example, the differences among agricultural regimes within Europe and within East Asia are distinct from the contrast between small-scale intensive cultivation in East Asia and the larger-scale mixed dry field arable and pasture across Europe. Yet we are unlikely to speak of regions as useful spatial units in the study of world history because they all too easily remind us of categories already rejected by scholars unhappy with 'area studies', or an earlier generation of scholars who rejected the grand comparison of civilizations by historians like Toynbee.

Were political critiques and anxieties about simplification of complex cultures the only reasons for failing to make more efforts to study world regions, we would likely have more work formulated in such terms as part of the effort to create world history. But the concept of region lacks the spatial precision we associate with cities, countries, or the world as a whole. The absence of any consistent criteria to define any particular region means that we discover scholars who have looked at what initially seems to be the same region in fact focus on similar but quite different spaces. Consider for example the multiple ways in which scholars of early modern Asia, who inspired Fernand Braudel's study of the Mediterranean, have studied quite different spaces and stressed overlapping features in their work.[2] Identifying various regional worlds in the early modern era that can be vantage points from which to look out at larger global patterns is one way to go beyond a European-centred world history. Just as there is more than one Europe and hence we have Braudel's Mediterranean world and an Atlantic regional world, there is more than one Asian regional world in the early modern era. There is a Chinese Mediterranean of the sort treated in Denys Lombard's three-volume study of Java entitled *Le carrefour javanais*.[3] The physical space is quite different since Java is an island at the crossroads of several sets of cultural influences rather than a body of water across which are set two very different cultures. But there is a methodological similarity between Lombard's work and Braudel's Mediterranean because both scholars create a picture of a social world located in a specific physical place that is made up by the connections forged between multiple groups and kinds of people. In Lombard's Java, different waves of influence wash

---

[2] The following discussion draws from R. Bin Wong, 'Between Nation and World: Braudelian Regions in Asia', *Review* 26/1 (2003), 1–45.
[3] Denys Lombard, *Le carrefour javanais: essai d'histoire globale*, 3 vols (Paris, 1990).

over the island, each living its imprint, beginning with Hindi and proceeding to Islamic, Chinese, and European. He argues that the cultural compound forged in Java is made up of elements from each of the outside influences combining with native practices, while at the same time there remain distinctive cultural differences in early modern Java. Quite separate from Lombard's view of Java in regional space is Anthony Reid's definition of early modern South East Asia as a Braudelian space. Different again is K. N. Chaudhuri's Indian Ocean as a maritime world with several subregions in this world stretching from the east coast of Africa to the Sea of Japan.[4] Among Japanese historians, there is Takeshi Hamashita's influential work on a maritime Asia defined by the agrarian empire's tributary relations as well as by flows of silver and of commodities.[5] Like Chaudhuri, Hamashita also divides his largest maritime space into smaller sections, each again defined by the character of connections and transactions giving them coherence. But Hamashita's overlapping maritime spheres within Asia are not the same as Chaudhuri's. The lack of uniform spatial definitions of regions makes them difficult for historians to use in more general ways.

Two further problems of generalizing from Braudel's Mediterranean to the identification of other world regions merit brief consideration. First, Braudel envisioned the Mediterranean as the centre of a much larger world defined by European maritime movements into Asia in search of economic riches and political power; Immanuel Wallerstein's modern world-system owes key elements of its intellectual inspiration to Braudel's Mediterranean. Such a Mediterranean was thus historically unique since no other region could, at this point in time, play a comparable role across such vast spaces; this condition again limits the apparent generality of regions as comparable spatial units within world history. A second problem about the generality of Braudel's Mediterranean is signalled by the author's evocative reference to Spain leaving the Mediterranean for the Atlantic in order to temporally bound the space he is studying. Spain's shift to the Atlantic was part of what made the Atlantic a regional space defined by connections among African, American, and European peoples and

---

[4] K. N. Chaudhuri, *Asia before Europe: Economy and Civilisation of the Indian Ocean from the Rise of Islam to 1750* (Cambridge, 1985).
[5] Takeshi Hamashita, 'Tribute and Treaties: Maritime Asia and Treaty Port Networks in the Era of Negotiation, 1800–1900', in *The Resurgence of East Asia: 500, 150 and 50 Year Perspectives*, ed. Giovanni Arrighi, Takeshi Hamashita, and Mark Selden (London, 2003), pp. 17–50.

places. The Atlantic becomes an important regional space but only as rulers of Spain and France shifted their focus away from the Mediterranean.

The example of Braudel's Mediterranean as an important work of regional history that inspired much work on Asia and the world more generally suggests the limits of regions as usable units to replace national units between the local and the global. The concept of a region can inspire great works of individual scholarship but it does not promote the easy integration of information and arguments across studies because the spatial units are not easily matched to each other. But is our expectation for precise spatial units in fact reasonable? Neither local nor global is particularly precise. The 'local' used by historians varies from topic to topic, and the 'global' that other historians address is rarely, if ever, truly the entire world but only some portion that is implicitly defined. 'Region' is no more varied in practice than either 'local' or 'global'. The fact that regions rise and fall in prominence and significance is not so different from the rise and fall of cities in earlier periods of history or countries in later periods. Since we know that the 'national' units are misleading categories for many themes in history, especially before the consolidation of national states, we have to consider whether observing the past with an eye to the various kinds of regional space might not be better than avoiding such categories.

Conscious attention to regional spaces promises the possibility of being more mindful of the ways in which different kinds of stability can be sustained and historical changes be multiple as well as common. The possibility that there are features present in one region of the world that are absent in another is implicitly assumed in earlier generations of scholarship who viewed all historical changes leading to the modern world as having begun in Europe. The empirical rejection of such views has been largely achieved through showing parallels and connections between European changes and those elsewhere. Europe is a region that shares some traits with other world regions but, like other world regions, also has traits more particular to itself. Said explicitly, the point is obvious, but learning how to deal with the differences we find across historical cases, be they regions or some other category, has attracted less consideration than the search for similarities. Conventional histories often assert the particularities of a case, while world history studies frequently stress common traits among different places. We are thus left with two kinds of scholarship that have little to say to each other. Increasing the study of world regions could prove a way to navigate between these conceptually distant activities.

The possibilities for comparison of world regions
c.1000–1800

World history is perhaps most widely noted for its bold identification of unexpected connections that cross oceans and continents, often with utter disregard for the social and cultural practices or the political and economic institutions of those people historians typically study. But world history also includes opportunities for making comparisons. By focusing on large areas that are far more than 'local' but far less than 'global' we can begin to take the measure of some spatial dimensions of history more effectively. Within a region people may share clusters of traits or connections that are different from those that they have with people beyond that region. The kinds of differences within a region may well be particular to that region and not the same as the types of variation found in another region.

Think, for instance, of the importance of the Catholic Church in medieval and early modern Europe and the changes brought about by the Reformation—the role of Church doctrine and institutions in shaping European notions of law and its political and social uses has no obvious and direct counterpart in East Asia. The varied roles of Catholic and Protestant Churches politically and socially across Europe are a feature of this world region.[6] Of course the development of European conceptions and uses of law depended on the aspirations and abilities of other social actors outside religious organizations to formulate and implement ways to use that law. European rulers created courts as part of their administrative centralization of power; in some circumstances royal power competed with other power-holders to supply law. European merchants contributed to the development of commercial laws through their rules governing guild activities as well as in their demand for courts and contracts, the provision of which by governments was a key feature of early modern European expansion of trade. Scholarship on early modern European history provides economists, political scientists, and sociologists with the kinds of law that they deem necessary for political and economic development into modern societies in other parts of the world. Historians have studied law outside Europe in order to explain the distinctive uses

---

[6] Harold Berman, *Law and Revolution: The Formation of the Western Legal Tradition*, 2 vols (Cambridge, MA, 1983, 2006).

for law politically, socially, and economically in other places.[7] But to observe law playing, in part, different roles outside of Europe does not in fact tell us that the purposes served by law in Europe go unmet elsewhere. Certainly, state building and economic expansion took place outside of Europe in the early modern era despite the absence of European ideologies and institutions.

Consider China—a region as large as Europe and with a far larger population which also happens to have a single state. Thanks to a recent generation of scholarship exploiting archival records little known three decades ago, we are aware of law, and in particular litigation, playing a much larger role in eighteenth-century China than we had previously imagined.[8] Yet this discovery of practices previously thought lacking in China, does not mean that all the purposes served in Europe are also found in China. Those scholars pointing out similarities to European practices do not always simultaneously consider the differences. It is typically scholars wishing to show how China failed to develop in ways parallel or equal to those in Europe that produce arguments about differences in Chinese law which are viewed as deficiencies and thus sources of failed development more generally. What we do not find is much discussion of whether or not the purposes served by law in early modern Western Europe might not have been met in other ways in China.

Consider, for example, the role of law in facilitating economic change. During the early modern era, China and Europe both experienced periods of commercial expansion. The same basic economic principles of areal specialization of production and exchange according to market prices determined by supply and demand were at work in both regions. There is therefore a basic similarity of economic growth that confounds earlier assumptions about European economic dynamism and stagnation. At the same time, features of commercial expansion in China and Europe differ. Europeans, and in particular north-western Europeans, developed formal institutions to lower transaction costs by using contracts and courts to

---

[7] E.g. Baber Johansen, *Contingency in a Sacred Law: Legal and Ethical Norms in the Muslim* Fiqh (Leiden, 1999); J. Mark Ramseyer, *Odd Markets in Japanese History: Law and Economic Growth* (Cambridge, 1996); Liang Zhiping, 'Explicating "Law": A Comparative Perspective of Chinese and Western Legal Culture', *Journal of Chinese Law*, 3 (1988), 55–91.

[8] Kathryn Bernhardt and Philip Huang (eds), *Civil Law in Qing and Republican China* (Stanford, CA, 1994); Madeleine Zelin, Jonathan Ocko and Robert Gardella (eds), *Contract and Property in Early Modern China* (Stanford, CA, 2004).

adjudicate commercial disputes. The importance of these developments has been stressed by Nobel laureate Douglass C. North and other economic historians; when these practices are contrasted with others it has been to suggest that certain European institutions are better at reducing transaction costs and hence better at promoting expanded exchange than institutions elsewhere. In fact, however, there are multiple ways in which transaction costs can be reduced in order to facilitate commercial expansion. China's commercial expansion, which reached higher volumes over greater distances earlier than achieved by Europe before the eighteenth century, relied far less on the formal institutions deemed so important in European history. Instead, the Chinese relied on a combination of kinship and native place ties to form networks of trust through which they transacted business. Appeal to government review to adjudicate merchant disputes existed but was used less frequently than in Europe where large and specialized commercial courts emerged sequentially in Bruges, Antwerp, Amsterdam, and London, none of which had counterparts in China. This example suggests two more lessons from regional comparisons in world history: (1) similar dynamics, in this case market-based growth, can be at work separately from each other in two world regions; (2) the specific ways in which these dynamics operate can be only partially parallel, and the differences, in this case the relative importance of formal law and contracts, which matter little at one point in history, can subsequently become more important in unanticipated ways.

If we look at Chinese political history we can see that in the same centuries as law began to develop in Europe, the ideology and institutions of China's expanding civil service bureaucracy had no real parallels in Europe. Indeed the bureaucratic capacities of the state in China, as well as its agenda for affecting domestic society, far outstripped the imaginations let alone the abilities of rulers grappling for control over more limited territories in Europe.

It would be surprising if the political priorities and possibilities of this bureaucratic system did not strongly affect the kinds of state formation and transformation trajectories China experienced in later centuries. We might find some parallels or similarities in other world regions, but we should also consider the likelihood of this bureaucratic tradition making for a set of capacities and challenges distinctive from those found elsewhere. These 'Chinese' possibilities were not limited to the geographical space of the Chinese mainland or to ethnic Han Chinese people. Chinese political ideology and institutions were utilized by non-Han Chinese, including those who ruled the Chinese mainland (most notably the Manchus who formed the last in a long line of imperial dynasties) and those who ruled areas beyond the agrarian empire's borders, including Korea, Vietnam, and the Ryūkyū kingdom.

What implications might we draw from evaluating the enabling features of Chinese bureaucratic rule? First, we might expect a different range of problems and opportunities for political action in a Chinese bureaucratic context than in a European political arena composed of would-be centralizing rulers whose menu of ideas and institutions included the Catholic Church and its laws. Second, we might wish to compare Vietnamese strategies of rule with those of other South East Asian kingdoms and polities which drew on other political and religious traditions. China's bureaucratic political tradition simultaneously offers us a large cluster of practices we can contrast with political concerns in a world region lacking this tradition, such as Europe, and a means to compare a polity that participated in this tradition with its neighbours that did not. We are able to address political variations within relatively small spaces and across very large distances according to the spatial locations of the phenomena we observe.

A third implication emerges when we compare the variety of state-making efforts made by leaders drawing upon the ideas and institutions crafted on the Chinese mainland with the kinds of state-making strategies developed elsewhere. What if we started with the assumption that certain traits found among the Chinese-inspired cases would be quite different from traits found elsewhere? We are comfortable making precisely this kind of assumption in studies of early modern European state formation. We conventionally assume that the political changes taking place in Europe were very different from those occurring in other parts of the world and deny, at least implicitly, the relevance of political differences elsewhere for subsequent patterns of political change. The European states that emerged in the early modern era became the models for what states in the rest of the world would (or should) become in the nineteenth and twentieth centuries. The main challenge to this particular Eurocentric view of world political history has been to signal the presence of political parallels outside of Europe to the exclusion of attention to those features that can distinguish Europe from other regions for fear of practising a kind of Eurocentrism. If Europe is the only region to be privileged in historical analysis as the key source of historical changes, the motivation to avoid differences between Europe and elsewhere is understandable. But if instead we take Europe as only one region and consider its traits as sharing some similarities with practices and processes in other world regions as well as having differences, we can avoid the costs of focusing solely on similarities or differences when making historical comparisons across the globe. If we ignore world regions it becomes more difficult to address variations across contiguous spaces and to compare larger areas with each other, as we will see below.

Early modern world history without regions

Perhaps the most ambitious and certainly the only such synthetic effort at early modern world history that makes South East Asian cases prominently part of its comparisons is Victor Lieberman's two-volume study of South East Asian mainland polities in this era.[9] The initial formulation of Lieberman's analytical framework identified parallel processes of territorial consolidation, administrative centralization, social regulation, and cultural integration in Burma, Siam, Vietnam, France, Japan, and Russia. The stress on similarities, in what Lieberman's 1997 article title refers to as 'six ostensibly disparate areas', undermined the notion of early modern Europe being so very different from Asia but it did little to prepare us for the political, social, and economic variations and differences across Asia and Europe, let alone attend to the possibility of different kinds of variation and difference within and across world regions. Instead, he offers an initial sketch of an ambitious vision of how Eurasia can be seen as a series of 'rimlands' bordering older core civilizations that were all more directly exposed to the dangers posed by nomadic invaders.[10] It is in the so-called rimlands where Lieberman first discovered his shared patterns of early modern historical change. This geographical division between core civilizations exposed directly to the threats from nomads and those areas protected from such predation suggests an explanation for the kinds of areas where we can expect to find parallels and possibly even connected dynamics of social, economic, and political changes, and those areas in which such changes would be absent. This possibility was subsequently undermined when Lieberman read the scholarship on Chinese history and

---

[9] Victor Lieberman, *Strange Parallels: Southeast Asia in Global Context, c. 800–1830*, 2 vols (Cambridge, 2003, 2009).
[10] Victor Lieberman, 'Transcending East–West Dichotomies: State and Culture Formation in Six Ostensibly Disparate Areas', *Modern Asian Studies*, 31/3 (1997), 463–546.

discovered that many of the economic and social changes he had assumed were present in the rimlands but absent in the older civilizations exposed to nomads were in fact basic features of early modern China. As he put the matter in a 2008 article:

> At a workable level of abstraction, moreover, the dynamics of political and cultural integration in the chief realms of mainland Southeast Asia, Europe, Japan and Qing China were comparable. In essence, I would argue, in each polity between *c.* 1650 and 1850 four phenomena—expansion of material resources, new cultural currents, intensifying interstate competition, and diverse state interventions—combined to strengthen privileged cores at the expense of outlying areas. Each dynamic had a certain autonomy, but all four constantly reinforced and modified one another.[11]

With his initial contrast of rimlands and civilizations exposed to steppe nomads no longer plausible, Lieberman went on to discuss other differences between Qing China and his rimland cases. China had Inner Asian conquest elites, formed its state in an earlier historical era than those in the rimlands, was far larger territorially, and did not see military imperatives play as salient a role in state formation as in the rimlands. Lieberman has moved from considering only parallels among rimland cases to noting the presence of these parallels in a different kind of case, which he then distinguishes from his initial rimland category by citing other kinds of differences between China and his rimland examples. Had the original distinctions been empirically true, he would have had an explanation based on protected rimlands avoiding the ravages of exposure to steppe nomads. Once Lieberman recognized that China shared important features he first believed were distinctive only to rimlands he lost his geographically based explanation for differences among early modern historical dynamics. In its place he posits four other contrasts between China and his other three sites of common historical changes. These obviously cannot explain why China shares certain traits with those three spaces, nor do these Chinese traits explain why China was different from the other three cases; rather, they describe some of the main differences.

Were Lieberman to have gone on to evaluate the similarities and differences among China and his rimland cases, explaining the parallels in terms of common causes, the differences in terms of distinct factors, or

---

[11] Victor Lieberman, 'The Qing Dynasty and its Neighbors', *Social Science History*, 32/2 (2008), 281–304.

engaging in some other kind of analytical exercise seeking to account for the mix of similarities and differences he highlights, we would likely have an example of a kind of world history that contributes to ordering the unruly spaces between local and global levels of study. But because Lieberman identifies his similarities and differences among radically different scales of space that are not always clearly defined, it is difficult to understand his units of comparison. His France represents Western European countries more generally.[12] Western Europe alone is smaller than the Chinese empire; however, if we combine Western Europe with Eastern European countries as far as Russia, then Europe is every bit as large spatially and at times even larger than early modern Chinese empires. In either case, his mainland South East Asia is but a fraction of the size of either China or Europe, and Japan of course is even smaller than any of his other cases. Two spaces are composed of multiple regimes, with one (South East Asia) housing just three governments and the other (Western Europe or Europe more generally) with some five to ten times that number. Two other spaces are two single polities (China and Japan) which differ demographically and territorially even more starkly than the European and mainland South East Asian cases. Amidst these differences in his units of observation it should not be too surprising to discover that Lieberman's strategy of accommodating China with his rimland examples of historical changes of the early modern era, with a subsequent series of qualifications about differences, leaves us without a clear taxonomy of cases and little guidance towards explaining the similarities and differences he observes across early modern Eurasia.

Early modern state transformations in world regional perspective

Let us return to the regional approach introduced earlier in this chapter in order to consider what such an approach can help us see with regard to both similarities and differences within and between world regions. A regional approach to state formation and transformation that began before

---

[12] 'Western Europe as typified by France (but which could have been represented as easily by Britain, Sweden, Portugal, Spain, Prussia, etc.).' Lieberman, 'Transcending East–West Dichotomies', p. 468.

the modern era of national states can identify major differences as well as some key similarities in state-making in Europe and other world regions. During the early modern era Chinese and European states developed different kinds of political capacities because they faced different kinds of challenges.[13] China faced the challenges of sustaining bureaucratic rule over a vast agrarian empire. The political response was to work out a wide range of policy choices for officials at local, provincial, and central government levels to promote social stability, material security, and cultural identification with a common set of beliefs and practices. Crucial to these efforts was a reliance on local elites sharing common concerns with officials in order to support the social order of which they were the leaders. The relative balance of competition and cooperation between elites and the state was very different from that found in early modern Europe, as were the ideological and institutional bases for the relationships between them. Also different from Europe and important to the character of Chinese imperial rule was the repeated reliance on extraordinary campaigns, not simply for military purposes but also for civilian ones. Large-scale water control projects as well as the building and expansion of the civilian granary system are examples of such campaigns which required special mobilizations of resources and manpower. Some government campaigns, like those for famine relief, were clearly a response to extreme conditions, but mounting campaigns was also a proactive way to expand government intensity and involvement in social matters that allowed the government also to retreat after major mobilizations had been implemented. The eighteenth-century political agenda for effective rule included the kinds of social welfare and cultural activities that European states would not consider until the second half of the nineteenth century, when European governments began to think more explicitly about civic morality and national cultural identity. The Chinese agenda for rule in the early modern era shared certain traits with emerging European states, but it was pursued on a far larger territorial and demographic scale and included techniques and priorities, the parallels of which would not appear until later in Europe.[14]

If we turn to consider the nature of political relations within Europe in the early modern era—a spatial scale that is 'domestic' within the Chinese

---

[13] R. Bin Wong, *China Transformed: Historical Change and the Limits of European Experience* (Ithaca, NY, 1997).
[14] R. Bin Wong, 'Did China's Late Empire have an Early Modern Era?', in *Comparative Early Modernities*, ed. David Porter (Basingstoke, forthcoming).

empire—we see that Europe's foreign relations within the region were dominated by different forms of competition for territory, people, and resources. Marriage alliances among rulers united discrete territories as a kind of personal property. At the same time, rulers engaged in chronic warfare which was costly even though it promised some gains for the victors. The formulation of some rules to govern relations among European rulers followed the termination of the Thirty Years War. Often viewed as the beginning of the modern system of sovereign states, the Treaty of Westphalia in 1648 can also be returned to its original historical context and recognized to be the political innovation of European states to improve the mechanisms they employed to deal with each other. These conventions were irrelevant to European adventures into other world regions. There was no set of early modern diplomatic conventions common to Europe and other parts of the world. Europeans developed various techniques to pursue multiple objectives in Africa, the Americas, and Asia. As the Portuguese, and subsequently the Dutch, eagerly imported Asian spices to Europe, they, as well as the English and other Europeans who followed them, exported new technologies of warfare to other world regions, making violence and force the basic elements of their strategies to achieve their goals of wealth and power.

Chinese maritime diplomatic relations did not export violence in the manner pioneered by Europeans. They did, however, include displays of grandeur to inspire awe and reflect the imperial state's great power in the early fifteenth century, when Zheng He led seven maritime expeditions in 1405 and 1431, stopping at ports in South East Asia and reaching as far west as the east coast of Africa. But these expeditions, the largest of which had 300 ships and some 27,000 men, were extremely expensive. They formed the largest naval contingents that anyone in the world would see until the twentieth century's First World War. The empire's northern frontier came to demand more military and diplomatic attention because Chinese leaders in the fifteenth century increasingly feared the possibility of Mongols once again invading the country. The cessation of the dramatic naval expeditions has long been invoked as an indicator of fifteenth-century Chinese leaders losing their curiosity about the outside world and turning introspective, but such pronouncements ignore the practical matters of organizing and paying for military defences against potential invaders from the steppe to the north, which trumped the continued pursuit of diplomatic adventures in the maritime south. At the same time, Chinese ships became increasingly important in maritime South East Asia as merchants extended and increased trade through the region. While the Chinese state did not send out any large fleets after 1431, it did continue to host missions coming from other countries that sought diplomatic relations, either as a framework for encouraging trade or as a means of obtaining Chinese political support for a particular regime embattled domestically. China did not become more isolated, politically or economically, when the extravagant naval expeditions of Zheng He ended.

Chinese diplomatic relations and foreign trade, ideologically and institutionally, did differ from the political forms and economic logics pursued by Europeans, even if the notion of changes in Chinese foreign relations in the fifteenth century is not best characterized as a cultural turn away from foreign involvements and curiosities. In contrast, European maritime expansion into other world regions no doubt prompted curiosity about strange and distant places more than it served to persuade European merchants and officials to launch expensive searches for valuable goods to sell back in Europe. European exploration for riches and resources in other world regions was in fact prompted by political and economic competition among European states for wealth and power. The sixteenth-century search for spices became, in the eighteenth century, a focus upon raw materials and a particular kind of trading relationship between a government and its colonies that allowed the European home country to produce goods manufactured with imported raw materials. Such efforts fit within a mercantilist competition among European countries, each seeking to produce more commodities than its neighbours and to support its economic expansion based on this manufacturing process. The mercantilism at the heart of European political economy of maritime empire was rooted in a political and economic competition within the European world region. This competition stimulated and guided European engagements with people and places in other world regions.

An alternative Chinese political economy of agrarian empire focused on promoting economic prosperity and social stability across the empire's many diverse settings as far more important than any political or economic agenda involving people and places in other world regions. The Ming and Qing imperial governments both dealt with two broad categories of foreign regimes. Those along China's northern borders posed potential military threats and relations with such groups depended on a shifting mix of ideological, material, and coercive strategies of engagement; the Qing state, itself formed by Manchus who had entered the realm of the Ming dynasty from their homeland, the realm becoming north-east China as a result of their conquest, created a separate bureaucratic organization to manage relations with peoples of the steppe. The second category of foreign regimes was located beyond the agrarian empire's other borders; it included those ruling the Korean peninsula, Japanese islands, and the South East Asian mainland, archipelago, and islands. Relations with these foreigners were overseen by the Ministry of Rites, a government body that also managed important domestic ritual activities. The conceptual linkages of proper behaviour by rulers towards Heaven, Nature, and governments from afar were in turn connected to a larger set of political sensibilities guiding domestic governance and an agrarian political economy. These entailed far greater levels of bureaucratic effort to promote a stable society through a mix of techniques designed to support social needs and exert social control than could be found in Europe in the same era.

We can draw contrasting linkages between relations within each world region and the people and places beyond them. In the Chinese case the conventional contrast of domestic and foreign allows us to make some initial contrasts among the government's relationships to different kinds of people because the empire has a domestic space defined by the area subject to bureaucratic rule. Relations with people not subject to the regular civil service bureaucracy are not simply 'foreign' however, since the Chinese empire, like empires more generally, engaged in various kinds of indirect rule over peoples whose leaders were subordinated in one way or another to imperial authority. The distinction between domestic and foreign might therefore be better considered a continuum rather than a binary contrast.

The construction of Chinese political space is quite different from what we observe for the European world region and its relations with others. European political competition drove marriage alliances among its ruling elites and war-making between regimes. Some territories came under different authorities according to shifts in political equilibrium. The Treaty of Westphalia in 1648, often heralded as the origin of modern international relations, was at the time a key development for defining norms of engagement among European rulers. European relations with others did not follow the same norms. Instead, they were driven initially by mercantilist competition. Two very different sets of norms distinguished relations among European rulers and their relations with others, neither of which resembles the approach adopted by the late imperial Chinese empire within the world region of China or the empire's relations with others beyond its borders.

If we briefly return to the European domestic level of observation, Europe's distinctive kinds of institutions and ideologies of law can be related not only to the important roles of organized religions, but also to the ways in which its rulers developed relations with the noble, clerical, and urban commercial elites of their societies. Rulers and elites developed political ideologies and institutions to structure their negotiations with each other, which were distinctive in early modern world history. Ideas of representation and the mechanisms enabling political voice extended from *ancien régime* elites to broader strata of modern European societies and eventually beyond the European world region to other parts of the world. But during the early modern period, these ideas and institutions were particular to this world region. The dynamics of state transformation in the early modern world were largely determined within world regions, even though some partial parallels can be observed across cases in different parts of the world. The significance of regions to the study of early modern world history can also be shown for economic change. We can of course find much important evidence of connection between world regions, but the significance of these connections can be exaggerated.

Early modern economic change within and between world regions

Early modern European aspirations to capture and control wealth from people in other world regions were not always achieved through a major and organized commercial presence backed up by military force. In fact the early trade between the Chinese and European world regions was a kind of market exchange lacking the colonial undercurrents that would be felt in the nineteenth century. Between the sixteenth and eighteenth centuries trade between China and Europe grew. Europeans developed a growing taste for Chinese silks, porcelains, and teas. Chinese manufactures and processed agricultural products made their way to Europe, but Europeans lacked any goods to exchange for these commodities, as the Qianlong emperor famously remarked to King George III when he explained his willingness to allow the English to continue trading at Canton:

> Hitherto, all European nations, including your own country's barbarian merchants, have carried on their trade with Our Celestial Empire at Canton.

> Such has been the procedure for many years, although Our Celestial Empire possesses all things in prolific abundance and lacks no product within its borders. There was therefore no need to import the manufactures of outside barbarians in exchange for our own produce. But as the tea, silk, and porcelain which the Celestial Empire produces are absolute necessities to European nations and to yourselves, we have permitted, as a signal mark of favour, that foreign *hongs* should be established at Canton, so that your wants might be supplied and your country thus participate in our beneficence.[15]

Sometimes taken as a sign of arrogant self-satisfaction, the Qianlong emperor's remarks in fact can also be seen as a simple statement of what he understood to be the basic principles for commercial exchange. His view would have made sense to Smith, Ricardo, and other classical economists. Smith expected markets to grow according to division of labour and Ricardo introduced the principle of comparative advantage. In addition, Smith recognized that trade between colonies and the mother country obeyed a distinctive logic according to which colonial raw materials were intended to support the growth of manufactures in the home country. Neither the market principles of exchange according to division of labour and comparative advantage nor the colonial trade principles could motivate the early modern trade between China and Europe. In the eighteenth century, in exchange for the teas, silks, and porcelains that they sold to the Europeans, the Chinese received silver bullion. But this silver was not a financial transfer to balance a foreign trade deficit as it would likely be seen in more modern times. Rather, silver was a commodity with a commercial value. The Chinese used the silver to expand their monetary supply which used a combination of silver and copper. The English grew increasingly concerned in the eighteenth century about the great outflows of bullion to China since mercantilist thought taught policymakers to view the outflow of silver with alarm. Indian-grown opium imports to China became the main commodity balancing trade flows between Europe, playing a deadly role in escalating tensions between Chinese and British officials in the nineteenth century. Even when the British found a good to substitute for silver, they had to choose a commodity they did not produce themselves.

---

[15] J. Mason Gentzler, *Changing China: Readings in the History of China from the Opium War to the Present* (New York, 1977), pp. 25–6.

Nothing in the economic relations between China and Europe in the eighteenth century would have prepared an observer for the subsequent economic divergence that marked Europe's economic take-off and China's stagnation. In his influential work *The Great Divergence*, Kenneth Pomeranz argued for economic similarities between China and Europe before the industrial revolution that were largely unknown except to a few scholars working on China.[16] The existence of these similarities sets the context for identifying the reasons why Europe subsequently industrialized and China did not until considerably later. His account of economic divergence has been understood by many readers to highlight coal and colonies—the latter providing easy access to energy sources to be used for industrial production and easy access to windfall gains from raw materials produced in overseas locations. The economic divergence between the two world regions turns on environmental differences in the two regions and the linkages built by one of these regions with other parts of the world. But the existence of coal and cotton in the colonies does not explain what created the demand for either of them. Without new technologies to create energy and power, as well as new technologies to produce machine-made cloth, coal and cotton could not have become so important economically.

To explain the advances in science and technology, historians have offered social and cultural explanations for the cluster of inventions in the late eighteenth and early nineteenth centuries that powered the expansion of English textile production and the development of steam power and the railways. European approaches to observing and explaining the natural world were geared to solving problems. People shared their findings and sometimes undertook projects in response to the offer of rewards and prizes. Scholars are quick to assume that identifying the particular social contexts and cultural sensibilities found among Europeans engaged in scientific and technological research explains a more general set of conditions necessary for scientific and technological changes needed for economic growth. The economic divergence between China and Europe then follows from the absence of the European social and cultural traits in China. An analogous identification of institutions particular to England that explains its early modern commercial expansion with institutions more generally necessary for economic growth has been made. But for this phenomenon we have examples in other places in the world, including

---

[16] Kenneth Pomeranz, *The Great Divergence: China, Europe and the Making of the Modern World Economy* (Princeton, 2000).

many parts of China, where commercial expansion took place without English-style institutions. We therefore can distinguish a contextual explanation plausible for England from what might be a more general explanation, which should have elements that apply to both English and non-English cases of commercial expansion. What made contracts and courts to resolve commercial disputes so important in England (and on the continent as well) was the reduction of risk associated with the uncertainty regarding a trading partner living up to the terms of an exchange. The Chinese were able to expand long-distance trade without the kind of legal infrastructure elaborated in Europe because they reduced risk in other ways, most importantly through social networks based on combinations of native place and kinship. For scientific and technological changes we do not have the same kind of parallel to commercial expansion in China that alerts us to the non-necessity of English-style institutions for early modern economic growth. It is thus difficult to know if there were comparable substitutes in China for the ways in which technological information was shared or the manner in which observations of the natural world led to improvements in production.

The cluster of inventions that together make up what historians of technology refer to as 'general purpose technologies' (GPT) occur infrequently in history, though their likelihood has increased in modern history because of the manner in which such improvements are pursued in recent times compared with the ways in which GPT emerged based on practices begun in the early modern era. Today, researchers are organized in laboratories within national contexts that vary in terms of funding, but also as members of international networks that make the transmission of knowledge across world regions easier than was possible a few centuries ago. Some historians of science, including Joseph Needham, creator of the 'Science and Civilization in China' project, remind us that scientific and technological knowledge likely flowed across Eurasia in the distant as well as not-so-distant past, but the existence of Chinese and European scientific traditions rooted within distinct world regions that may have shared some ideas and practices but largely worked independently of each other forms a reasonable contrast with contemporary conditions. Once the nineteenth-century expansion of European economic and political power spread across the globe, knowledge of Western science and technology, as well as their economic and political applications, became increasingly common, even if people's capacities to take advantage of the economic possibilities unleashed by European changes were not shared equally by all. It becomes very difficult to find the economic applications of science and technology anywhere in the world without observing the conceptual frameworks developed in Europe; this empirical situation makes it unlikely that we can even imagine some scenario in which science and technology could have developed differently. But how plausible or implausible an alternative scenario of science and technology developing under a non-European basis is cannot be reasonably estimated. The example of medicine does, however, remind us that some of the scientific traditions developed in China and Europe have persisted to the present, with the flows of knowledge between them beginning at different times—Western medicine began to disseminate to China well before knowledge of Chinese medicine moved to the West, but today the flows are in both directions and increasingly connected.

Given the difficulties of concluding confidently that only European social practices and cultural norms could have produced the kinds of science and technology necessary for an industrial economy, we can consider an alternative approach to explaining English industrialization as being at the core of the economic divergence between China and Europe which is one key marker of the uneven entrance of these two world regions into the modern era. Rather than focusing on the non-economic factors affecting the supply side of science and technology advances, about which we know too little, we could turn instead to consider the economic demand for scientific and technological change. Jean-Laurent Rosenthal and I argue in *Before and beyond Divergence: The Politics of Economic Change in China and Europe* that differences in the relative prices of capital and labour in China and Europe meant that the likelihoods of developing economically useful technologies with market advantages became higher in European than in Chinese settings.[17] This follows from the relatively higher proportion of craft manufacture in European cities than in China. This contrast is typically considered to be an indicator of Chinese backwardness but the causal linkage may well run in the other direction: because Chinese craft production was situated in the countryside, it became more backward. Between the sixteenth and eighteenth centuries, it made more sense economically to produce goods in the countryside since labour costs were high relative to capital costs and therefore labour was cheaper when located in rural settings. Food was more expensive in cities because of transport costs and the workers' productive life was shorter because of a higher death

---

[17] Jean-Laurent Rosenthal and R. Bin Wong, *Before and beyond Divergence: The Politics of Economic Change in China and Europe* (Cambridge, MA, 2011).

rate due to disease. But Europeans faced chronic threats of warfare given their fragmented and competing polities, which made urban locations safer places in which to produce crafts behind city walls. There is a venerable tradition of arguing that political competition is good for economic development, much as market competition is generally healthy. But such views neglect the higher costs of producing in cities as well as the smaller markets caused by divisions among different political regimes usually seeking to tax trade even when they don't actively disrupt trade through warfare. Moreover, when and where peace broke out, some forms of craft manufacture, in particular different kinds of textile production, expanded in different parts of the European countryside, including important cases in England.

The differences in demand for commercially useful technologies occasioned by relative factor prices made the emergence of industrialization more likely in Europe than in China, whatever the supply side differences for creating new technologies may have been in China and Europe. Coal and colonies could only play their roles in the European industrialization narrative once a new kind of demand for them was created. Deposits of coal would obviously have continued to exist whether or not they were exploited as intensively. For political rather than geological reasons, colonies would likely have continued to evolve in the absence of industrialization since they were a product of a politically motivated competition among European countries, a competition made possible by the fragmented political structure of the region—a feature absent in China's politically integrated world region. Apart from the question as to whether coal and colonies would have existed separately from the industrial uses to which they were put, were either necessary to explain the economic divergence? Certainly coal as a source of energy was necessary, though this may explain more why industrialization began in England and not in Europe, rather than why Europe and not China diverged economically. Both China and Europe had coal which was used in both world regions once the technologies to exploit it became available in each. Colonies certainly mattered as a source of cheap raw materials. Without these, industrial production costs would have increased, but would this have prevented the economic divide that opened between China and Europe from occurring? It would likely have reduced the rate at which the gap opened, but not the creation of the basic divergence. Once the industrialization process begun in Europe gathered momentum in the early nineteenth century, new economic possibilities and problems emerged in other world regions. At stake for political and economic leaders around the world were not the sources of initial divergence but the factors promoting economic differences across the world and those supporting movement towards convergence.

As in the case of political transformations, we can gain considerable insight into the dynamics of early modern economic change by examining dynamics within different world regions, attentive to both similarities and differences that might emerge in the consideration of any particular problem or process. Ignoring world regions as useful constructs within which to assess comparisons and connections in world history may leave us a more singular and precise set of ideas about what happened in the global past and allow us to avoid imprecise and multiple units of observation and analysis. But at least some of what we think about early modern world history based on such approaches will miss the bases of difference and variation in the past, which in turn matter to ordering and understanding what historians with more conventional concerns and approaches usually consider unique. Taking seriously world regions may help us bridge the gap between newer and older historical scholarship. This possibility alone makes it worthy of pursuit.

7
Institutions for writing the economic history of the global

JAN LUITEN VAN ZANDEN

Since the 1990s, world, global, and 'big' history have become familiar, if not fashionable, concepts. The *Journal of World History*, which set the new trend more than a decade ago, and its new competitor, the *Journal of Global History*, are representatives of these trends. This interest in global history is a complex phenomenon, and the number of approaches that can be pursued is perhaps as large as the number of scholars working in the field. Nevertheless, it is still possible to distinguish between a number of broad approaches.

The largest group of world historians consists of specialists of non-Western regions who are studying the interaction of their region with the rest of the world, often focusing on the period before 1800. Interaction in all spheres of life—from trade and bullion flows to academic exchange and the spread of microbes—forms the prime interest of these historians.[1] The message often is that all parts of the world were closely interconnected from a very early stage—and that we cannot understand the events in one region without studying its inter-exchange with other regions. Since the world is one complex, interconnected whole, Eurocentrism is from this point of view a rather shallow way to conceptualize the history of the world. Kevin O'Rourke and Jeffrey Williamson have developed an economic version of this approach in their analysis of the process of globalization during the nineteenth and twentieth centuries.[2] They study the growing interaction

---

[1] W. H. McNeill, *Plagues and Peoples* (Oxford, 1977); J. L. Abu-Lughod, *Before European Hegemony: The World System AD 1250–1350* (Oxford, 1989).
[2] K. H. O'Rourke and J. G. Williamson, *Globalization and History: The Evolution of the Nineteenth Century Atlantic Economy* (Cambridge, 1999).

Institutions for global economic history

between different parts of the world, which, however, before the age of steam did not lead to the integration of world markets (in fact they argue that between 1500 and 1800 the degree of integration was quite weak). Only after about 1870 did the first steps in the process of globalization—of worldwide integration of markets for goods, labour, and capital—occur. The Great War of 1914–18 interrupted this process, resulting in a backlash, which in effect meant that these processes were to a large extent reversed in the decades following 1914. Only in the final quarter of the twentieth century did a similar, second wave of globalization take place.

A different branch of global economic history concentrates on internationally comparative studies, again mainly concerning the period before 1800. The focus is on the economic success and failure of different parts of the world—most often Europe versus other (Asian) regions.[3] The view emerging from this literature is that before the industrial revolution—which is taken as an important break in the economic history of Europe—other parts of the world, in particular parts of China, India, and Japan, were quite well developed and experienced similar patterns of Smithian growth to those in Europe.[4] In this sense it argues against the Europe-centred view of the history of the world, which considers that everything of importance in the world since, say, the fourteenth century has happened in (Western) Europe (or, in slightly more extreme versions, in England).[5] More radical versions of the same story argue that until the industrial revolution, East Asia was in fact the core of the world economy and that Europe was situated on its periphery.[6]

A phenomenon that is perhaps related is the growing number of publications covering global economic history. Since the publication of Rondo Cameron's *Concise Economic History of the World* in 1989,[7] a still growing number of 'world histories' have been published by representatives of the generation of scholars who dominated the profession in the 1960s and 1970s. Their impact, also outside strictly academic circles, is sometimes quite large—the best example being David Landes's *The Wealth*

---

[3] An early example is E. L. Jones, *Growth Recurring: Economic Change in World History* (Oxford, 1988).
[4] Kenneth Pomeranz, *The Great Divergence: China, Europe, and the Making of the Modern World Economy* (Princeton, 2000).
[5] A. D. J. MacFarlane, *The Origins of English Individualism: The Family, Property and Social Transition* (Oxford, 1978).
[6] A. G. Frank, *ReOrient: Global Economy in the Asian Age* (Berkeley, 1998).
[7] R. E. Cameron, *A Concise Economic History of the World* (Oxford and New York, 1989).

and Poverty of Nations.[8] There is apparently a growing demand for these kinds of global visions of the long-term development of the world economy; the popularity of Angus Madison's *The World Economy: A Millennium Perspective* is another case in point.[9] Supply factors also seem to play a role: those pioneers of the renewal of economic history in the 1960s and 1970s apparently wish to conclude their careers by publishing world histories that synthesize the ideas they have worked on during a lifetime. In many other respects these books are rather traditional, however: they stress, for example, European exceptionality in the centuries before the industrial revolution.

It is perhaps a cliché that these trends—the emergence of world history and the growing demand for economic histories of the world—are linked to the process of globalization. During the past two decades or so we have increasingly become aware that we are living in a global 'village' and we therefore need (like smaller human communities before us) a historical perspective of our common roots, to make sense of our common history. Globalization induced economic historians to start thinking of the economic history of the world as one interconnected process, which is more than, and therefore different from, the mere sum of the economic histories of individual states and regions. The underlying question appears to be: if the world is one integrated whole, can we then interpret its history as one unified process? What are the big questions of 'global economic history' if we see the world as 'one global village'? And how can we answer them?

From questions to data

In another study I have suggested that this new global economic history should focus on two issues.[10] First, what can be called the 'success' of mankind: why are there so many people inhabiting this globe, and why are they so rich—that is, producing and consuming so much more than is strictly necessary for survival? And secondly, what can be seen as the 'failure' of mankind: why is global inequality so extremely high—why are

---

[8] D. S. Landes, *The Wealth and Poverty of Nations* (New York, 1998).
[9] Angus Maddison, *The World Economy: A Millennial Perspective* (Paris, 2001).
[10] Jan Luiten van Zanden, 'Global Economic History: A Personal View on the Agenda for Future Research', in *Explorations in Economic Growth: A festschrift for Riitta Hjerppe on her 60th Birthday*, ed. Sakari Heikkinen and Jan Luiten van Zanden (Amsterdam, 2004), pp. 365–84.

some countries rich and others poor? These are—since Adam Smith—the fundamental questions of economics and economic history, but what is new now is that we can start to pose these questions on a truly global scale, and can start to think of these changes towards the wealth and poverty of nations as global, interconnected processes of economic change. But global questions require global data. We want to know when and where 'modern economic growth' began—and why. The rise of new theoretical approaches in economics—new growth theory (or unified growth theory), new institutional economics, and new economic geography—also means that an up-to-date analysis of these global trends cannot concentrate on the narrow economic indicators only, on GDP and its components, as in the Angus Maddison synthesis. These new theories suggest that human capital formation, knowledge accumulation, institutions, and distance all matter—but also that their effects may change in time and may be different from place to place. Moreover, the concept of institutions introduces a lot of variables that are not easy to measure, such as trust, property rights, and governance. In a similar way, unified growth theory speculates about links between demographic and economic behaviour at the micro level of the household, which introduces a large range of 'variables' that are not easy to quantify—in particular not on a global scale.

Global datasets are required to answer the big questions of global economic history. The fundamental problem is, however, not that we do not have the knowledge to, for example, create a global dataset of the age of marriage of women and men in the past, or of the real wages of unskilled labourers in different pre-1800 societies, but that this knowledge is fragmented. There are specialists on eighteenth-century Chile (or on real wages in eighteenth-century Chile), on nineteenth-century Indonesia, or on fifteenth-century England, who know the local sources, and who have often already published important research related to the concept that is to be measured. The big problem is to bring this knowledge together, and standardize concepts and methods of measurement. It is, fundamentally, a problem of creating the right institutions for cooperation, in order to create the global datasets that are needed. In the past, a few very influential scholars, such as Angus Maddison, managed to organize a network on a specific theme (in his case, national accounting) in such a way that they were able to produce the kind of global datasets required. The point of this chapter is that we as a profession have to develop the institutions to pool and standardize our data on a more systematic basis.

The collaboratory[11]

Over the past two decades, the natural sciences have established collaboratories to fulfil these needs. A collaboratory is a more or less standardized way of working together as a group of scholars specialized in a certain field, with the aim of realizing some kind of common project, or benefitting from a large instrument (a telescope for example). After providing some theoretical background about the possible risks of collaboratories, I will show how research on the functioning of what is now being described as an 'information commons' may offer some guidance in the construction of such a framework. A transparent institutional design can create the right incentives for researchers to cooperate and contribute to the common good: to encourage high quality scientific output. To illustrate these ideas about collaboratories, we use an example of a collaborative project that is close to the ideal of a true collaboratory: the Global Price and Income History Group,[12] in cooperation with the Historical Prices and Wages initiative at the International Institute of Social History (IISH).[13]

The term 'collaboratory' first appeared in the scholarly community in the late 1980s. A collaboratory is 'a laboratory without walls, where scientists are connected to each other, to instruments, and to data independent of time and location'. It can be regarded as 'an organizational entity that spans distance, supports rich and recurring human interaction oriented to a common research area, and provides access to data sources, artefacts and tools required to accomplish research tasks'.[14] Collaboratories can provide communication environments and tools for scientists, they can serve as a communication tool for students, allow the collection of data, give online access to data to members and in some cases non-members of the collaboratory, and create the means to share scientific instruments within research or learning communities.[15] The idea was originally

---

[11] This section is based on T. de Moor and J. L. van Zanden, 'Do ut des Collaboratories as a "New" Method for Scholarly Communication and Cooperation for Global and World History', *Historical Methods*, 41/2 (2008), 67–78.
[12] See <http://gpih.ucdavis.edu/>.
[13] See <http://www.iisg.nl/hpw>.
[14] A. Finholt, 'Collaboratories', *Annual Review of Information Science and Technology*, 36 (2002), 465–91; at 467.
[15] The science of collaboratories project has several different names for different types of collaboratories. There are about six different types, according to their classification: distributed research centre: Biocore: <http://www.ks.uiuc.edu/Research/biocore/> (accessed 10 April 2007), virtual learning community, virtual community of practice, shared instrument

developed for the joint use of instruments, but has now been applied to many other forms of collective work.[16]

Notwithstanding the many variations in objectives of current collaboratories, they all have several common features:[17]

- *Boundary crossing*: a collaboratory is first and foremost a tool to bridge gaps and distances of: (a) geography, by providing international access through the Internet; (b) time, by supplying both synchronous and asynchronous communication technologies; (c) institutions, by allowing groups access to tools and materials of common interest; and (d) disciplines, by enabling the participants to decide what resources are most relevant to a topic, without regard for traditional understandings of what constitutes a particular discipline.
- *Shared enquiry*: participants not only share common goals in for example data collection, but also a common set of problems or issues that interest them, which they study in depth.
- *Intentionality*: a collaboratory is a joint venture; there is a shared consciousness of the status of its website as a mutual project.
- *Active participation and contribution*: the success of a collaboratory is to a large degree decided upon by the extent that its members use and add to its resources.
- *Members only*: although the data collected by a collaboratory can become freely accessible over time (this usually means after publication of the research results), participation in a collaboratory is generally for members only. Membership is usually restricted to peers in the research field.

(Earthscope, <http://www.earthscope.org>, accessed 10 April 2007), expert consultation (TeleMedicine <http://www.telemedicine.arizona.edu>, accessed 10 April 2007), and community data systems (see, e.g., <http://research.umbc.edu>, accessed 10 April 2007)).

[16] Besides their diverging objectives, the scale of collaboratories can also vary significantly. Most collaboratories that manage to survive for at least a few years are on a grand scale, as in the Human Genome Project, or the ATLAS Project at the European Organization for Nuclear Research (better known as CERN). ATLAS coordinates 1,800 particle physicists in thirty-four countries. They also can include many formerly separate threads of research. For instance, the Space Physics and Aeronomy Research Collaboratory, based at the University of Michigan, gives researchers simultaneous access to both observations and predictive models so they can predict 'space weather' (such as the geomagnetic storms that produce aurora borealis events) and then see what actually happens.

[17] These features are partly based on: K. J. Lunsford and B. C. Bruce, 'Collaboratories', *Working Together on the Web*, 45/1 (2001), 52–9.

- *Access to shared resources*: collaboratories provide unique information (data, links, research findings) and tools needed by participants.
- *Technologies*: collaboratories involve technologies. These vary from scientific instruments shared by sophisticated communities, to the unique symbol systems used among participants, or the information technologies necessary to communicate.
- *Limited in time*: collaboratories are set up to reach certain research goals (creating a dataset, answering certain research questions). Once these goals have been attained, the collaboratory is dissolved, though in some cases its results remain available via the collaboratory's website.

Collaboratories differ in several ways from WIKIs which are increasingly being established on the Web. Though these can play a valuable role in offering free and unrestricted access to information, the user has no guarantee that the data are reliable. If the author's credentials and validity are unknown, the quality of the information cannot be judged. Although collaboratories can be as free as a WIKI for the dissemination of data (if the authors of the data allow it), access to the input side is restricted to peers. In this way the quality level is controlled, and collaborators dare to trust one another's data.

The development of collaboratories along the above given common set of features stems from a trend that has developed over the last half-century towards large-scale projects or so-called 'big science', which requires more collaboration among scientists, not only in the natural sciences but also in the social sciences and the humanities (cf. the increasing importance of global history). The natural sciences have an advantage in that they also have a common scientific language, such as chemical or mathematical formulas, and most of the data used for research are newly created, thus allowing the researchers to start from a consensus about which data to collect and how to input them in the database (the structure of which can be agreed on in advance). In the case of history, data must be derived from what has been left by our predecessors. The Historical Prices and Wages database shows that this is not a straightforward task. First, its information is derived from a multitude of very different sources, with varying accuracy and applicability. Some sources tend to under- or overestimate the situation, depending on the purposes of the archival documents. Some of the data refer to hourly wages, other data to daily wages, weekly or even annual wages, with varying numbers of hours attached to each time entity, and differences from place to place. Wages may also vary, with differences in experience, education, gender, age, task, or function of the receiver, or they may be supplemented with wages in kind. And what about estimating the cost of labour in societies where wage labour was still a rare phenomenon? All in all, extensive meta-knowledge is necessary before wages across countries and over time can be compared. The Global Price and Income History Group of UC Davis in collaboration with the Historical Prices and Wages Initiative in Amsterdam, with the help of many researchers associated with other universities, has managed to bring together a multitude of such data, along with working papers that contain extensive meta-knowledge. One of the aims is to measure systematically the development of real wages in the centuries before and during the Great Divergence of the nineteenth century. This is based on a methodology developed for large parts of Europe by Robert Allen,[18] which has now been applied to the Ottoman Empire, Japan, India, China, South Africa, and Latin America, resulting in a near global overview of this aspect of the standard of living (and of economic performance) in the economies involved. Other, related work is concentrating on the changes in relative prices in different parts of the world, on interest rates, and premiums for skilled work—all features of economies that can be studied systematically in this way.

The concept of a collaboratory has even more potential than this initiative shows, however. It does not fully exploit the potential of the collaboratory idea. For example, the Historical Prices and Wages database could be improved by paying more attention to metadata standards and to the future of the dataset in the long term. An important element is also the accessibility to the collected data. In principle, while a collaboratory is not specifically designed to do this, once the data have been used by scientists, there is no reason to keep the public from having access to the datasets. Global Price and Income History Group publishes all its results on two websites.[19] These data collections, which were developed by leading researchers, can provide added value to society as a whole, as well as encouraging other researchers who may not yet be on a peer level in that field of science (e.g. young researchers) to use the data and develop their own line of research, or a new collaboratory.

---

[18] Robert C. Allen, 'The Great Divergence in European Wages and Prices from the Middle Ages to the First World War', *Explorations in Economic History*, 38 (2001), 411–47.
[19] See <http://gpih.ucdavis.edu/> and <http://www.iisg.nl/hpw> (accessed 4 June 2012).

The research infrastructure project CLIO INFRA, an initiative of the International Institute for Social History in Amsterdam, is an attempt to bring such collaboratories together and create a global framework for this kind of work. The idea is to construct a large number of datasets covering the main economic, demographic, and institutional features of the world economy in the period since 1500. The collaboratory is the main instrument for doing this. It will consist of a central datahub where all datasets will be made available, in combination with a number of specialized hubs, such as the datahub on wages and prices of the Global Prices and Incomes Project and the datahub on historical national accounts of the Gröningen Growth and Development Center. Other datahubs (on biological standard of living, on human capital formation, on demography, and on institutions) are under construction as well.[20]

---

[20] For further details see <http://www.clio.infra.eu/index.php/Main_Page>.

Part III
Shaping Global History

8
Writing about divergences in global history: some implications for scale, methods, aims, and categories

KENNETH POMERANZ

'Divergence in global history' is a slightly odd topic. It was assigned to me phrased in general terms, as if it could just as easily be 'divergences in world history'. It has, however, become strongly associated with a particular case: the opening of a large gap in both wealth and power between several North Atlantic countries, on the one hand, and just about everybody else on the other—in other words, what has often been called 'the rise of the West'. Presumably, I was asked to write about 'divergences' because I have written a book about precisely that topic called *The Great Divergence*, but therein lies a tale about writing: I had intended for that book to be called *A Great Divergence*, and did not notice that the definite article had crept in until it was too late.

Certainly, I have no desire to minimize the importance of that episode, or the value of framing it as a 'divergence'—a perspective that keeps both comparisons and connections between Western Europe and other parts of the world in the picture in a way that many accounts framed as 'the rise of the West' do not. But we should also recognize that the way we think about or write about that particular divergence may not be a model for writing about divergences in general. When we move to a general level, various issues come to mind.

First, since divergences are necessarily something recognized through comparisons, it may seem that they belong primarily to that axis of world history, rather than to that which emphasizes connections or a third dimension that we might call 'comprehensiveness'.[1] But while divergence must have a comparative dimension, and doesn't *require* connections, connections can figure in multiple ways. There can be divergence attendant upon a process of disconnection (so that A and B diverge when ideas, resources, or whatever no longer flow between them, the way that subgroups within a single species may experience genetic drift when they no longer have contact with each other). There can be divergences that occur in a context of *increased* connection and inequality, as two entities that were separate are brought together in a hierarchical relationship conferring very unequal benefit (or negative benefit for one)—as in, for instance, a Wallerstinian view of the world economy.[2]

There can also be increased non-hierarchical diversification within some increasingly connected body or network in which that body holds together. Under those circumstances, the divergence is real but limited—in other words, the trend of increasing difference stops at some point, either on its own or through outside influence—and the chances of at least partial re-convergence are relatively high. Here we might think of the difference between simple overseas expansion of a religious group, in which the original group is simply gaining adherents elsewhere without those new recruits either changing the original group much or adopting all of its views, and what sometimes happens as the new adherents gain voice in governing bodies and insist that their visions are of equal status with what has been popular in the religion's older centres.

Second, historical divergences are provisional unless we specify the time frame, and no time frame is a priori the correct one. If whatever gap we are talking about eventually closes, is the interesting way to frame things as an enquiry into why there was a time lag in getting to the same place (in which case we tend to look for barriers of one sort or another that were later overcome), or is the issue of timing ultimately less important than explaining the spread of whatever we're talking about?

---

[1] By 'comprehensiveness', I refer to attempts to generalize about states or trends characterizing the world in general at some moment, rather than statements about one or more human groups in contrast to others: a bit like what one might imagine a Martian observer would try to do. Such efforts are obviously very tricky, but they should have some place in global history. For an attempt to make such statements the *main* focus of world history, see David Christian, *Maps of Time: An Introduction to Big History* (Berkeley, 2004).
[2] Immanuel Wallerstein, *The Modern World System*, 3 vols (New York, 1974, 1980, 1989).

An example that is not global, but illustrates the principle with familiar material, is the way that economic history comparisons between France and England have changed in the last thirty-five years. Before the work of scholars like Crafts and Harley and O'Brien and Keydar, most such comparisons focused on explaining 'why France failed'; but as a gap of a few decades in initiating modern growth came to be seen as much less important in light of very similar contemporary living standards, French economic history came to be more commonly framed as part of a shared (Western) 'European miracle'.[3] Naturally this raises questions about whether a similar reframing makes sense for Japan—where much of the literature has already shifted that way, even though Japan showed no signs of independently initiating modern growth (suggesting that it may have had some of the necessary conditions, but not all of them), and the gap of a few decades before it followed parts of Europe into modern growth had major historical consequences (as it did for continental Western Europe, too). And if we can reframe Japanese history that way, what about the Yangzi Delta, where the Human Development Index (HDI) is now roughly equal to that of Italy, Austria, or the UK, and just below France, Finland, and Iceland, and rising steadily?[4] It is tempting to assert that the same principle applies, but here the relative delay in initiating modern growth was significantly longer than in Japan, the short and medium-term historical consequences of that delay considerably larger, and the country as a whole (as opposed to the region) still a very long way from any convergence to the living standards of the early industrializers. What criteria do we employ in deciding those questions?

Third, historical divergences are never total, and are always, at least in part, a matter of perspective. One can construct, for instance, a series of

---

[3] For instance, N. F. R. *Crafts, British Economic Growth during the Industrial Revolution* (Oxford, 1985); Patrick O'Brien and Caglar Keydar, *Economic Growth in Britain and France, 1780—1914* (London, 1978); Eric Jones, *The European Miracle: Environments, Economies, and Geopolitics in the History of Europe and Asia* (Cambridge, 1981).

[4] Provincial data for China are available at <http://en.wikipedia.org/wiki/List_of_Chinese_administrative_divisions_by_Human_Development_Index> (accessed 10 June 2012). If one combines Jiangsu, Zhejiang, and Shanghai, one gets a population-weighted average of 0.850; this figure should understate Jiangnan's HDI, since both Zhejiang and Jiangsu contain substantial regions that are less well off than any part of Jiangnan. For comparison, the following are official figures for 2010: France 0.872; Iceland, 0.86; Italy, 0.854; UK, 0.849. For the European data see Jeni Klugman, *Human Development Report 2010 the Real Wealth of Nations: Pathways to Development* (New York: 2010), p. 139 <http://www.undp.org.ua/downloads/HDR_2010_EN_Complete.pdf> (accessed 15 June 2011).

comparisons that would bring out many differences among nineteenth-century US expansion, the Russian move into Siberia, and Qing expansion into what is now China's far west—differences that would grow ever wider with time, as a 'divergence' should—but from the standpoint of the Hopi, the Miao, and the Yakuts it might well be the similarities that matter.

Fourth, as this suggests, we need to think not only about divergences and convergences, but also about parallels—or, for that matter, oscillating distances that never completely disappear.

Fifth, any story framed in terms of a divergence raises the issue of 'origins'—and all the problems with designating and emphasizing historical origins that Marc Bloch pointed out long ago.[5] If we have a specific thing that we think we can pinpoint as key to creating a divergence, but it only developed slowly, what do we do with the original event? This is, of course, hardly a problem unique to studies of divergence. It comes up all the time, for instance in studying scientific or technological innovations that spread slowly at first. Is the important moment—and the important object of explanation—the invention of, say, the original steam engine, which for over one hundred years, was largely confined to pumping water out of British mines, or the subsequent changes that eventually made it suitable for many other uses and places?[6] Or what about a change in circumstances which makes some existing difference have a new impact? Or cases where some difference that eventually comes to be an important advantage had long been present, but had been outweighed by something else until something happened to shift its relative importance? There are also questions of when differences (which are always present) become 'divergences'—something that is complicated even for the *relatively* measurable area of economic history. Consider for a moment that if we accept the revision to Maddison's figures suggested by Van Zanden in 2004, then per capita GDP in the Yangzi Delta *c*.1750 trailed that in England (and per capita GDP in China that of Europe) by only about 10 per cent.[7] That is considerably less than the margin by which most of the EU trails the US

---

[5] Marc Bloch, *The Historian's Craft*, trans. Peter Putnam (New York, 1953), pp. 29–35.
[6] This difference is, among other things, at the heart of Robert Allen's recent use of a distinction between 'macro-inventions' and 'micro-inventions' to understand the Industrial Revolution as both a British and a global event: see Robert C. Allen, *The British Industrial Revolution in Global Perspective* (Cambridge, 2009), pp. 135–55.
[7] Jan Luiten van Zanden, 'Estimating Early Modern Economic Growth', working paper, International Institute of Social History, University of Utrecht, 2004, pp. 22–3 <http://www.iisg.nl/research/jvz-estimating.pdf> (accessed 17 December 2007).

today, or that by which the US trails Luxembourg, but nobody expects that these contemporary incomes represent the early stages of a gap that will ever approach the 12:1 difference in per capita GDP that the US and China reached before significant reconvergence began.[8] So if we proceed strictly by tracking outcomes, we have no 'great divergence' in 1750; but at the same time, clearly the things that had created big differences by 1800,[9] and enormous ones by 1900, weren't entirely absent in 1750.

So this, too, reminds us of the importance of experimenting with multiple timescales even within a single enquiry. When, for instance, should we bring in the role of the Americas as a source of primary products and an outlet for migrants? Should we bring it in only when it starts to have an unmistakable statistical impact (after 1730, and very strongly after 1830, as in some of O'Rourke and Williamson's work)?[10] Or when the institutional foundations for this impact were being laid?

Part of any answer, as we've seen, depends on what else we think was necessary to make this 'foundation' matter and/or could have prevented it from mattering. Ultimately, then, we can't avoid questions of causality, or questions of (at least implicit) counterfactuals, much as many historians profess to avoid them.[11] And if counterfactuals are part of our thinking, we may as well make them explicit, and more rigorous than they tend to be when they are only implicit.

It is also worth noting that insofar as divergences are an important topic for us, a history of humanity as a species (*à la* David Christian, among others[12]) cannot be a *sufficient* account of global history. Of course this doesn't mean that such histories don't have their own importance—among other things in helping to give us a context in which to decide which divergences really matter—but such stories can also obscure important divergences unless we make an effort to treat them as just one of various simultaneously important frames.

---

[8] Penn World Tables for 2008: <http://pwt.econ.upenn.edu/php_site/pwt_index.php> (accessed 15 June 2011).
[9] Li Bozhong and Jan Luiten van Zanden, 'Before the Great Divergence? Comparing the Yangzi Delta and the Netherlands at the Beginning of the 19th Century' CEPR Discussion Paper No. DP8023 (1 October 2010). Available at SSRN: <http://ssrn.com/abstract=1711016> (accessed 15 June 2011).
[10] Kevin O'Rourke and Jeffrey Williamson, 'From Malthus to Ohlin: Trade, Industrialisation, and Distribution since 1500', *Journal of Economic Growth*, 10/1 (2005), 5–34, at 18–25.
[11] For a discussion of the necessity of dealing with causation, even in disciplines that prefer not to, see Judea Pearl, *Causality: Models, Reasoning, and Inference* (Cambridge, 2000).
[12] David Christian, *Maps of Time*.

Trying to keep both these very large stories and ones in which divergences among human groups remain crucial in view raises complex issues of representation; these may show up especially strongly in stories that have a large environmental history component, since environment is quite obviously both global and inescapably local. I can live almost anywhere and participate in an intellectual world centred thousands of miles away—and to some extent, this was already possible a long time ago. But the air I breathe and water I drink are inevitably local, and often unaffected by trends elsewhere. Yet at the same time, environmental history is quite clearly global in scope, and—especially so when we think about its larger temporal and spatial timescales—can encourage a viewpoint in which divergences are collapsed or elided.

An interesting example of this issue is evident in Alfred Crosby's *Ecological Imperialism*. Crosby's story is essentially that of European overseas colonization, but he shifts the focus sharply away from European institutions or culture. Instead he argues that any group of people from a densely populated part of Eurasia would have come to dominate the temperate zones of the Americas and Australia once they came upon them, because the diseases, plants, domesticated animals, and so on that they brought with them would have devastated their counterparts from the rest of the world, as European ones did in fact do. Furthermore, Eurasian domesticates, freed from the predators that had co-evolved with them in the Old World, attained remarkable yields in their new settings, helping to make the neo-Europes both very prosperous in themselves and very valuable to the original Europe as trading partners and outlets for 'surplus' people. That the people who wrought this havoc and reaped these gains happened to be from Europe, rather than China, India, or Persia was, as Crosby sees it, partly a matter of their geographic location, partly of skills in blue water sailing, partly of the fact that Europeans needed to find a way to get to Asia and/or the sub-Saharan gold fields much more than Asians needed to find a way to reach them. It did not result from Europeans having some much more general advantage, such as being freer or more rational or more motivated to transform the world.[13]

But in Crosby's conclusion, he steps back to take a broader view. At least temporarily, his story stops being one about how Europeans, their accompanying biota, and their descendants gained an advantage over

[13] Alfred Crosby, *Ecological Imperialism: The Biological Expansion of Europe, 900–1900*, 2nd edn (Cambridge, 2004).

others—or, as Crosby's introduction memorably phrased his guiding question, 'What in heaven's name is the reason why the sun never sets on the empire of the dandelion?'[14] Instead this section of the conclusion glosses the book as a tale of how humans, *as a species*, became able to generate vast food surpluses in the 'neo-Europes' which allowed us to greatly increase our numbers and prosperity. Crosby compares this process to a military conquest and occupation.[15] The people we now call 'indigenes', who arrived in the Americas and Australia millennia ago, are likened to the marines storming a beach; they took enormous casualties and did not remain masters of the territory in the long term, but they were a critical part of the human conquest (wiping out indigenous megafauna, for instance, which left ecological niches that Eurasian quadrupeds would later occupy). The early European and African arrivals Crosby likens to the rest of an invading army: much better off than the first wave, but still arriving under strict discipline and enduring great privation. (For the purposes of this argument, it does not matter that the Africans suffered far more and benefited far less—yet another case in which a divergence that is enormously important on one scale disappears on another.) The vastly larger wave of post-1840 migrants represent the civilian occupiers: whatever hardships they bore, their lives were nonetheless strikingly free and secure compared with those of their predecessors, and they reaped by far the greatest material benefits.

This metaphor—placing all humans on the same team in a struggle to get the most out of the planet—is not misleading from a certain Olympian and biological perspective, though whether the grain surpluses of the neo-Europes—undoubtedly crucial c.1850–1960—are actually more important in the longer run than the dramatic gains in food production by Europe, China, and India in the second half of the twentieth century is another matter. But because the metaphor minimizes the struggles among groups of humans that are central to most history, it also poses serious problems—epistemologically and, potentially, even ethically—if not balanced by attention to the origins and present reality of global inequality.

Essentially, attempts to write history on a global scale highlight a more general problem that arises as soon as we try to explain historical events or patterns (on any level) that are neither completely unique nor ever exactly replicated. Events are examples of convergence, divergence, parallel

[14] Ibid., p. 7.
[15] Ibid., p. 295.

development, or parts of a single, larger process by virtue of the labels we attach to them, and those labels are themselves derived in part from the researcher's agenda.

Trying to impart some order to these choices, Jack Goldstone has argued that we should choose our explanatory framework for any event in part by looking at the frequency of events like it and the range of circumstances in which it recurred.[16] An outcome that emerged repeatedly (though not necessarily universally) from varied initial conditions (what we are calling a convergence) might well recur because it was an optimal (or at least equilibrium) outcome, and the path to it might therefore be well traced by rational choice theory. Or it might recur because it represents some fundamental constraint that human efforts can relax only temporarily. (The two can even go together, if we assume that a particular outcome is the best possible one given certain constraints that prevail widely.)

On the other hand, an outcome that occurs relatively infrequently, and always in a situation where certain initial conditions prevailed, might lead us to search for a general law like those of physics (noting here that general need not mean applicable to a broad range of cases, simply invariant given certain conditions). Finally, a unique outcome should lead us to look for a truly path-dependent story, in which it is not initial conditions, but a particular sequence of exogenous early events that lock in a later outcome: something that is especially likely to appear to us as a highly significant 'divergence'.

This is a useful beginning, but we then run into serious trouble trying to categorize events. Is British economic growth in the late eighteenth century a unique instance of 'first industrialization' and a new era of thus-far sustained growth, or a more common temporary growth spurt of the kind that Goldstone has called an 'efflorescence', which was later followed by industrialization? (In a 2009 essay, I argue at some length against Goldstone's claim that you can cleanly separate the two in this case, but the ideal types are clearly distinguishable.[17]) Is the peopling of North America just one example of a relatively common phenomenon of 'frontier

---

[16] Jack Goldstone, 'Initial Conditions, General Laws, Path Dependence, and Explanation in Historical Sociology', *American Journal of Sociology*, 104/3 (1998), 829–45.

[17] Kenneth Pomeranz, 'Le machinisme induit-il une discontinuité historique? Industrialisation, modernité précoce et formes du changement économique dans l'histoire globale', in *Histoire globale, mondialisations, capitalisme*, ed. P. Beaujard, L. Berger and P. Norel (Paris, 2009), pp. 335–73.

expansion', with certain more or less similar features, or as Alfred Crosby saw it, the centerpiece of a once in many millennia story of 'closing the seams of Pangaea' with more or less unique biologically driven dynamics, repeated in just a few other cases (such as Australia)? The examples could be multiplied indefinitely. The appropriate labelling will very often rest on the timescale we employ, and the extent to which we observe either return to equilibrium/convergence or increasing returns/continuing divergence over that time frame. And sometimes we will see bits of both, depending on which variables we look at. There has been considerable reconvergence of life expectancies since 1945, after the period 1830–1945 opened up unprecedented differences, and significant reconvergence of literacy rates, but incomes have continued to diverge between the pre-1930 North Atlantic core and most of the rest of the world, except for coastal East Asia, the fringes of Europe (e.g. Scandinavia and Iberia), and a few small oil states and financial centres elsewhere.[18]

David Kracauer, an evolutionary biologist, has suggested that historians might deal with some of these difficulties by defining their topics so as to make them amenable to the use of the best tools available. Though he does not say so, this would often involve eschewing, at least provisionally, many of the topics that intuitively seem the most important, including many dramatic, complex events that are central to national and other identities. Moreover, Kracauer's approach is in this respect more or less the reverse of Goldstone's. Goldstone, like most of us, begins with big events that are self-evidently worth explaining, and then tries to place them in groupings that will suggest what the best explanatory tools are. Kracauer, by contrast, suggests that we move our focus—at least for now—away from 'The French Revolution', where we are stuck with the N =1 problem, and look at the sub-events that happened multiple times—meetings of the Estates General, confiscations of church property, etc.[19]

This approach also has its uses, but since it relies heavily on decomposing large unique events into smaller and less unique components it is unlikely to be sufficient for the task of 'writing the global'. An alternate, perhaps complementary, strategy would be to try to get categories with a

---

[18] See data in Angus Maddison, *Monitoring the World Economy, 1820–1992* (Paris, 1995), Table I:4, and Penn World Tables for 2008: <http://pwt.econ.upenn.edu/php_site/pwt_index.php> (accessed 15 June 2011).
[19] David Kracauer, 'The Search for Patterns in Meta-History', *Santa Fe Institute Bulletin*, 22/1 (2007), 32–9; 36.

reasonable number of items in them by resorting to generalized categories *imposed by the investigator*, rather than those most legible either to the participants in an event or to supposed 'heirs' who profess a great stake in it. With this strategy, we would not go from 'French Revolution' to 'confiscations of church property, etc.', but to categories like 'collective violence', 'state collapses', centre-out' and 'periphery-in' revolutions, etc.[20]

Many social scientists—especially non-historians—have, of course, been doing this for many decades. So far, they have done so without finding many generalizations that are agreed to hold across a wide variety of historical circumstances; but the process of reasoning involved is nonetheless essential to thinking about divergences in global history. At the very least, proposed generalizations of this sort generate a set of expectations which, when frustrated, give us new problems to explain and lead us to local differences in either initial conditions or subsequent events which may explain a growing divergence.

Sometimes the explanation for a proposed generalization not holding in a different society will be very simple. For instance, R. Bin Wong has pointed out that while proletarianization seems to have lowered the age at first marriage in various parts of Europe—since it made it easier to start a new household without parental consent—one would not expect the same thing to happen as wage labour spread through parts of Qing and Republican China, since marriage there often did not involve setting up a new household, and since the age at first marriage was already very young.[21] In fact, we could note that in some Chinese cases, wage labour for young women facilitated marriage resistance, raising the average age at first marriage.[22] Rather than giving up on generalization, one might proceed from these observations to rewrite the hypothesis as 'the availability of wage labour reduces parental control over marriage', and see whether that claim holds up more generally. At least it seems promising, though the extent, pace, and nature of the change have clearly varied.

---

[20] See Kenneth Pomeranz, 'Labeling and Analyzing Historical Phenomena: Some Preliminary Challenges', *Cliodynamics: The Journal of Theoretical and Mathematical History*, 2/1 (2011), 3–27; 126–7; on centre-out and periphery-in revolutions, in particular, see Charles Tilly, 'Town and Country in Revolution', in *Peasant Rebellion and Communist Revolution in Asia*, ed. John W. Lewis (Stanford, CA, 1974), pp. 271–302.

[21] R. Bin Wong, *China Transformed: Historical Change and the Limits of European Experience* (Ithaca, NY, 1997), pp. 37–8.

[22] Janice Stockard, *Daughters of the Canton Delta: Marriage Patterns and Economic Strategies in South China, 1860–1930* (Stanford, CA, 1989), pp. 52–5, 134–86.

In other cases, the intervening factors that cause a hypothesis generated from one case to not hold in others might be so numerous, and the paths along which they act so complex, that they are hard to specify—much less to incorporate into a more broadly applicable rule. Still, if we want to get beyond simply shrugging and saying 'well, A and B were different', we need some kind of sorting principle.

Here it is important to remember that historians never produce a one-to-one map of exactly how *anything* happened; but, unlike disciplines where the holy grail is a simple model that has strong predictive power, we generally don't want—even on a global level—to accept arguments that things happened 'as if X were driving the story' when we know that X does not even approximate the actual dynamics. As I have argued elsewhere,[23] one useful rule of thumb for explaining social phenomena is that the mechanisms invoked to explain why something happened in some places, but not in others with which they shared at least some basic similarities (without which 'divergence' isn't interesting), must involve a plausible path by which those mechanisms would *influence* human *intentions*; it need not, however, rely on reproducing the actor's actual thought processes. Thus it makes sense to argue that rivers with wild seasonal fluctuations and heavy silt loads would inhibit the implementation of known technologies for water mills,[24] even if we cannot find a single document in which somebody says 'Gee, I'd build a water-powered mill here if only the current were more regular.' It also seems a permissible simplification to 'explain' a low rate of urbanization at least partly on the basis of wage rates having been lower than tenant earnings,[25] even if it was probably only a few tenants who ever explicitly framed the problem in those terms. On the other hand, McCloskey's famous argument that medieval English villagers had roughly the same scattering of plots that *they would have had* had they been consciously maximizing the number of standard deviations separating their average yield from the yield that would bring starvation—a calculation nobody at the time could have done[26]—is a very interesting observation about convergent outcomes, but it does not dispense with the

---

[23] Pomeranz, 'Labeling and Analyzing Historical Phenomena', especially pp. 138–9.
[24] Terje Tvedt, 'Water Systems and the History of the Industrial Revolution', *Journal of Global History*, 5/1 (2010), 29–50.
[25] Kenneth Pomeranz, 'Chinese Development in Long-Run Perspective', *Proceedings of the American Philosophical Society*, 152/1 (2008), 83–100.
[26] Donald N. McCloskey, 'English Open Fields as Behavior Towards Risk', in *Research in Economic History*, ed. P. Uselding (Greenwich, CT, 1976), vol. 1, pp. 124–70.

need to look at custom, inheritance law, and social conflict to *explain* that fact. Since no individual could have made this calculation (and individuals often had very little choice about what plots they worked, anyway), any forces that were somehow guiding the situation towards such an optimal equilibrium must have operated through this broader set of institutions; thus an adequate explanation must reckon with the way those institutions shaped actions. Moreover, when we are dealing with humans, we will rarely be able to come up with plausible mechanisms without at least some attention to the categories through which they saw their world, and the goals they pursued—even if the mechanism we then describe relied on unintended consequences of their actions. So despite my earlier suggestion that we might best begin with etic categories self-consciously imposed by the historian, we must eventually deal with emic ones.

Finally, it is also worth noting that understanding the emic categories of others will generally involve some juxtaposition with our own; we grasp the significance of others' world views when we compare the actions they lead to with those which first occur to us. Thus an analysis that became completely divorced from our own society's everyday labels for social phenomena—if that were even possible—would probably cease to be recognizable as history, and would certainly seem less relevant to urgent questions. Moreover, those everyday categories are also tied to a wide variety of political, moral, aesthetic, and other reasons for thinking about history, which in turn suggest a broad range of topics, timescales, and divisions of humanity to write about. Consequently, any account of divergences will always need to be considered in juxtaposition to convergences, parallels, and so on involving related phenomena; and it is the self-conscious movement back and forth among those varied optics that will continue to generate some of our most interesting histories.

9
The European miracle in global history: an East Asian perspective

KAORU SUGIHARA

Global approaches to comparative history

This chapter discusses the ways in which the 'European miracle' has been interpreted from the perspective of Asian (especially East Asian) economic history, and the potential of such an approach to set new research questions and stimulate history writing. The European miracle is treated here mainly in the context of economic history, that is, a regional economic development that led to the industrial revolution in England.

In reviewing the literature on comparative historical development, I do not propose to go back to the works of Simon Kuznets and W. W. Rostow, as they formulated their framework essentially without worrying about the rise of Asia.[1] Their primary concern was to compare the United States with the Soviet Union, or the free or liberal institutions with socialist ones. Reflecting such terms of reference, they were interested in investment (and savings), capital-intensive technology, research and development, economies of scale, mass consumption, and the rise in the standard of living. Peasant family economy, small-scale production, industriousness and the quality of (unskilled and uneducated) labour, labour-intensive technology, and the social capacity to hold a vast population with limited resources were not the sort of topics central to them.

---

[1] Simon Kuznets, 'Toward a Theory of Economic Growth', in *National Policy for Economic Welfare at Home and Abroad*, ed. Robert Lekachman, Columbia University Bicentennial Conference Series (New York, 1955), pp. 12–85. Reprinted in Patrick O'Brien (ed.), *Industrialisation: Critical Perspectives on the World Economy*, vol. 1 (London, 1998), pp. 3–72; W. W. Rostow, *The Stages of Economic Growth* (Cambridge, 1960).

A fundamentally different approach was proposed by Eric Jones. When he wrote *The European Miracle* in 1981 (by which time the term 'Japanese miracle' was in circulation), he compared Western Europe with the three Asian empires (the Ottoman, Mughal, and Ming-Qing) to argue for the global importance of economic development in Western Europe between 1400 and 1800, eventually leading to the industrial revolution.[2] He was interested in the role of institutions, especially the states system, and their capacity to deal with environmental disasters in Europe, on the one hand, and the prevalence of rent-seekers and the rigid and unequal social systems in Asia, on the other. Judging by the more recent historiography, his characterization of the three Asian empires reads rather out of date, but it is important that he thought that the comparative empirical investigations into the four regions was a valid intellectual exercise, to establish the uniqueness of the European development.

Jones also developed the idea of 'recurring growth' in his *Growth Recurring* (1988), in which he suggested that growth can be observed across major civilizations and over a very long period of time.[3] In some ways this conceptualization goes beyond the comparative history with methodological focus on the European miracle, although the term has not been elaborated in a concrete manner any further. Thus the foundation of comparative global history was laid in its present form, which acknowledges large regions of the world, of which Europe is one, as basic units of comparison. Meanwhile, Braudelian approaches have been widely adapted to global history, especially in the history of maritime regions.[4] Although the contributions of this literature have not quite been communicated to the thinking of economic development, it has a strong non-diffusionist, multipolar orientation, and its impact on historical writings has overlapped with the development of comparative global history.

Of course, traditional comparative histories, for example the comparison between England and France, have not lost their relevance to the study of comparative economic development, nor should we ignore the growing

---

[2] E. L. Jones, *The European Miracle: Environments, Economies and Geopolitics in the History of Europe and Asia* (Cambridge, 1981).
[3] E. L. Jones, *Growth Recurring: Economic Change in World History* (Oxford, 1988).
[4] K. N. Chaudhuri, *Trade and Civilisation in the Indian Ocean* (Cambridge, 1985); Anthony Reid, *Southeast Asia in the Age of Commerce 1450–1680*, vol.1: *The Lands below the Winds* (New Haven, CT, 1993); *Southeast Asia in the Age of Commerce 1450–1680*, vol. 2: *Expansion and Crisis* (New Haven, CT, 1993); Takeshi Hamashita, *China, East Asia and the Global Economy: Regional and Historical Perspectives*, ed. Mark Selden and Linda Grove (London, 2008).

literature on European regional integration.[5] But, from the perspective of comparative global history, these developments are to be integrated into the more global set of comparisons, for example by comparing the experience of European integration with regional integration processes in other regions. The literature on the Atlantic economy should also be compared with the more recent growth of the Asia-Pacific economy, in order to place its significance in global history.[6] In other words, the intra-regional comparisons within Europe or the West alone could no longer provide a methodology for global history. Karl Marx and Max Weber, while addressing the issue of how to understand the non-European world, were both inclined to create key typologies within Europe rather than comparing Europe and the rest of the world. This way of thinking should be firmly rejected if the main concern is global history.

Another major development is a shift in focus to the early modern period, but with a keen interest in bringing the early modern comparisons to the present. Thus, compared with the earlier literature based on the theory of modern economic growth, current literature highlights the long-term 'path' of economic development (usually covering at least a few centuries). The scope and utility of the term 'path dependency' have been broadened dramatically, compared with the usage in the history of the Atlantic economy, as it must deal with a far wider set of environmental, technological, and institutional diversities.[7] This development reflects the advancement of empirical research, especially in the non-European world,

---

[5] Patrick Karl O'Brien, 'Path Dependency, Or Why Britain Became an Industrialized and Urbanized Economy Long Before France', *Economic History Review*, 49/2 (May 1996), 213–49; Sydney Pollard, *Peaceful Conquest: The Industrialization of Europe, 1760–1970* (Oxford, 1981); Alan Milward, *The European Rescue of the Nation State* (London, 1992).

[6] Timothy Hatton and Jeffrey Williamson (eds), *Migration and the International Labor Market, 1850–1939* (London, 1994); Kaoru Sugihara, *Ajia Taiheiyo Keizaiken no Koryu* [The rise of the Asia-Pacific economy], (Osaka, 2003). For a brief summary, see Kaoru Sugihara, 'Oceanic Trade and Global Development, 1500–1995', in *Making Sense of Global History: The 19th International Congress of the Historical Sciences Oslo 2000 Commemorative Volume*, ed. Solvi Songer (Oslo, 2001), pp. 55–70.

[7] H. J. Habakkuk, *American and British Technology in the Nineteenth Century: The Search for Labour-Saving Innovations* (Cambridge, 1962); Paul A. David, *Technical Choice, Innovation and Economic Growth: Essays on American and British Experience in the Nineteenth Century* (London, 1975); Kaoru Sugihara, 'Gurobaru Hisutori to Fukusu Hatten Keiro' [Global history and the multiple paths of development], in *Chikyuken, Seimeiken, Ningenken: Jizokuteki na Seizonkiban o Motomete* [Geosphere, biosphere, humaosphere: in search of sustainable humanosphere], ed. Kaoru Sugihara, Shuichi Kawai, Yasuyuki Kono, and Akio Tanabe (Kyoto, 2010), pp. 27–59.

which has made it possible to discuss global comparisons in serious academic terms, both with the use of a better set of quantitative estimates and by bringing the information from other disciplines (on geography, environment, and diseases, for example) into consideration.

What implications do these recent global approaches have for the understanding of the European miracle? The rest of this chapter is devoted to the discussion of this question. The next section introduces the 'two paths thesis', which is the idea that the 'East Asian path' had a distinct technological and institutional route, based on its regional ecological characteristics, and that this path interacted with the 'Western path' over the last two centuries to push global industrialization forward.[8] The third section examines the possibility of reinterpreting the European miracle, not as the beginning of the 'Western path', but as the generator of a longer and larger 'global miracle', that is, a sustained growth of world population and world GDP in the last two centuries. By recognizing divergent development paths in different regions of the world, we can identify the ecological specificities of the European experience, on the one hand, and the nature of the contributions of its technological and institutional development, the hard core of the miracle, on the other. The final section raises the question of whether such technology and institutions contained the seeds for threatening global environmental sustainability.

The two paths thesis

It was Bin Wong who compared Chinese and European experiences in his *China Transformed* (1997), demonstrating much more explicitly than anyone else what it entails to say that the comparison should not assume the European yardstick.[9] The significance of this work lay in the legitimization of the 'two paths thesis', that is, to regard (in this case) Chinese history as

---

[8] Kaoru Sugihara, 'The East Asian Path of Economic Development: A Long-Term Perspective', in *The Resurgence of East Asia: 500, 150 and 50 Year Perspectives*, ed. Giovanni Arrighi, Takeshi Hamashita, and Mark Selden (London, 2003), pp. 78–123. For a discussion on this thesis, especially on labour-intensive industrialization, see Gareth Austin and Kaoru Sugihara (eds), *Labour-Intensive Industrialization in Global History* (London, forthcoming). The term 'two paths thesis' was coined by Gareth Austin. See Gareth Austin, 'The Developmental State and Labour-Intensive Industrialization: "Late Development" Reconsidered', *Economic History of the Developing Regions*, 25/1 (2010), 61–9.

[9] R. Bin Wong, *China Transformed: Historical Change and the Limits of European Experience* (Ithaca, NY, 1997).

fully comparable to European history, and actually show the usefulness of asking reverse questions, for example by reviewing the history of European attempts to create larger political units, from Rome to the European Union, and by asking why such attempts did not last long in the ways they did in China.[10] Many other attempts to 'provincialize' European history have emerged.[11]

We then saw the publication of Ken Pomeranz's *The Great Divergence* (2000), which argued that it was Europe, not the rest of the world, that diverged from the general trend of 'Smithian growth'.[12] Smithian growth is defined here as the growth of the market accompanied by proto-industrialization and the commercialization of agriculture, but not necessarily accompanied by the growth of the factor markets of land, labour, and capital. Until the late eighteenth century the 'core' areas of East Asia, India, and Europe were roughly on a par in terms of the standard of living and the degree of economic development measured in Smithian growth terms. Then came the discovery that coal and a vast land and other resources of North America, only part of which had been brought into the economic orbit of Western Europe, could be fully exploited to support the industrial revolution. The growth of the fossil fuel-based economy became global in the second half of the nineteenth century, led by the first transport revolution with the introduction of railways and steamships. The 'resource-gobbling' type of economic development, most typically in the United States, laid the foundation for an Atlantic-centred world economy, with the result that capital- and resource-intensive technology and the accompanying institutions became widespread, causing environmental strains and conflicts over resources.

Pomeranz's book stirred the imagination of many historians, but so far the debate has focused rather narrowly on the comparison of living standards between the core regions of the world. I do not propose to discuss this debate in detail here, except to state that, in spite of the partially critical conclusion drawn by some of the main participants of the debate that Pomeranz overestimates the level of living standards in China, these comparisons are widely recognized as a useful way of comparing different

---

[10] Roy Bin Wong, 'Comparing States and Regions in East Asia and Europe: Is Southeast Asia (Ever) Part of East Asia?' *Southeast Asian Studies*, 48/2 (2010), 115–30.

[11] Dipesh Chakrabarty, *Provincializing Europe: Postcolonial Thought and Historical Difference* (Princeton, 2000).

[12] Kenneth Pomeranz, *The Great Divergence: China, Europe, and the Making of the Modern World Economy* (Princeton, 2000).

regions of the world.[13] In the course of the debate, it also became clear that we need to be sensitive to the comparability of the categories, without assuming the Western path as a norm.[14]

However, the significance of Pomeranz's thesis does not end with the standard of living debate. It raised the question of how to locate the industrial revolution in relation to the history of global allocation of resources, perhaps more explicitly than any previous works. And this had major implications for the establishment of the 'two paths thesis'.

First, Western Europe and East Asia had very different resource endowments before industrialization.[15] While the Western path sought to raise labour productivity in the early modern period, East Asia held a much larger population with a relatively small amount of land and very little pasture. It focused on the increase of land productivity rather than labour productivity. The result was the development of labour-intensive technology and labour-absorbing institutions in agriculture and proto-industry. Centred on rice farming, the number of working days per year became greater, with the diffusion of double-cropping and proto-industrial by-employments. Although clearly targeting different goals, both Western and East Asian societies became seriously concerned about raising productivity.

Japan had a strikingly similar environmental profile to Western Europe, except that the amount of arable land was much smaller.[16] Thus the

---

[13] Robert C. Allen, Jean-Pascal Bassino, Debin Ma, Christine Moll-Murata, and Jan Luiten van Zanden, 'Wages, Prices, and Living Standards in China, 1738–1925: In Comparison with Europe, Japan, and India', *Economic History Review*, 64/S1 (2011), 8–38.

[14] For example, it may be more sensible to compare the living standards of Chinese tenant farmers, rather than Chinese agricultural workers or urban dwellers, with those of English agricultural workers, since tenant farmers were the mainstay of Chinese society, while agricultural workers often failed to form a decent household. Pomeranz argues that the real wage of the latter was about a third of that of the former. See Kenneth Pomeranz, 'Land Markets in Late Imperial and Republican China', *Continuity and Change*, 23/1 (April 2008), 101–50. Agricultural workers as a class did not exist in Japan.

[15] Although Pomeranz's book does not acknowledge this, it is consistent with his thesis. See Kenneth Pomeranz, 'Is There an East Asian Development Path? A Long-Term Comparisons, Constraints and Continuities', *Journal of the Economic and Social History of the Orient*, 44/3 (2001), 322–62.

[16] Japan is a relatively small country with considerable climatic and geographical diversity. Four main and many smaller islands form a long chain along the western side of the Pacific Rim. The difference of latitude between the furthest north and south is about 10 degrees, being larger than any Western European nation situated on a similar latitude. The mountains take up some 80 per cent of the land and divide the habitable parts of the main island into the warmer and sunnier Pacific side and the colder and snowier Sea of Japan side. Each area of habitable land of a relatively small size naturally tended to form a region, often along the coast, separated by surrounding mountains. There are great seasonal differences in rainfall and temperature.

dynamics between population growth and the expansion of arable land through geographical specialization in Western Europe did not occur nearly as much in Japan. On the other hand, the Japanese control of epidemics was far more successful than the European counterpart in the seventeenth and the eighteenth centuries,[17] while her battle against fire, flood, and typhoons was less so. This difference in the nature of response to the environment must have reinforced differential technology paths, Europe towards labour-saving and Japan towards labour-intensive. Blessed with water and wood (hence paper was available), as well as precious metals and sand iron, Japan developed a sophisticated system of rice farming and went through the 'industrious revolution' without the expansion of foreign trade.[18] Although China as a whole had taken a very different institutional path from Japan, economies of the lower Yangzi, one of the most advanced regions, followed a similar path to Japan's, with the 'East Asian' type of labour-intensive technology and the 'industrious revolution'.[19] Unlike other major rivers, the lower part of River Yangzi became relatively stable by the early modern period, and a broad ecological stabilization was achieved in the delta. Meanwhile, epidemics were not a major element in Chinese population trends of the early modern period.[20] By 1820 East Asia's share in the estimated world population exceeded 40 per cent, and its share in world GDP was 37 per cent; both figures are much larger than those for Western Europe and North America combined.[21]

---

[17] Ann Bowman Jannetta, *Epidemics and Mortality in Early Modern Japan* (Princeton, 1987).

[18] Kaoru Sugihara, 'Higashi-ajia ni okeru Kinben Kakumei Keiro no Seiritsu' [The emergence of the industrious revolution path in East Asia], *Osaka Daigaku Keizaigaku*, 54/3 (2004), 336–60. The usage of this term is different from that coined by Jan de Vries. See Jan de Vries, *The Industrious Revolution: Consumer Behavior and the Household Economy, 1650 to the Present* (Cambridge, 2008), pp. 78–82. There was also a recent exchange between Osamu Saito and Jan de Vries on the subject. Osamu Saito, 'An Industrious Revolution in an East Asian Market Economy? Tokugawa Japan and Implications for the Great Divergence', *Australian Economic History Review*, 50/3 (2010), 240–61; Jan de Vries, 'Industrious Peasants in East and West: Markets, Technology and Family Structure in Japanese and Western European Agriculture', *Australian Economic History Review*, 51/2 (2011), 107–19.

[19] The development of labour-intensive technology was a long incremental process, but was especially remarkable in seventeenth-century China and in eighteenth-century Japan. While the former had a greater impact on other regions, the Japanese path was more sharply focused on the labour-intensive technology, hence arguably more 'typical'.

[20] For north China, see Lillian M. Li, *Fighting Famine in North China: State, Market, and Environmental Decline, 1690s–1990s* (Stanford, CA, 2007).

[21] Angus Maddison, 'Statistics on World Population, GDP and Per Capita GDP, 1-2008 AD' <http://www.ggdc.net/maddison/> (accessed 27 February 2010).

It seems possible to argue that the two most successful paths of economic development in the early modern period diverged, while both benefited from stable environmental conditions, relatively free from natural disasters and epidemics. Serious attention to long-term productivity growth occurred under these circumstances, while land, the key resource, became scarce relative to population. It was against this background that what was later called the Malthusian and Boserupean framework emerged, in which population changes were discussed in terms of the dynamic relationships between land and labour.[22]

Second, the Great Divergence produced a situation of an extremely uneven allocation of resources, which accelerated divergent regional patterns of development. Thus the Atlantic economy was given a much better chance to develop capital- and resource-intensive technology (such as mass production) and institutional arrangements (such as the exploitation of economies of scale), while East Asia, with limited access to land and foreign resources, restricted chances of emigration to high-income regions, and relatively small inflows of capital, developed labour-intensive technology and labour-absorbing institutions in the manufacturing sector. Thus Japan, the first industrial nation in the non-European world, pursued labour-intensive industrialization, in which the efficient use of labour and the improvement of the quality of labour were attempted. While the growth of factor markets led to the replacement of labour by capital in Western Europe, substitution occurred in Japan in the opposite direction; Western technology was introduced with as much substitution of capital by labour as possible. This labour-intensive path was followed by China in the interwar period and by many other East and South East Asian countries after the Second World War. Today, most manufacturing employment is located in developing countries where factor endowment conditions are similar to the East Asian path, with abundance of labour relative to capital.

Meanwhile, Japan's resource constraints became more and more acute in the pre-war period, eventually leading to territorial expansion and war. On the other hand, the energy intensity (measured by total primary energy supply divided by GDP) of the Japanese economy remained low. In addition, the development of energy-saving technology began in the 1920s

---

[22] Boserup described the ways in which population growth led to land intensification. Ester Boserup, *The Conditions of Agricultural Growth: The Economics of Agrarian Change under Population Pressure* (London, 1965).

and was actively pursued in the 1950s.[23] The energy intensity of other Asian countries (except for socialist ones) was also low. In this way the East Asian path retained distinct technological and institutional characteristics. Put another way, global industrialization created divergent technological and institutional paths.

The European miracle as part of the global miracle

The standard account of the diffusion of industrialization is that it began in England and spread to continental Europe and the United States, where capital- and resource-intensive industries were developed further, while the labour-intensive path thesis deals with the second wave of diffusion, beginning in Meiji Japan and spreading among other Asian countries and beyond. If the replacement of labour by capital started the process of global industrialization, it was the labour-intensive path that diffused industrialization among poor countries, contributing to the reduction of global income inequality. Thus I have argued elsewhere that, if the European miracle was a miracle of production, the East Asian miracle was a miracle of distribution. In the sense that together they raised the standard of living of the majority of the world population, the two miracles (and the connections between them) can be seen as a single miracle.[24]

Viewed in this light, the European miracle was not just the beginning of the Western capital-intensive path. It was simultaneously the beginning of the global miracle and the first experiment in human history to create a modern industrial society. The experiment took place in a society that was surrounded by a relatively stable environment, endowed with rich technological and institutional heritage, but held a relatively small population. The industrial revolution was then to be diffused to the rest of the world, involving most of the world population, for the next two centuries. The process continues to this day.

---

[23] Satoru Kobori, *Nihon no Enerugi Kakumei: Shigen Shokoku no Kingendai* [The energy revolution in Japan: the modern and contemporary history of a resource-poor country] (Nagoya, 2010).
[24] Kaoru Sugihara, 'The European Miracle and the East Asian Miracle: Towards a New Global Economic History', *Sangyo to Keizai*, 11/2 (1996), 47. Reprinted in Kenneth Pomeranz (ed.), *The Pacific in the Age of Early Industrialization*, vol. 11: *The Pacific World: Lands, Peoples and History of the Pacific, 1500–1900* (Surrey, 2009), vol. 11, p. 22.

In what ways did the European experiment determine the subsequent global path? I suggest that European regional economic development from 1500 to 1800 contained elements of both a capital- and resource-intensive path and a labour-intensive and resource-saving path, and that the industrial revolution in England and subsequent European industrialization occurred, not as a result of the former path, but as a fusion of the two paths.

First, many institutional arguments about the European miracle have been informed by factor-endowment considerations, but the comparison with East Asia has not featured largely in them. One fundamental point is that Europe was characterizd by mixed farming, while in the rest of the world this was not the norm.[25] Mixed farming, a combination of crop production and cattle-raising, is inherently more capital-intensive and land-using (its usage was extensive rather than intensive) than the typical East Asian rice farming, which was labour- and land-intensive. Thus the basis for the institutional development was different. From the perspective of most of the world's population, the European pattern was biased towards the capital-intensive path.

Europe's institutional development was dependent on factor-endowment conditions within this framework. Thus enclosure helped make both land and labour available to capitalist agriculture, and accelerated capital accumulation, while the development of the capital market lowered the interest rate, which facilitated capital accumulation in manufacturing and service sectors and large-scale investment in infrastructure and war efforts. Frequent wars destabilized the countryside, which gave the urban manufacturing sector a chance to develop capital- and skill-intensive industries.[26] Meanwhile, wages went up relative to capital, as the integration of the labour market took longer. This encouraged the development of labour-saving technology, compared with the regions where the growth of the capital market was slow. These factors account for the favourable conditions for capital accumulation and the development of labour-saving technology.

If one institutional condition for the industrial revolution is the presence of such a sequence, however, it follows that a reverse loop could also be

---

[25] The institutional integration of pasture into arable crop production in Europe goes back to the Middle Ages at least. B. H. Slicher van Bath, *The Agrarian History of Western Europe, AD 500–1850* (London, 1963), pp. 164–6, 178–9.

[26] Jean-Laurent Rosenthal and R. Bin Wong, *Before and Beyond Divergence: The Politics of Economic Change in China and Europe* (Cambridge, MA, 2011), pp. 99–128.

present. If the capital market did not develop while the labour market was integrated to a certain extent, the same logic would predict the development of labour-intensive technology. In East Asia, while interest rates were relatively high, efficient institutions for labour absorption were present. This is the 'industrious revolution path', with an extensive use of family labour and the in-house combination of rice farming and proto-industry. The direction of the accompanying technological path was towards double-cropping rather than crop–pasture rotation. A speculation from this is that there is no reason why a labour-intensive path similar to the East Asian path did not exist in regions of Western Europe where labour-absorbing institutions developed better than capital-absorbing ones. Relative price signals would often favour the labour-intensive path. This was the case with many proto-industrial areas in Europe, as well as in most resource-poor developing countries in the second half of the twentieth century.

While 'coal and North America' biased the direction of technological development in early nineteenth-century England towards the capital- and resource-intensive path, the Smithian dynamic simultaneously developed a strong element of the labour-intensive path across Europe. In particular, proto-industrialization in continental Europe (as well as in England), which was substantially based on peasant societies, retained this tendency, and helped boost population growth. Geographical specialization developed between fertile grain-producing regions and those which were either mountainous or had poor soils and engaged in pastoral husbandry. Over time, the former regions expanded productivity, earning a good surplus from grain sales, and cottage industry tended to reduce, while in mountainous regions cottage industry was combined with pastoral agriculture, and eventually began to produce industrial goods for sale. Access to the sea, which does not easily freeze, big rivers (like the Rhine), which seldom flood, and resources from the surrounding mountainous areas and forests, all helped the growth of trade. This is a vision of Smithian growth under what E. A. Wrigley has termed the 'high organic economy'.[27] And this process was linked to a regional development of urban networks and the growth of consumer demand.[28] It developed the market economy, which became the basic economic system of today.

---

[27] E. Anthony Wrigley, *Continuity, Chance, and Change: The Character of the Industrial Revolution in England* (Cambridge, 1988).

[28] Franklin Mendels, 'Proto-Industrialization: The First Phase of the Industrialization Process', *Journal of Economic History*, 32/1 (1972), 241–61; Jan de Vries, *European Urbanisation, 1500–1800* (London, 1984).

On the other hand, it is important to remember that this was happening within the framework of mixed farming, which placed a greater emphasis on capital and more extensive land use than East Asian agriculture did. The mixed farming path produced a less densely populated landscape, a greater opportunity to deploy cattle for transport, and an economy more familiar with the concept of 'fixed capital'.[29] The labour-intensive proto-industries in Europe were characteristically embedded in the regional economy more prone to the capital-intensive path than their much larger counterparts in East Asia.

Second, resource endowments in Europe must have worked in both ways too. Of course, releasing resource constraints helped to develop resource-intensive technology, but the persistence of local resource constraints, especially when the competition from modern industry arrived, must have encouraged the development of resource- and energy-saving technology at the same time. Wrigley emphasized that the local availability of coal was largely a matter of chance.[30] In early nineteenth-century England the price of coal near coal fields was very low, and the price difference compared with other areas of Europe was significant enough to encourage the rapid development of coal-operated industries. And this factor may have been more important than the high wages enjoyed in England as an explanation for the country's lead.[31] Likewise, however, the lack of availability of specific resources (such as coal) could direct society to longer, more persistent efforts to overcome local resource constraints by developing resource- or energy-saving technology (such as charcoal). If so, they must have contributed to the sustainability of the European miracle in a more Smithian fashion.

The resource issue also has the dimension of uncertainty. Once the international system of free trade and security was established in the nineteenth century, local resource constraints (especially the relatively immobile factors of production such as land and labour) would in theory have been mitigated by trade. On the other hand, the weather, prevalence of epidemics, or threat of natural disasters could be important in

---

[29] John Hicks, *A Theory of Economic History* (Oxford, 1969), pp. 142–3. Hicks refers to fixed capital in modern industry, in contrast to merchant circulating capital. A parallel can be drawn in the contrast between mixed farming and elaborate annual crop cycles in East Asian agriculture.
[30] Wrigley, *Continuity, Chance, and Change*, pp. 114–15.
[31] R. C. Allen, *The British Industrial Revolution in Global Perspective* (Cambridge, 2009), pp. 80–105.

determining the profile of local resource endowments. As Jones suggested, Western Europe developed a better technique of disaster management than other regions, and became relatively disaster-free.[32] This helped the accumulation of social overhead capital, such as buildings and roads, well before the industrial revolution raised labour productivity, while the rest of the world continued to suffer from chronic destruction of infrastructure caused by monsoons, earthquakes, and fire. This might have biased Europe's technology path towards investment in physical rather than human capital. It might also have created an environment favourable to scientific experiments aimed at the use of motive power. Meanwhile, the control of epidemics, and hence the decline of the mortality rate, lagged behind a little, although population pressure came from increasing birth rates.

The emphasis on contingency by Wrigley and Pollard is a step towards an appreciation of the role resource endowments played,[33] and the Great Divergence story carried it to the level of global history. But we need to go further by linking the local response to all sorts of contingencies, not just in the geosphere (for example, where coal was deposited) but also in biosphere and human society (for example, access to forest resources and threat of animal and human diseases), to the long-term technological and institutional development path. By identifying European specificity in this way, we will be able to understand to what extent England formed an industrialization path that was sustainable in principle, and how much the country diverged from it.

Inclusion of the labour-intensive, resource- and energy-saving path as an essential element of the European miracle would broaden the research agenda, by making the comparison with the rest of the world easier and, in so doing, by making the study of the European miracle more relevant to that of global industrialization.

The global miracle and environmental sustainability

What did industrialization do to environmental sustainability? Environmental sustainability is defined here as a state where the path of economic

---

[32] Jones, *The European Miracle*, pp. 22–41.
[33] Pollard, *Peaceful Conquest*, pp. 4–5, 120–1.

development is consistent with the logic of nature, especially with the logic of the geosphere (energy and material circulation, movement of water and air, etc.) and the logic of the biosphere (the conservation of the ecosystem with appropriate food chains and biodiversity). The assessment of the European miracle requires the examination of whether it was regionally sustainable, while the assessment of the global miracle requires the examination of whether it has been globally sustainable.[34]

Generally speaking, population growth to around 1800 did not cause major problems of environmental sustainability, if we define it in terms of whether nature was basically governed by forces of the geosphere (smooth energy and material flows are maintained in accordance with the circulation mechanism of the earth) and the biosphere (the ecosystem and food chains are functioning by incorporating human interventions rather than vice versa). Humans depended for their food on their own labour on arable land, and Malthusian or Boserupean dynamics were at work. Meanwhile, they depended for their energy on (mainly forest-derived) biomass, as well as humans, animals, water, and wind. Burning biomass was the basic technology for heating and lighting, as well as for clearing the land. But energy consumption per capita increased very slowly, while population growth was yet to reach the point of exhausting the land frontier in most parts of the world.

A massive increase in the use of fossil fuels (especially coal and oil) since the industrial revolution fundamentally altered the relative importance of the geosphere and the biosphere, as the balance between geosphere-derived and biosphere-derived energy sources changed dramatically. Today, the commercial value of land- and forest-derived products in world trade is much less important than that of fossil fuels. Biomass remains an important source of fuel in developing countries (it is often vital to the livelihood of local communities), but it is, in relative terms, much less valued today than two centuries ago. In this respect the world economy

---

[34] This section is based on Kaoru Sugihara, 'Kaseki Shigen Sekai Keizai no Koryu to Baiomasu Shakai no Saihen' [The emergence of a fossil-fuel-based world economy and the reorganisation of the biomass society], in *Koza Seizon Kiban-ron*, vol. 1: *Rekishi no nakano Nettai Seizonken: Ontai Paradaimu o Koete* [Lectures on humanosphere, vol. 1: The tropical humanosphere in global history: beyond the temperate zone paradigm], ed. Kaoru Sugihara, Kohei Wakimura, Koichi Fujita, and Akio Tanabe (Kyoto, 2012), pp. 101–32. On the definition of geosphere and biosphere, see Kaoru Sugihara, 'Jizokugata Seizon Kiban Paradaimu towa Nanika' [What is the sustainable humanosphere paradigm?], in *Chikyuken, Seimeiken, Ningenken*, pp. 1–22.

became much less organic, and much more urbanized and globally connected through man-made materials, transport, and infrastructure. The main agent of this change was global industrialization. The land frontier was exhausted, and population growth became increasingly dependent on modern industry and services. The long-standing relationship between humans and biosphere, which had been the basic mechanism of sustaining the local population, was broken, and was replaced by an invisible web of contacts through trade and technological and institutional transfers without a recognized method of evaluating their environmental consequences.

Thus the course of human society diverged significantly from the previous pattern of human–nature interface. The impact of fossil fuels on the structure of the world economy has been so great that the direct interactions between human society and the biosphere have become rather peripheral to global resource and energy security issues as we see them today.

This divergence has not been a linear, inevitable course of human history, however. In East Asia, land was scarce relative to population by the early modern period, and labour-intensive technology and labour-absorbing institutions developed. When Japan, China, and other parts of East (and South East) Asia industrialized a little later than Western Europe, the region created a labour-intensive industrialization path. By and large the region depended on biomass for its energy much more than Western Europe did during industrialization. It also had a tendency for choosing relatively less energy-intensive industries and energy-saving technology.

The West also eventually directed its attention to energy intensity. Prior to the two oil crises of the 1970s, heavy and chemical industrialization, with military industry leading energy-intensive technology, made the level of energy intensity of the leading powers (the United States and the Soviet Union) very high, while many countries under a labour-intensive path maintained a steady level. However, there was a remarkable convergence after the 1970s, through the reduction of intensity in the United States and Western Europe, as well as in China, and eventually in the (former) Soviet Union. The traditional distinction between capital-intensive industrialization and labour-intensive industrialization became skewed to some extent, as the focus on energy-saving technology began to dictate the direction of global technological innovation.

It is therefore possible to suggest that the global industrialization path began to shift from an energy-intensive to an energy-saving one. Looking back, the two centuries of energy-intensive industrialization path as a whole may be seen as a great divergence from the more balanced, environmentally sustainable path. I wish to suggest that the latter path began in the European miracle, survived the Great Divergence largely because it was countered by the East Asian path, and is eventually becoming a global path.

Of course, the story of energy intensity is only part of a larger narrative of the establishment of a global environmentally sustainable path, which must include a change in the relative importance of a geosphere-derived and biosphere-derived (and 'clean') energy source, a fuller respect for the logics of geosphere and biosphere (e.g. the development of science and technology should be directed more clearly towards sustainability concerns), and the reorganization of human society in accordance with sustainability needs demanded by nature. When such a perspective is established, industrialization will be accepted as a truly positive agent of global history.

Part IV
Knowledge and Global History

10
Technology and innovation in global history and in the history of the global

DAGMAR SCHÄFER

In the origins of the history of the global, technology and innovation have played a major role. Reviewing the issues, concepts, frameworks, interests, and perspectives that have shaped histories of the global thus far, technology and innovation indeed emerge as pivotal agents. In its basic forms, and with apparent general applicability, technology is perceived as a global phenomenon. Farming and textile production, metallurgy and ceramics, hydraulics and architecture can be found in many cultural spheres. Furthermore, technology and its advances gave the world its global nature: the telescope discovered it, navigation verified it, and cartography manifested it. The development of some technologies made it possible for the world to become what modern minds generally define as 'global': through enhanced transportation and communication, societies and individuals, continents and regions interacted with increasing intimacy, first materially and intellectually, via trade and travel, and then virtually using digital technology.

It is instructive to pause here to point out how insidiously the cross-cultural history of technology has become, within one short paragraph, an inter- (or trans)cultural history of technology, shifting from a view of technology in many cultures to its dissemination from one culture to another. This focus on the cross- and intercultural formats of technology serves the agenda of grand historical accounts in two ways. They are used, first, as tools to indicate comparative levels of development or stagnation, and, second, to argue for either diversity or unity. Put into a chronology, these two functions of technology make the world historically explode from a few original, yet flat, joint features (namely basic skills and attitudes) into an orb of diversity, before then imploding again into a new global world of uniform features: in this way the global world becomes the world of globalization.[1]

Against the rise of global history, the history of technology has undergone a significant methodological shift: in the wake of social constructivism, historians have become increasingly aware of the situated and negotiated character of technology. Yet, while the phenomena of technology, and in particular their innovations, thus emerge as historically and culturally multidimensional endeavours,—which might, as David Edgerton asserts, be detached from each other in both global and globalized contexts[2]—they remain one-dimensional on the conceptual level. Histories of both technology and innovation tend to adhere to a general 'Western' perspective that was centred around, and has been represented by, a particular group of countries (usually France, Germany, Britain, and Italy) since the nineteenth century.

When the history of science began to scrutinize the historicity of its conceptual basis in early modern Europe and ponder on the interaction of artisans and natural philosophers in the production of scientific knowledge, various studies located shifts in the identification of fields of practical learning and theoretical knowledge, crafts, arts, and *scientia*. The same studies also emphasize that these shifts were crucial for the subsequent emergence of Western concepts of science and technology, their growing dominance, and the development of both fields of knowledge into global categories.[3] Although cultures such as ancient Chinese, Indian, or Mayan did not develop a recognizably 'European' concept of science, each possessed scientific knowledge and each produced, expressed, and processed knowledge distinctively. The same can be said about practical fields of knowledge, where technology is considered to be 'knowledge about how to do things' and innovation is defined as issues and ideas emerging within this context and being perceived as new. This raises questions such as what were the reasoning and rhetoric strategies of Chinese, Persian, or Indian

---

[1] Pierre-Yves Saunier and Shane Ewen, *Another Global City: Historical Explorations into the Transnational Municipal Moment, 1850–2000* (New York, 2008). See also Pierre Yves Saunier, 'Going Transnational? News from Down Under', *History: Transnational* (published online 13 January 2006) <http://geschichtetransnational.clioonline.net/> (accessed 16 July 2008).
[2] David Edgerton, *The Shock of the Old: Technology and Global History since 1900* (Oxford and New York, 2007).
[3] Lissa Roberts, Simon Schaffer, and Peter Dear, *The Mindful Hand: Inquiry and Invention from the Late Renaissance to Early Industrialisation* (Amsterdam, 2007).

cultures? What role did these cultures assign to texts, artefacts, and people in the formation, evaluation, and transmission of technological knowledge? How did they phrase these issues and what impact did the chosen formats and notions have historically? Seen from this point of view, the history of technology still lacks local experience and concepts as well as a basic understanding of the cultural appearances and implications of both technology and innovation—in other words, it lacks an intra-cultural perspective to account for a history of the global. Conversely, this suggests that academics considering the history of the global should be more interested in what our theories do *not* tell us than in what they do. This chapter, in attempting an intra-cultural perspective, examines how original concepts of technology and innovation can be traced in Chinese history.

Although I have already used the terms 'culture' and 'cultural' several times, they can have rather ambiguous meanings in discussions on the global, especially when combined with the prefixes 'cross-', 'trans-', or 'inter-'. Here I use the term 'culture' in all its flexible vagueness, as a definition of a particular group of people who shared an elementary body of knowledge and values at a particular time. By this definition 'culture' blurs any identification of empires, nations, tribes, people, or regions, and concomitantly presupposes that a society ruled by or affiliated with the Song, Yuan, Ming, and Qing dynasties (roughly the period from the tenth until the eighteenth centuries) by tributary relationships or for ethnic, geographical, or other reasons, agreed on a basic understanding of what 'technology' was and how it should be assessed (to make dissemination, sharing, or exchange possible). At the same time, when it comes to a closer identification of 'shared knowledge and values', I argue that distinct cultures can be formed by the people inhabiting a particular geographical region or place, such as the city of Hangzhou in sixteenth-century Ming China, or a specific social group within a society, such as the craftsmen or a local community of oil pressers. In accord with Pamela O. Long and others, I thus prefer to refer to 'cultures of knowledge', rather than 'cultures' per se.[4] This distinction is necessary because the last decade of Chinese studies has brought about an increasing awareness of the changing content and local character of what global accounts generally summarize as 'Chinese' (referring to a seemingly coherent society ruled by one dynasty and in which the elite at least used a common language for written

---

[4] Pamela O. Long, *Openness, Secrecy, Authorship: Technical Arts and the Culture of Knowledge from Antiquity to the Renaissance* (Baltimore, 2001), p. 100.

documentation).[5] Studying the ways in which this part of the world dealt with technology, how they conceptualized it in writing, or the practices and ideals they developed, produces a notion of a Chinese culture made up of multifarious cultures of knowledge whose basis was subject to quite individual definition—a landscape of diversity that has not yet been given its rightful role and place in the history of the global.

Keeping this in mind, my method is to look at the way in which knowledge about items and their production—'technology' in its broadest sense—was discussed, treated, and appropriated in the various cultures of China. I then outline conceptual approaches to this history. In this process, I include practices that signify a major concern with technologies and that assign technology a place and function in statecraft, public and individual life, or scholarly achievement—as a body of fact and hypothesis, the product of a specific labour, or a belief. I assert that Chinese culture developed an idiosyncratic set of tools to discuss practical know-how and strategies of appropriating practical knowledge which are manifest in material culture as well as in written texts. Emperors and elites laid claim to artisanal skills by inscribing an object. They organized production and documented this organization on the product itself. Practices surrounding objects reveal elites' evaluation of materials and professions. The focus on appropriation is also intended to provide a view of an individual's relation to, and notion of, technology, by revealing the way in which a craftsman made use of his skills and knowledge. I thus presume that a craftsman had an essential interest in protecting the skills and knowledge that secured his or her livelihood, even if the documentation only reveals traits such as a reaction against state, elite, or administrative intervention. Another view of the individual is provided because the scholars, that is, the elite and literate class, chose to include technologies, practical knowledge, and its innovations in their written accounts.

The state and technology

Historically, the most visible signs of technological development in Chinese culture are the activities and attitudes of the state and its powerful repre-

---

[5] Nicola DiCosmo (ed.), *European Technology and Manchu Power: Reflections on the 'Military Revolution'* (Oslo, 2001). Peter Kees Bol, *'This Culture of Ours': Intellectual Transitions in T'ang and Sung China* (Stanford, CA, 1992).

sentatives. Presiding over a waning and waxing sphere of influence, all dynastic rulers engaged in a huge variety of technologies to defend and maintain their power, including those based on the military, hydraulics, agriculture, silk, and porcelain production. Each of the Chinese ruling houses enforced exclusive rights of ownership on technologies and their products, their usage and dissemination, mostly through a subtle combination of formal and informal institutions, ritual, social, or political patronage, rather than legal coding. These settings and practices are an important indication of the continuities and shifts in imperial notions of technology, and thus its use as a means and expression of power. Song (960–1279) (i.e., the Liao and Jin), Yuan (1271–1368), Ming (1368–1645), and Qing (1645–1911) rulers, for instance, all used silk and porcelain as a means of retaining power. As one of the most highly valued tributary goods, silk was used to obtain obedience from the empire's servants (the officials), it served to appease hostile border tribes, and it cemented relationships with neighbouring realms. In this way, silk traded in peace on the Asian continent. On a more metaphorical level, porcelain transmitted the reputation of Chinese imperial power far beyond its immediate sphere of geographical influence. Traded as far as the Arabian world and the European continent, china effectively exported an image of political and cultural identity under an enlightened sovereignty. Ottoman records explicitly categorize Chinese blue and white ware as 'faghfuri' (imperial), and Persianate states (states run by mostly Turkic military elites, but with a Persian language court culture, e.g. the Ottomans until the 1500s, Safavids, Timurids, etc.) in effect 'clothed' their realms in blue, turquoise, or blue and white ceramics.[6] Within French, Italian, German, and British court culture, teacups made of whitish kaolin clay strengthened the perceived significance, the quality and value, of the Chinese empire without the need to ever approach these countries physically. Acknowledging this influence, all Chinese dynasties between the tenth and nineteenth centuries incorporated silk and porcelain production into systems of state governance, treating silk and porcelain as political tools and means of power. The *Ming Shilu* 明實錄 (Veritable records of the Ming) documents that the emperor and his ministers discussed the management of silk and porcelain, its production rate, and best usage for negotiating power almost weekly at the court, similar to the

---

[6] Yolande Crowe, *Persia and China: Safavid Blue and White Ceramics in the Victoria and Albert Museum, 1501–1738* (London, 2002) gives a good introduction to these pieces.

way that rulers of European principalities or kingdoms discussed military armaments or the maintenance of city walls.[7]

In Chinese history, administrative reforms manifest different dynastic and individual approaches to the political role of technological endeavour, but some generalizations can be made to provide an overview of the kind of changes that took place. Emperor Huizong 徽宗 (1082–1135, reign 1100–26) of the Northern Song established a court workshop for jade carving, thus signifying that this was strictly a court technology, something that satisfied both the genuine needs and the desires for luxury of the palace inhabitants. The Ming state controlled jade production within state governance, sharing responsibility for it among the ministries of Works (*gongbu* 工部), Finance (*hubu* 戶部), and Rites (*libu* 吏部). Emperor Qianlong 乾隆 (Gaozong 高宗, 1711–99, reign 1736–96) of the Qing dynasty, however, drew responsibility for jade design and production back into the inner court. Raw jades from Xinjiang had to detour via the capital where artists developed a design that carvers in Suzhou then implemented.[8] Many of these stones came from Southern Xinjiang, whose entire annual production was monopolized by the Qing military of the imperial court. East Turkistan labourers transported the stones in lots weighing thousands of kilograms to Suzhou or Yangzhou, where they were carved.[9] Qianlong's attempt to make himself pertinent to the trade was not entirely selfish, however. By obliging these messengers to come to his court, he succeeded in linking their regions together while retaining control of the production process. Jade also became a symbol of power: Qianlong rewarded subsidiary states and his own officials with polished and carved jade ornaments and he furnished his palace with huge carved jade stones to impress tributary delegations and guests. One, for example, reproduced a prominent Song dynastic representation of a hydraulic engineering project. By flaunting such massive carved jade stones at the major entrance halls of the Forbidden City in Beijing, Qianlong was not merely vaunting his political

---

[7] Excerpts of the discourse were included in Chen, Zilong 陳子龍, *Huang Ming jing shi wen bian* 皇明經世文編 [Collected writings about statecraft from the Ming dynasty]: [*504 juan, bu yi 4 juan*] (Shanghai, 2002). See, for instance, ch. 112, p. 3a. For a discussion of these debates, see Dagmar Schäfer, *Des Kaisers seidene Kleider: staatliche Seidenmanufakturen in der Ming-Zeit (1368–1644)* (Heidelberg, 1998).
[8] Jean-Pierre Desroche, 'Le jade ancien: modification et contrefacon sous l'empereur Qianlong', *Orientations*, 29/10 (1998), 70–4.
[9] James A. Millward, *Beyond the Pass: Economy, Ethnicity, and Empire in Qing Central Asia, 1759–1864* (Stanford, CA, 1998), pp. 1,801–91.

power over a peripheral region, but was also manifesting his approach to technology as a universal one, embracing all the areas of the world he was interested in.

Institutional organizations indicate different and changing political agendas. For instance, the Northern Song installed offices such as the Water Mill Office (*Shuimo wu* 水磨務) within the court, whereas the Ming rulers left such responsibilities in the hands of the locals.[10] Equally, the Song allocated major responsibilities for controlling manufacturing institutions to the court, through units such as the Directorate for Imperial Manufactory (*Shaofu jian* 少府監) which ran silk production, or the Directorate for Armaments (*Junqi jian* 軍器監), which was in charge of army supplies. While the Southern Song maintained this basic structure after its defeat by the Jurchen Jin and the retreat to the South, it drastically changed its attitude towards silk and porcelain. Institutionally the Southern Song paid respect to the dual functions of these two technologies—as both court supplier and imperial means of power—by doubling manufacturing institutions, giving each the purpose of either serving palace needs or acting as a manufacturing unit for official use.

The first Ming emperor Zhu Yuanzhang 朱元章 (1328–98, reign *Hongwu* 1368–98) detached major manufacturing institutions from direct court influence and placed them directly under the control of central state administration, allocating the management and financial control of porcelain and silk to the various ministries. The ministries installed a complex structure of state-owned silk and porcelain manufacturing institutions that spread throughout the empire. Specific centrally directed bureaus produced silk for imperial (*shanggong* 上供) and tributary-imperial (*gongyong* 供用, *shangyong* 賞用) use, whilst sixteen local workshops produced silk bolts for public (*gongyong* 公用) purposes. Later emperors of the Ming repeatedly subverted these institutional restrictions and their exclusion by dispatching their favourite eunuchs

---

[10] Li Cho-ying 'Evolutionary Statecraft: The Ming State and Local Elites in the Field of Hydrological Management in the Lower Yangtze Delta' (Cambridge, MA: Harvard University, 2007), unpublished PhD dissertation, p. vii. The institution's staffing is described in Tuo Tuo 脫脫, Song shi 宋史 [Song history] (Beijing, 2000) , chap. Zhiguan zhi 5 職官志五. For a discussion of the Song system of incorporating fields of astronomy, silk, etc., see Sun Xiaochun, 'State Control and Peer Competition: A Study of Song Calendar Reforms', in *Science and the State in the Song Dynasty China*, ed. Zeng Xiongsheng and Sun Xiaochun (Beijing, 2007). pp. 30–49.

to the manufacturing sites where they oversaw production of special requests.[11]

In an attempt to circumvent the restrictions set by the first Ming emperor's institutional constraints, the third Ming emperor, Taizong 太宗 (1360–1424) (better known by his reign title *Yongle* 永樂 (1402–24)) initiated the dissemination of silk technology 'throughout the world (*tianxia* 天下)' (more accurately the Ming sphere of political power) in the year 1403.[12] Yongle established new state-owned production units in places with no tradition or experience of silk weaving. Nothing is known about the technical side of this endeavour, but clearly many of these newly established bureaus did not produce high quality wares. In some cases it is doubtful whether they were ever materially existent or actually produced anything. Instead the officials in charge of weaving bureaus outside these provinces purchased silk from private workshops situated in South Zhili, Jiangnan, and Sichuan provinces where silk was traditionally produced. On the practical level, Yongle had thus failed. But on the conceptual level the expansion was nevertheless a huge success. Yongle had managed to bring almost all the regions under his control into the silk network. Ming rulers after him could truthfully claim that silk technology was an enterprise characterizing the total civilized sphere and an endeavour that had spread *tianxia*, that is 'throughout the world'.

As well as this type of institutional appropriation, Chinese states also employed rituals to control technologies, which were often complementary to, and supportive of, the administrative management structure. Such ritual appropriation demonstrates the state's ideological backing of silk technology. The Song and Qing dynasties, for example, invested time and money into bringing local silk rituals under the state's auspices. Both dynasties promoted the construction of temples for silk goddesses, and the Qing made further efforts to urbanize these cults by relocating temples from the countryside into towns and cities.[13] Moreover, they attempted to gain better control over raw material production and its distribution. Andreas

---

[11] Dagmar Schäfer and Dieter Kuhn, *Weaving an Economic Pattern in Ming Times (1368–1644): The Production of Silk Weaves in the State-Owned Silk Workshops* (Heidelberg, 2002), pp. 20–1.

[12] Zhang Tingyu 張庭玉 (1672-1755), Ming shi 張庭 [Ming history of the year 1736] (Beijing, 1997), juan 82, shihuozhi 6, p. 2003. Schäfer and Kuhn, *Economic Pattern* (2002), p. 22.

[13] Dieter Kuhn and Joseph Needham, *Science and Civilisation in China*, vol. 5, pt. 9: *Textile Technology: Spinning and Reeling* (Cambridge, 1988), pp. 101–5; Philip S. Cho, 'Sericulture Songs and the Urbanization of Silkworm Temples in 18th Century Jiangnan', paper presented at the 12th conference of the International Society for the History of East Asian Science, Technology and Medicine (ISHEASTM), Johns Hopkins University, Baltimore, 18 July 2008.

Janousch's study of salt production at the Xiechi 解池 salt lake in Shaanxi province suggests that officials of the Ming and Qing dynasties deliberately substituted the loss of institutional control with a promotion of ritual endeavour. A stele inscription at the Temple of the Salt God in the lake district of Yuncheng 運城 reveals a campaign by Jiang Chunfang 姜春髣, the Salt Commissioner responsible for the district, to extend the temple site.[14] Jiang Chunfang's encouragement of salt traders' ritual performance coincided with the state's administrative reforms (single whip reform) in the 1570s which passed the risky tasks of transportation, packaging and sales on to private merchants. These rough sketches provide a broad outline of the changing ideological backing that Chinese states gave to technologies.

Individuals and technological enterprise

Officials such as the salt administrators recorded the economic success or failure of technologies and products in management records. In records such as steles, they communicated the values they considered relevant for the local anchoring of technologies and manifested their relevance for society, state, and self. Stele inscriptions thus complement the official documentation that provides basic contemporary information on the number of workers, their organization, and the architectural arrangement of the manufacturing site. Publicly displayed stelae are an important source of evidence on the contemporary role states assigned to material production. Most of the Ming state-owned silk workshops (and imperial porcelain kilns) were equipped with such commemorative steles. Placed at the entrance of a state workshop, these stelae also functioned as an information board or signboard. Individuals and officials erected stelae at temples or places such as bridges to commemorate important events, thus leaving a guide to the changing spatial contextualization of technological efforts.[15] Other stelae exemplify the associative practices of weavers and

---

[14] Andreas Janousch, 'Salt Production Methods and Salt Cults at Xiechi Salt Lake in Southern Shanxi', paper presented at the 12th meeting of the International Society for the History of East Asian Science, Technology and Medicine (ISHEASTM), Johns Hopkins University, Baltimore, 18 July 2008.

[15] Suzhou li shi bo wu guan, Jiangsu shi fan xue yuan, Li shi xi, and Nanjing da xue, Ming Qing shi yan jiu shi. *Ming Qing Suzhou gong shang ye bei ke ji* 明清蘇州工商業碑刻集 [A collection of inscriptions concerning crafts and trade in Suzhou in the Ming and Qing dynasties] (Nanjing, 1981).

dyers, paper-makers, lacquer producers, and coppersmiths, providing a record of (1) the election of association members, (2) rules governing participation in a group, or (3) the handling of stolen goods, and (4) rules as to the marking of wares. Stelae hence reveal the local and individual appropriation of technologies and their innovations, and demonstrate that although Chinese culture had only one court and centralized power, it had assorted cultures of knowledge—especially in the vast field of technology that served several functions at the same time.

Practices of marking objects are revealing because they indicate how imperial and court technologies featured in relation to private enterprise and how they functioned as commercial goods. The marked object itself shows that the definition of what was an imperial, court, or commercial technology was subject to individual recognition and purposeful application, exposing the tension between local and central power, their co-existence, cooperation, and competitive relationships during periods of change, such as the seventeenth-century commodification and commercialization of Chinese society. The great variety of markings on objects—in form, function, and interpretation—indicates how concepts of knowledge appropriation changed and diversified throughout Chinese culture.

The history of artisanal marks in China and their relation to the state has received little attention from historians of science, technology, or economy as yet. Most historians assume that production marks mainly served administrative purposes, as explained in written accounts. Imperial rulers appropriated marking in China indeed early on already as a managerial practice in state-owned contexts for the purpose of tax collection and as a way to control quality (*yi kao qi cheng* 以考其成). In accordance with its first mention in the *Lun yu* 論語 (*Analects*), this was identified as the *wule gongming* system 物勒工名, which means literally the 'carving of craftsmen's names'. How this practice related to the emergence of seals, stamps, or colophons which artists, owners, or those commissioning wares added to art or craft works is still open to debate. Repeating this quote with slight variations, official accounts and government handbooks from the Song until the Qing portray a rather simple and fixed history in which the state restricted the usage of marks to this function: marks were used to trace the maker, allowing for the slight variation that the Song distinguished between markings naming the craftsmen (*gongming* 工名) and those naming the official responsible (*guanming* 官名).[16] Art studies

[16] Xu, Song 徐松 *et al*, *Song hui yao ji gao* 宋會要輯稿 [Edited manuscript of Song dynastic institutional records] (Beijing, 1957), ch. 101, p. 6b.

classify colophons and seals as a different category, used by elites to appropriate high-quality artefacts rather than a standard part of craft production.

In contrast to this written account, however, objects themselves reveal dramatic shifts in the application of marks, most obviously in the porcelain sector. The Yuan dynasty, for example, applied marks that named the production unit responsible: *shu fu* 樞府. These were probably linked to the Mongolian Yuan state (1271–1368) Bureau of Military Affairs, which supervised the kilns in Jingdezhen, which would also verify the belief that the Mongols considered porcelain a means of warfare rather than simply a luxury item. The subsequent rulers of the Chinese cultural sphere, the Ming, mainly applied year marks (*nianhao* 年號), such as 'produced by the great Ming (*Da Ming zhizao* 大明製造)'. In both cases, the official account stated that these markings were used as a way to facilitate tax calculation, although a generalized mark like 'Great Ming' would not enable the actual production unit to be identified, even when the third emperor *Yongle* started to enforce the requirement to name the specific reign, a trend established by the Xuande reign (1426–35) so as to distinguish each emperor's wares from those of his ancestor and predecessor. Instead it added a new quality: the proprietary claim was subtly transposed from the dynasty as such to the individual ruler.

One important backdrop to this development is that both the Yuan and the Ming dynasties had already incorporated the production process into their own administrative apparatus. Since they occupied and ran the kilns themselves, there was no need to specify the maker on the product, as such information was available from official documentation. These reign marks now became a badge of ownership: only the court and the state were allowed to produce and use such wares. Unlike the Ming, the Yuan (at least in principle) still adhered to the concept of tax accounting and collection, embedding the proprietary claim into this original purpose. In both cases, however, the mark served to communicate to the subjects of their empires and other rulers of Asia, the tributary states, that only the Chinese dynasties of the Yuan and Ming upheld the right of production and usage. Both dynastic houses enforced this claim simply through applying these marks without needing any further legislative regulations in their general statutes. Nevertheless, the rulings were binding—at least as binding as equivalent measurements in the geographically much smaller frameworks of contemporary European principalities, such as Venetian patents of the fifteenth and sixteenth centuries which retained the exclusive rights of production throughout European, American, or Asian countries.[17]

As Anne Gerritsen's research shows, porcelain wares bearing the *shu fu* mark, in varying quality and produced at different kilns, appeared in regions far away from the Yuan dynastic centre of power, such as Japan, Korea, and the Philippines.[18] Entrepreneurial merchants or clever potters faked not only particular styles but also markings, to assign higher quality and status to the product. Little is known about the prosecution of such violations. However, I suggest that the state may have carefully weighed profit against expenditure before starting any such initiative for punishment. As long as its power was not being challenged, the state could even profit from such actions, both economically and politically. Economically, the mark itself added value, thereby inflating even mediocre wares into valuable trade goods. Qianlong, for instance, once asked Tang Ying to sell inferior wares with marks of the imperial porcelain kilns on private markets to raise further funds, assuming that these marked wares would achieve higher prices.[19] Japanese traders and elites explicitly promoted the Chinese reign marks as a sign of quality when introducing Chinese wares to the global market. Distributing such wares to its neighbouring states as tokens in bargaining for peace, the Chinese states may have traded on their reputation by way of adding false marks as a sign of quality. Politically, even such faked wares, whatever their quality, carried the reputation of Chinese imperial rulership to places far away from its actual region of influence.

In the case of *shu fu* wares and Qing porcelains, the reign mark became a mark of quality. This shows that the mark was a flexible entity that became embedded into systems of thought, and as a cultural practice subject to political and social concerns. Its proprietary claim could pertain

---

[17] See Luca Molà, 'States and Crafts: Relocating Technical Skills in Renaissance Italy', in *The Material Renaissance*, ed. Evelyn Welch and Michelle O'Malley (Manchester, 2007), pp. 133–53; Luca Molà, 'Il mercato delle innovazioni nell'Italia del Rinascimento', in *Le technicien dans la cité en Europe Occidentale (1250–1650)*, ed. Mathieux Arnoux and Pierre Monnet (Rome, 2004), pp. 215–50.

[18] Duncan MacIntosh, 'Shufu Wares, Jingdezhen Wares, The Yuan Evolution', in, *Oriental Society of Hong Kong and Fung Ping Shan Museum Exhibition Catalogue* (Hong Kong, 1984); Anne Gerritsen, 'Fragments of a Global Past: Ceramics Manufacture in Song-Yuan-Ming Jingdezhen', *Journal of the Economic and Social History of the Orient*, 51 (2009), 117–52.

[19] Wang, Guangyao 王光堯 (ed.), Qianlong shiqi yuyao chan de guanli tizhi he guanyang zhidu 乾隆時期御藥廠的管理和官樣制度 [The management of kilns and the organization of official templates during the Qianlong era] (Beijing, 2010).

either just to the object itself, or it could extend to the skills and knowledge required for its production as well as its usage and disposal. Its function is subject to definition. Reappearing in different contexts, the practice can achieve new functions or become incorporated into changes in actual practice. While we can trace how goods and raw materials circulated, and look at the commodities that crossed borders, we know very little about how Chinese culture originally established, used, and conceived of these practices, and how they varied with regard to locality and technology or material of production. Initial investigations suggest that they were not arbitrary: producers' names were written, carved, engraved, sealed, or stamped into lacquer or silver and woven into textiles from the Song to the Qing, often elaborating on the relation between the object and its producer or owner, rather than obscuring it. Porcelains as well as ceramics, lacquerware, sculptures, wall paintings, silver, furniture, silk bolts, bricks, belts, and buckles are signed with the names of institutions and individuals (such as 'produced by Zhang Demin' 張德民造), family marks (such as 'made by the Zhang clan' 张氏造') or, in accordance with changing fashions, with characters such as 'longevity' (*shou* 壽) or 'luck' (*fu* 福).[20] Material traces and some stelae show that the usage of marks was subject to empire and local trends that the written accounts almost entirely neglect (or discuss in ways that we have yet to understand).[21] Yixing wares from the late sixteenth century, for example, imitate stamps, whereas Dehua porcelain marks—even those mentioning individuals or referring to familial enterprise—imitate the form of imperial marks. The importance of contextual understanding is vital when investigating such practices and their historical recognition. The Ming dynasty saw pronounced differences in the range of attitudes and ideas about its function as the state became increasingly involved in production (and then later retracted from it). Studying the practices of marking objects, porcelains, lacquerware, or silver, provides a new insight into the varied attitudes of Chinese dynastic rulers towards the appropriation of craft know-how, a story which also produces a more detailed picture of the ups and downs of political control,

---

[20] For an overview on the usage of hallmarks on porcelain etc., see Xiong Yulian 熊玉莲 and Teng Haisheng 滕海生, Tang ming gong jiang kuan bian = Tangming gongjiang kuan bian 堂名工匠款編 [Compilation of the hallmarks and craftsmen signatures] (Jiangxi, 2005).

[21] Jiangsu sheng bowuguan, Jiangsu sheng Ming Qing yilai beike ziliao xuanji 江蘇省明清以來碑刻資料選集 [Selected stele documents from Jiangsu in the Ming Qing periods] (Beijing, 1959). Shanghai bo wu guan. Tu shu zi liao shi, Shanghai bei ke zi liao xuan ji 上海碑刻資料選輯 [Selected stele documents from Shanghai] (Shanghai, 1980), pp. 54, 80–1.

the changing roles of emperor and state, and the relation between local and central power than a written account of the same area is likely to provide. This reality of objects—and practices attached to objects—can disturb the official account of a continuation of rules and regulations, challenging historians in their quest for comparability and also with regard to the construction of linear accounts.

Individual marks indicate that the potter or lacquer carver used the opportunity to promote his craft, distinguishing his skills against competitors. These individual and often idiosyncratic markings illustrate crucial historical changes in Chinese knowledge culture. In the first period of the Ming, hardly any porcelain products have individual craftsmen's names, but such markings appear increasingly after the Mid-Ming, around 1533. At the same time, individual names appear on other products, such as lacquerware (a prominent example is provided by the wares of Wang Ming 王明 (n.d.). Wang preferred to carve his name on highly visible places instead of the more usual underside). Lacquerware shows these changes most explicitly, but we can also find carvings on interior design features (for example pillars, archways, and carved reliefs), jewellery, belts and buckles, silverware, and textiles. How such traditions prevailed often affected attitudes throughout whole craft sectors. A change of practice may have anticipated the scholarly recognition of a huge range of individual craftsmen within one branch, rather than any sudden scholarly interest initiating these changes. The object is central to the research of conceptual changes in technological knowledge culture, as well as to obtaining a deeper understanding of technological choices.[22]

Whereas scholars rarely discussed marking practices and changing meanings, collectors recognized such marks as an important way to identify products as 'authentic (zhen 真)', 'copies (chao 抄)', or 'false (jia 假, wei 偽)'. Because of this, art lovers also mentioned artefacts' makers and their specializations, locating them in the urban centres of seventeenth-century Chinese culture.[23] Similarly, literary accounts focus on extraordinary craftsmen as a suitable subject, featuring artistic tasks such as

---

[22] George Basalla, *The Evolution of Technology* (Cambridge, New York, Melbourne, and Sydney, 1989), p. 208.
[23] Meng, Yuanlao 孟元老 (c.1090–c.1150), *Dong jing meng hua lu* 東京夢華錄 [The dream of Hua in the Eastern Capital]. (Huhehaote Shi: Yuan fang chu ban she, 2001: 15). discusses urban sceneries and several lacquer shops in Wenzhou. See also Cao, Zhao 曹昭 and Wang, Zuo 王佐, Xin zeng Ge gu yao lun: shi san juan 新增格古要論 [Guide to the study of antiquities] (Nanjing (Beijing), [1368] 1987), ch. 8, p. 3a.

sculpting and painting. By the end of the Ming era, local gazetteers featured representatives of crafts such as pottery, lacquerware, or tailoring as a local characteristic.[24]

Both marks and administrative records only very rarely name craftsmen, which indicates that elites valued creativity and labour differently from modern standards, according to which the individual counts. So it is hard to tell if certain craftsmen actually existed. It is equally difficult to judge the value of the biographical information, since biographies of craftsmen were often written after a long delay (in relation to the appearance of the product). Biographical information on Zhang Cheng 張成, a lacquer carver attributed to the Yuan dynasty, appears in the *Jiaxing Fuzhi* 嘉興府志 (Local monograph of Jiaxing) of 1678 in a note by Wang Zuo 王佐 (js. 1427) who mentions his existence in his addition to *Gegu yaolun* 格古要論 (Essential criteria of antiquities) published in Nanjing around 1388 by Cao Zhao 曹昭. Both authors who identified an artist by name were not acknowledging any artisanal individuality: Cao highlighted authenticity and criticized contemporary crafts in order to promote the value of antiques, whilst Wang aimed to provide full information on the historical development to explain his contemporary era. A century earlier Zhao Guanzhi 晁貫之 (c.1100), in the *Mojing* 墨經 (Book on ink), similarly drew a genealogical tree of the ink trade up to his own time. Such passages show that historicizing and tradition building was an important strategy that scholars used in their accounts of technological affairs and products, whereas the identification of individual craftsmen was not. Documentation of the production process and artistic changes lent credibility to the object and scholars constructed a continuous account of development as a way to enhance the value of an art or craft object.

In constructing histories around things, whether concerning social affairs and political institutions or innovative products and technologies, Chinese scholars sometimes promoted the past while at other times they argued for change and innovation. Novelty was a 'bon mot' in Song-dynastic identifications of literary knowledge—from 'new editions' to 'new recipes'. Chinese scholars who collaborated with Jesuits on Western technologies in the seventeenth century preferred to invoke the past in

---

[24] See Wang Zuo's commentary to this passage in the *Gegu yaolun*. Zhang Cheng was from Zhejiang Jiaxing Xitang, Yanghan 浙江嘉興西塘楊匯人 (Modern Zhejiang Jiashan county 浙江嘉善县).

order to validate their efforts.²⁵ In both cases the technologies were implemented—in the case of Song China, new block printing methods; in the case of Ming and Qing dynastic efforts, enamel techniques and glass manufacture. As John Staudenmaier suggests, this is one sign of how 'progress talk' generated technology, as also did 'stasis talk' or 'cyclical talk'. Rhetoric strategies and forms of validation can vary and their effect is little understood.²⁶

Historical entitlement was a general strategy used in writing on Chinese culture to enhance reputation, and changing fashions and idiosyncratic viewpoints are also evident in these. In his *Tiangong kaiwu* 天工開物 (The works of heaven and the inception of things) from 1637, for example, Song Yingxing 宋應星 (1587–1666?) evoked the sage kings as ancient ideals of wise men engaging in craft know-how. Song's enquiries into technology reveal that he was not particularly interested in innovation, but neither was he backwards-looking; for him high antiquity was simply an abstract standard of validity and a useful way to claim truth. For this reason, he began the first chapter of his book by stating that it is irrelevant '[whether] the clan (*shi* 氏) of the Divine Agriculturalist actually existed or not, because it is the connotation of his title (i.e. divine (*shen* 神) and agriculture (*nong* 農)) which endures up until today'.²⁷

Applications of the past and the construction of a long tradition connect to the Chinese idea that tracing the origin of a thing or an affair (*wu yuan* 物原), knowing a thing's relation to other issues, was, similar to knowing about its moral implications, a prerequisite for 'knowledge (*zhi* 知)' in general. Taking this seriously means to understand that Chinese connoisseurs also used this perspective to determine the value of antiques: 'authentic' meant in this context that they could identify and verify an object's origin, and whether or not it was a copy.²⁸ But this understanding

---

²⁵ Joachim Kurtz, 'Framing European Technology in Seventeenth-Century China: Rhetorical Strategies in Jesuit Paratexts', in *Cultures of Knowledge: Technology in Chinese History*, ed. Dagmar Schäfer (Leiden and Boston, 2011).
²⁶ John M. Staudenmaier, *Technology's Storytellers: Reweaving the Human Fabric* (Cambridge, MA, 1985), p. 165.
²⁷ Song Yingxing 宋應星, Tiangong kaiwu 天工開物 [The works of heaven and the inception of things] (Guangzhou, [1637] 1976), ch.1, no. 1, p. 1a.
²⁸ Bruce Rusk, in his investigation on forgery, suggests focusing on the deployment of arguments based on authenticity. 'Artifacts of Authentication: People Making Texts Making Things in Ming-Qing China', in *Antiquarianism and Intellectual Life in Europe and China, 1500–1800*, ed. François Louis (New Haven, CT, forthcoming).

also allowed a copy to equal an original and meant that scholars regarded 'innovation' or 'originality' as being of minor importance. The importance given to an item's origin and development was also central for the scholarly conceptual approach to 'technology'. Scholars approached innovation from an awareness that it was always emerging from already apparent, pre-existent bits of knowledge and was never unconnected to what was already there. This is another insight that modern innovation studies have just started to emphasize.

Outright references to techniques or descriptions of technologies were often anticipated and accompanied by much more subtle strategies of bringing technological endeavour and the knowledge contained in it to the forefront of scholarly activity. Philosophy gave differing weights to technical, administrative, and creative ability within cultural evolution, and thus altered technology's place within nature and thought. Politics slightly shifted the emphasis from protagonists, thereby allocating and relocating technology's function within society. Society and individuals varied their understanding of things and events, new and old, defining and redefining their significance for historical evolution. In due consideration to such developments, scribes fashioned biographical accounts of craftsmen, artisans, and engineers, or scholars, philosophers, and politicians. They venerated practical knowledge or brushed such skills and talents aside; they gave technical products and technological events a history and either noted regional diversity in Chinese material culture or conspired in silence.

What strikes me is the fact that the field of non-Western technology in global history is either inhabited by anthropologists or discussed by historians of economy, not by historians of science and technology, philosophy, epistemology, or thought, as if there is a qualitative distinction between the technology that was described in seventeenth-century Europe compared to what Chinese, Arabian, Japanese, or other scholars at the same time wrote down about their crafts, agriculture, and technology; or as if those who research such issues with a regional focus are refusing to engage with contemporaneous global accounts. Most of the Chinese writings were grounded in administrative and managerial practice, but there was also a diverse 'elite' (in the sense of literate people) who discussed and commented on technology and innovation in their writing for private, scholarly, or professional interests—which is not so different to European early modern writing. The concepts that informed such authors, as well as how and why they wrote their work, have to be taken into account to understand the impact such works had on contemporary culture of knowledge. They need to be understood before crosscultural comparisons can be made.

To conclude, I suggest that a better understanding of Chinese concepts of knowledge production and circulation could provide a new view on when, where, and why technology and innovation actually happened. I concede that writing the history of the global from the perspective of these questions offers a less structured development than traditional Eurocentric or modernist accounts, and no easy solutions or direction. Yet such a research would reveal the huge range of historical possibilities and choices made in human knowledge production, both those that were taken and those that were eventually (or only temporarily) dismissed.

11
The art of global comparisons

CRAIG CLUNAS

It might be thought that a distinctive change in art history in recent decades has been an increasing attention to work from outside the European canon. It is the major selling point of Julian Bell's ambitious *Mirror of the World: A New History of Art* (2007), that it 'Takes a truly global picture, connecting different cultures across time and space'.[1] The fact that it is possible for the present writer, whose scholarly work focuses largely on China, to hold jobs within the British academic world which are simply titled as jobs in 'History of Art' might be thought to be a symptom of such a development. But it might also be argued counter-intuitively that the global or the 'non-Western' has *always* had a place in the history of art; indeed, that putting that Other in its place has always been one of the acts that made the constitution of a history of art, particularly a singular story of art, possible. And it could further be argued that this goes back a long way. Over sixty years ago now, Michael Sullivan drew attention to the place of Chinese art in one of the foundational texts of non-Italian art writing, Joachim von Sandrart's 1675 survey, *Teutsche Academie der Bau- Bild- und Mahlery Kunst.* Here, in this first European description of Chinese painting, Sandrart (1606–88) principally does two things, for the first time but certainly not for the last time. He tells us what Chinese painting is, and he tells us how it compares with European work:

> They set everything down singly in outline only, without shadows or modelling, but washed over quite simply with colours of their kinds. They do not know how to set off each figure according to its true quality, whether it is before or behind, or how to observe such other aspects of naturalism, upon which the European painters reasonably devote great diligence . . . It

[1] <http://www.thamesandhudson.com/9780500287545.html> (accessed 13 September 2010).

is not a little to be wondered at that such otherwise clever people have no knowledge whatever of the art of Perspective...[2]

Sandrart then goes on to tell us about four actual 'curious pictures, which I have obtained from the Chinese themselves, with ridiculous archaic figures'. Four may not be a large number, and their authority is further diminished by the fact that what Sandrart was looking at may well not have been Chinese paintings at all, but engraved illustrations in the volumes on China by such Western writers as Athanasius Kircher (1601/2–80) and Olfert Dapper (1636–89), but it is enough.

Sandrart may be distinctive in touching so early upon Chinese art, but he is in no sense unique among European writers down to the nineteenth century in his invocation of art from outside the Western tradition as the negative example that sets off what 'we' do so well. The *locus classicus* of this strategy can be found perhaps in the writings of Johann Joachim Winckelmann (1717–68), for whom the inferior art of the ancient Egyptians is the necessary foil to the achievement of the Greeks.[3] Partha Mitter, in his classic *Much Maligned Monsters*, has demonstrated how for a range of writers in the eighteenth and nineteenth centuries it was India above all which produced an art that served to define what true art was, by falling so far short of it.[4] He shows too how early attempts to account for what was seen in Europe as 'realistic' strands within early Indian art (in the style known as 'Gandharan') invariably evoke a global and diffusionist history whereby it is the influence of the Greeks, in the form of the armies of Alexander the Great, that was responsible for this 'higher' strand within the art of the East.[5] Such diffusionist accounts, which sought to write a global history of art while still retaining the centrality of the Greeks as the point of origin of everything good, were not uncommon in the age of imperialism, as conscientious scholars sought to understand the wider (if still extremely limited) visual field and range of examples with which they now had to deal. As is well known, the intellectual genesis of art history as

---

[2] Michael Sullivan, 'Sandrart on Chinese Painting', *Oriental Art*, 1/4 (Spring 1949), 159–61, at 159.
[3] Johann Joachim Winckelmann, *History of the Art of Antiquity*, trans. Harry Francis Malgrave (Los Angeles, 2006), p. 128.
[4] Partha Mitter, *Much Maligned Monsters: A History of European Reactions to Indian Art* (Chicago and London, 1977).
[5] Mitter, *Much Maligned Monsters*, pp. 274–5, also Stanley K. Abe, 'Inside the Wonder House: Buddhist Art and the West', in *Curators of the Buddha: The Study of Buddhism Under Colonialism*, ed. Donald S. Lopez, Jr. (Chicago and London, 1995), pp. 63–106.

an academic discipline lies largely within the German-speaking world, and the absence of a large-scale colonial enterprise on the part of that world might therefore be thought to correspondingly diminish the purchase which the ideas of Edward Said (drawn largely from French and British examples) might have on this issue. Put crudely, since Germans had no empire in Asia, their scholarship on it is free of the taint whereby learning served in essence as a tool of the colonial enterprise. Yet to take this position is perhaps to misunderstand the degree to which 'orientalism' acted not *only* in this instrumental way, but also as a pervasive mode of thought which, however explicitly generous and humanistic its *aims*, acted to write the art of the East into a text which had Western chapter headings. So, in what is perhaps the first attempt to write a fully global history of art, the *Handbuch der Kunstgeschichte* of Franz Kugler (1808–58), first published in 1841/2, a conscientious attempt is made to include the art of a wide range of nations beyond Europe. This is done often on the grounds of extremely narrow bases of knowledge, and manages for example to include East Asia only by the expedient of equating 'art' principally with 'architecture', which takes up three-quarters of the four pages allotted to China.[6] The placing of buildings at the highest point of a system of material culture forms would have been utterly meaningless in, for example, China, and the total exclusion of those forms (principally calligraphy and painting) which *were* the objects of elaborated discourses there means that Kugler is of necessity imposing on his material a set of values that were deeply Eurocentric (using that term not as one of abuse but simply descriptively).

What is often striking about early academic art history is that it clearly felt the need to be global, in a way that other forms of history perhaps did not. Franz Wickhoff (1853–1909), holder of the extremely prestigious chair in art history at Vienna, was a man of broad and attractive sympathies, much more attuned to and engaged with the art of his own times than many scholars were (are!). As such, the phenomenon of the contemporary arts' appropriation of Japan (in Impressionism and Art Nouveau, as well as in the work of contemporaries like Gustav Klimt) was of great interest to him. In an essay of 1898 entitled 'On the Historical Unity in the Universal Evolution of Art', Wickhoff attempted to account for this 'coming together in the nineteenth century of the Western and the Far Eastern styles', by first insisting on the precedence of the Chinese art from which Japanese art in

---

[6] Franz Kugler, *Handbuch der Kunstgeschichte*, 5th edn, 2 vols (Stuttgart, 1872), vol. 1, pp. 32–6.

turn derived, and then by resolutely refusing to countenance that this same Chinese art 'could have evolved independently'.[7] He is extremely complimentary about Chinese painting, which he sees as never having gone though a Middle Ages, but rather as having sustained throughout all time a type of classical illusionism which was lost in Europe after the Romans, only to be regained in the Renaissance and after. Yet the *source* of that quality cannot, for Wickhoff, be indigenous, rather, 'It truly is a single tradition that came full circle, and all art of the modern civilized nations can be traced back directly to the Greeks, whose influence spread in all directions.'[8] The confidence with which this opinion is advanced is in absolutely inverse proportion to the empirical evidence on which it is based. Wickhoff cites two actual examples of 'Chinese art'. One is a reproduction of an eighteenth-century Chinese woodblock print illustrating a vessel of the Bronze Age; the other is a seventeenth-century Japanese painting in the Louvre, possibly a copy of an earlier Chinese work. The basis of the evidence is somewhat thin. But this does not matter, since the point in work like that of Wickhoff is not to investigate 'Chinese art'; rather it is to deploy it as a category which is already *totally* known *prior* to its investigation. Here the argument of the Vienna professor is no different from that of Joachim von Sandrart; the minimal number of examples is irrelevant.

Another example, gone into in more detail, may make clearer the way in which this 'pre-existent knowledge' has operated. It touches again on the art of China, though it is highly likely that equivalent case studies could be drawn from other material, and other parts of the globe. One of the more intriguing 'what ifs' of European art history emerges in a letter from the Lithuanian-born but American-educated Bernard Berenson (1865–1959), who became a dominant figure in the connoisseurship of Italian Renaissance art, and who wrote from his Tuscan villa I Tatti in 1914, 'I look forward with zest to seeing what the dealers have of Chinese art to show me. Would I were young or at least well, & I'd chuck everything to go to China.' The following year he reiterated, in another letter, 'How I wish I were now starting out in life! I should devote myself to China as I have to Italy.'[9] Berenson was himself an enthusiastic acquirer of Chinese art up to

---

[7] Franz Wickhoff, 'On the Historical Unity in the Universal Evolution of Art', in *German Essays on Art History*, ed. Gert Schiff, The German Library: Volume 79 (New York, 1988), pp. 165–72, at p. 167.
[8] Wickhoff, 'On the Historical Unity', p. 171.
[9] Laurance P. Roberts, *The Bernard Berenson Collection of Oriental Art at Villa I Tatti* (New York, 1991), p. 8.

the First World War, and his collection—a fairly typical mix for the period of interesting problems and highly optimistic early attributions—remains in I Tatti to this day. An engagement with Chinese art appears in his scholarly work also. In 1903, he published in the principal London art journal, *The Burlington Magazine*, an article entitled 'A Sienese Painter of the Franciscan Legend'.[10] This is devoted to the work of the Italian painter Sassetta (1390–1450/1), several of whose works Berenson himself owned. In the heightened style that won him so many admirers, but which perhaps reads less smoothly in less confident times, Berenson opens with an extended meditation not on achievement but on failure, the failure of European visual art to engage effectively with the spiritual world, by comparison with the effectiveness of literature in this regard. But then he engages in a more daring comparison:

> Are the figure arts incapable of conveying a sense of things spiritual? If we confined our attention to European art alone, it would seem so, for our painting is apparently powerless to get out of the human figure more than an expression of heroism, of grandeur, of the superhuman—always something in the nature of the physically impressive. But if we turn to the extreme orient, we find that their arts of design do convey a sense of spiritual things . . .[11]

He goes on to drive this point home through a specific example, comparing Albrecht Dürer's woodcut of St Gregory saying mass, to 'a Chinese painting of the twelfth century'. Significantly the Dürer is not illustrated (a Burlington reader could be expected to look it up, if not conjure it up), but the Chinese painting is. It is one of a celebrated group of paintings of *luohan*, or Buddhist saints, which had been brought from Japan for exhibition in the Boston Museum of Fine Arts in 1894, and subsequently sold.[12] After an extensive ekphrasis of the scene, Berenson launches the full force of his rhetoric:

---

[10] Bernhard Berenson, 'A Sienese Painter of the Franciscan Legend, Part I', *Burlington Magazine*, 3/7 (1903), 2–35; Bernhard Berenson, 'A Sienese Painter of the Franciscan Legend, Part II', *Burlington Magazine*, 3/8 (1903), 171–84.
[11] Berenson, 'A Sienese Painter of the Franciscan Legend, Part I', p. 7.
[12] *Catalogue of a Special Exhibition of Ancient Chinese Buddhist Paintings, Lent by the Temple Daotokiyi, of Kioto, Japan* (Boston, 1894). The painting discussed by Berenson is now catalogued as 'Zhou Jichang (active 2nd half of 12th c.), "Lohan demonstrating the power of the Buddhist sutras to Daoists", Chinese, Southern Song dynasty, about 1178, ink and colour on silk. Acc. no. 06.290.'

> Here we feel an ecstasy of devotion and vision, here we behold a transubstantiation of body into soul, whereof we rarely get as much as a vanishing glimpse in our own art. Beside this design the most religious achievements of a Dürer grow sterile or commonplace...[13]

Significantly, Berenson raises the obvious and then-widespread orientalist explanation, that 'orientals' are intrinsically more mystical and spiritual, only to dismiss it. And he goes on:

> Among the reasons, therefore, to be given for the great superiority as religious expression of Buddhist to Christian art, we must place to the front the fact that Sino-Japanese design is almost exclusively an art of contours, of values of movement, and, in its own way, not ours, of space-composition. And if this be so, we are led to wonder whether of European schools of design that one which approached oriental art closest in its means of expression would not be most successful in conveying a sense of the spiritual.

The language is somewhat convoluted, but the meaning soon becomes clear: the art of Siena, and within it the oeuvre of Sassetta, and within *that* a painting which Berenson himself owned, is precisely that European school of design which approaches oriental art most closely in its means of expression, and hence is most successful in conveying a sense of the spiritual. To put it bluntly: 'Of European schools of design none comes so close to those of the far east as the school of Siena during the fourteenth and earlier decades of the fifteenth centuries.'[14] However, Siena's success in the achievement of spirituality is still seen as limited, is still on the weaker end of the ongoing comparison:

> Far be it from me to claim for them that they have extracted out of the events presented all their spiritual significance. A great Chinese master would have been more on a level with the high inspiration of the subject. My only claim for Sassetta is that he has dealt with these themes much more spiritually than any other European artist I can recall...[15]

The 'great Chinese master' may be great, but he is here still nameless, although in fact the paintings *are* signed. And the terrific confidence in the language can easily stop us from pausing to remember just how little Chinese or Japanese art someone like Berenson had actually seen in 1903; scarcely any more than Wickhoff had seen five years earlier. The sweep of

---

[13] Berenson, 'A Sienese Painter of the Franciscan Legend, Part I', 8.
[14] Berenson, 'A Sienese Painter of the Franciscan Legend, Part I', 12–13.
[15] Berenson, 'A Sienese Painter of the Franciscan Legend, Part I', 26.

the rhetoric can also hinder us from paying attention to what Berenson is saying here, and, significantly, to what he is *not* saying. Nowhere does he use the word that Michael Baxandall has taught all art historians to be wary of—'influence', with its misjudging of where agency lies in any cultural interaction.[16] Nowhere does he say that there is any causal connection between Sienese and Oriental painting. He says something much more radical than that, which is that Chinese painting is simply better at 'the spiritual', just as Wickhoff had praised it for retaining the illusionistic manner. But in making these comparisons Berenson, like Wickhoff, is above all making a judgement of quality, and it is the centrality of such judgements to the aesthetic enterprise that underpins art history which renders the act of comparison never an innocent one.

In a wary engagement with the whole issue of what comparison as 'the central form of engagement with art' does, Mieke Bal has written that 'It quickly becomes a ground for (relative) judgement and establishing hierarchies, and it distracts from looking.'[17] The centrality of comparison is nowhere more evident than in the ways in which—Berenson being a prime example—the art of China and of Europe have been spoken of together, whether explicitly or implicitly. However flimsy the evidence base, 'Chinese art' *begins* as a known and a coherent entity—and this remains so whether we are talking about Sandrart or Wickhoff or Berenson or Ernst Gombrich (1909–2001), who lists three eccentrically chosen Chinese painters in *The Story of Art* (1950), a book which famously begins, 'There is no such thing as art, there are only artists.' All of them were familiar with a pathetically small number of actual individuated works of Chinese art. And so it has remained.

It may be hard now to think ourselves into the decade before the First World War, when it still made sense to publish in *The Burlington Magazine* an unashamed paean to the 'Chinese master' who was a better artist than Albrecht Dürer (never mind Sassetta). But such types of comparison had even then a global reach, and are not simply an orientalist conspiracy. The year after Berenson wrote this, in 1904, his slightly older contemporary, the politician and thinker Kang Youwei (1858–1927) made his first visit to Italy, and wrote extensively in his diary of the art he was seeing there for the first

---

[16] Michael Baxandall, *Patterns of Intention: On the Historical Explanation of Picture* (New Haven and London, 1985), pp. 58–62.
[17] Mieke Bal, 'Grounds of Comparison', in *The Artemisia Files: Artemisia Gentilleschi for Feminists and Other Thinking People*, ed. Mieke Bal (Chicago and London, 2005), pp. 129–67; p. 129.

time. For Kang, preoccupied as he was with images of China's decline and its threatened position in the face of rampant imperialism, schema of global comparison came naturally to mind. In a manner that would have gladdened Giorgio Vasari's heart, he divided the history of Western painting into a stiff, lifeless 'before', and a vital 'after', which was both realistic and, more importantly, *scientific*, based on the laws of perspective. Kang knew only a bit more about the history of painting in Europe than Berenson did of that in China. But they shared a confidence in their own understanding which made sweeping pronouncements all too easy. Kang Youwei placed the turning point at Raphael, for him the first great European master, in front of whose achievements he was moved to exclaim, 'The painting of our country is shallow and desultory, far inferior to his, it must be reformed.'[18] But the roots of China's failure were also the source of that reform and revival. Kang believed that both veristic representation and the technique of oil painting were themselves Chinese inventions, transmitted to Europe from East Asia by Marco Polo.[19] All Chinese art had to do, then, was to return to its own more remote past in the Song and Yuan periods, that is, before the fourteenth century, when it had been far superior to the then 'stiff and lifeless' art of Europe.

It is perhaps worth considering the wider intellectual currents in which Berenson's and Kang's totalizing comparisons between West and East in art can be situated. One obvious point of reference lies in the writings of Josef Strzygowski (1862–1941). In 1901, two years before Berenson wrote, 'Of European schools of design none comes so close to those of the far east as the school of Siena during the fourteenth and earlier decades of the fifteenth centuries', Strzygowski published his book *Orient oder Rom?* ('Orient or Rome?'), with its trenchant exposition of non-Mediterranean, indeed 'Eastern', points of origin for the art and architecture of late antique and early medieval Europe. Although intellectually Berenson was probably closer to Strzygowski's great foe, Alois Riegl (1858–1905), and it would be banal to suggest any direct causal connection, not least because of

---

[18] Cao Yiqiang, 'Unintended Consequences of Tourism: Kang Youwei's Italian Journey (1904) and Sterling Clark's Chinese Expedition (1908)', in *Raising the Eyebrow: John Onians and World Art Studies*, ed. Lauren Golden (London, 2006), pp. 341–51; at p. 345.

[19] Cao, 'Unintended Consequences', p. 344; Kang was building on an argument of Xue Fucheng (1834–94), one of the first Qing imperial envoys to Europe, about the European perfection of originally Chinese inventions. *The European Diary of Hsieh Fucheng: Envoy Extraordinary of Imperial China*, trans. Helen Hsieh Chien, intro. and anno. Douglas Howland (New York, 1993), p. 22.

Strzygowski's notorious anti-Semitism, Berenson did have *Orient oder Rom?* in his library, and at the least these two very different men shared a willingness to see significant developments in European art as having not entirely autochthonous points of reference.[20] Kang Youwei is very unlikely to have encountered the work of Strzygowski. Perhaps much more important is the wider tendency within the humanities and nascent social sciences in the late nineteenth and early twentieth centuries for what has been called 'an especially ambitious kind of generalised historical comparison', in the search for 'a single intelligible global process'.[21] Monuments of this world history would include once well-known names like Winwood Reade, author of *The Martyrdom of Man* (1872), as well as H. G. Wells, Oswald Spengler, Toynbee, and of course Marx himself.[22] Closer to Berenson (Harvard class of 1887) was Ellsworth Huntington (1876–1947), a student at Harvard of the geographer William Morris Davis (1850–1934), and author of *The Pulse of Asia* (1907), a title also to be found in the Bibliotheca Berenson.[23] The 1930s and 1940s have been proposed as the high point of 'highly relativist, comparative cross cultural models of history', seen (perhaps largely under the impact of Marxism) as 'scientific'.[24] But it is worth considering whether, just as art history was arguably the first form of cultural history, it is in art history well *before* the 1930s that some of these global comparative constructions were first given their fullest forms.

The problem for art history then is not, as I am quite often told, that 'we know nothing about Chinese art'. The problem is that we already know *everything* about it. It is entirely a known quantity. As the Macedonian

---

[20] Strzygowski has a growing critical literature of his own: Suzanne L. Marchand, 'The Rhetoric of Artifacts and the Decline of Classical Humanism: The Case of Josef Strzygowski', *History and Theory*, 33/4 (1994), 106–30; Margaret Olin, 'Nationalism, the Jews and Art History', *Judaism*, 45/4 (1996), 461–82; Jas Elsner, 'The Birth of Late Antiquity: Riegl and Strzygowski in 1901', *Art History*, 25/3 (2002), 358–79.

[21] William T. Rowe, 'Owen Lattimore, Asia, and Comparative History', *Journal of Asian Studies*, 66/3 (2007), 759–86; 759–60; also Raymond Grew, 'The Case for Comparing Histories', *American Historical Review*, 85/4 (1980), 763–78.

[22] For a recent discussion, which also emphasizes the role of geography in the writing of universal histories, see Kitty Hauser, *Bloody Old Britain: O. G. S. Crawford and the Archaeology of Modern Life* (London, 2008), pp. 43–9.

[23] Rowe, 'Owen Lattimore', 761–2: Marchand, 'Rhetoric of Artifacts', 128, cites Spengler, 'Today we think in continents.'

[24] Rowe, 'Owen Lattimore', 781.

scholar Suzanna Milevska has put it, in the context of a debate on 'Is Art History Global?', published in a volume of that name:

> Perhaps the reason art history is not global now (and I believe it would be naïve to think it is) is the result of earlier art history, which had all the answers ready at hand before it was even written, and was based on the limited experience of its writers.[25]

And therein lies the central issue. Far from simply arguing for the inclusion in the art-historical canon of hitherto neglected or disregarded material, we need to lay down the discipline's claim that we already know everything about Chinese art (and by extension about Indian, African, Macedonian, 'world' art) if we wish to learn anything at all. But this conceit can perhaps be taken one step further. For although Chinese art is fully 'in place' as an object of art-historical knowledge, it has been one of the conditions of that knowledge's possibility that it needs to *forget* that it already knows everything. This is a process observable in writing from the first half of the twentieth century, associated with the professionalization of the disciple, and strikingly visible in the person of Bernard Berenson himself. If we revisit the ancient sage Berenson of 1950, the place of China has shifted considerably from the one it held for him fifty years earlier. In a short essay entitled 'Exotic arts', that place has become a marginal one:

> Compared with our art of the last sixty centuries with its endless variety of subject matter, of material, of kind and quality, every other art, Chinese included, is limited ... The exotic arts soon weary. As is the case with Yogi theosophies, Mazdanianism, and similar appeals, it is craving for mere otherness that draws us to them rather than any unique superiority of their own.[26]

I would insist that it is hard not to see in this progress from enthusiasm to weary disdain a psychological process of repression. This process parallels the way 'proper' art history came to be less open to the kind of grand comparative gesture that had seemed meaningful before about 1939, as it became professional and specialized. The inclusion of Chinese art and archaeology in the syllabus of the Courtauld Institute from 1933 to the Second World War, for instance, and its consequent exclusion after that date, is a fact now little known and not sufficiently acknowledged.[27]

---

[25] Suzana Milevska, 'Is Balkan Art History Global?', in *Is Art History Global?*, ed. James Elkins, The Art Seminar (New York and London, 2007), at pp. 214–22; 221.
[26] Bernard Berenson, *Aesthetics and History* (London, 1950), p. 227.
[27] Stacey Pierson, *Collectors, Collections and Museums: The Field of Chinese Ceramics in Britain, 1560–1960* (Oxford and New York, 2007).

As we all know, that which is repressed has a way of returning. This basic fact has been drawn on by the art historian Stanley Abe, in his work on the ways in which it was necessary for the success of abstract impressionism in post-war America that the empirically verifiable engagement on the part of several artists with what he calls an 'oriental mode' (principally via the medium of calligraphy) be systematically denied and refused. He sees fantasy, in its technical sense not as a mistake but as 'a failure to recognise which is fundamental to our subjectivity as well as the structuring of what we call reality', as central to the way in which the Chinese script and Chinese visual signs functioned as part of the conditions of possibility for modernist poetics and modernist art in the mid-twentieth century.[28] This fantasy is constructed from the long (very long, if we go back to Sandrart) history of repression expressed in Chinese art and, by extension, all the 'exotic arts' as simultaneously utterly inscrutable, unknowable, *and* at the same time totally known. That knowledge has always provided the grounds for comparison, more powerful when it is implicit, or even denied. But does it have to be so? Mieke Bal has written of the possibility that 'There are, however, other forms of comparison, not built on a logic of oppositional judgement. Comparison can be a tool for analysis as long as one of its terms is not established as normative', and argued that if this is done, 'Instead of an instrument of judgement, it becomes a source of differentiation.'[29] Examples of this are still thin on the ground, but one project which interestingly attempted something along these lines was the exhibition *Empire interdit*, 'Forbidden empire: Visions of the world of the Chinese and Flemish masters', held in Brussels and Beijing in 2007, and conceived by the Belgian painter Luc Tymans (b.1958) and the Chinese art historian Yu Hui.[30] In the exhibition, and the catalogue that records it, a very wide range of types of juxtaposition of Chinese and Flemish paintings was attempted; some were obviously iconographical, some formal, some deliberately devoid of obvious similarities at all. The larger point being made by the range and quantity of comparisons in 'Forbidden empire' is that no *single* type of comparison will do; the

---

[28] Stanley K. Abe, 'To Avoid the Inscrutable: Abstract Expressionism and the 'Oriental Mode', in *Discrepant Abstraction*, ed. Kobena Mercer (Cambridge, MA, and London, 2006), pp. 53–73; 54. See also now Alexandra Munroe (ed.), *The Third Mind: American Artists Contemplate Asia, 1860–1989* (New York, 2009).

[29] Bal, 'Grounds of Comparison', pp. 130 and 167.

[30] Luc Tuymans and Yu Hui, *L'empire interdit: visions du monde des maitres chinois et flamands* (Brussels, 2007).

relationship between a range of diverse Chinese images and diverse Flemish ones cannot be reduced to a comparison of stable identities. Bal's hope for comparison as the grounds of differentiation, rather than judgement, has possibly been glimpsed on the horizon, if not yet actually reached. There is a lot more of this sort of work to be done, since only when a full acknowledgement is made of the fundamental and foundational role of its fantasies of global knowledge, can art history begin the task of thinking about how to use comparison in this possibly utopian but still desirably productive and non-judgemental way.

12
Global objects: contention and entanglement

GLENN ADAMSON AND GIORGIO RIELLO

For those seeking to chart a global history, artefacts might seem a last resort. Most functional items were never intended to communicate explicitly, and extracting information from them can be difficult. They rarely survive in accurate samples; the material culture of the elite is vastly over-represented in the world's museums. And with some exceptions (like archaeological remains, architecture, and tombstones), they are decontexualized. Reconstructing the original place and time of their making and use is often a matter of guesswork. For historians, the interpretation of an object is dependent upon a prior understanding gained from documents, images, and other sources of information.

Sometimes one wonders: when we do history through objects, is that because it produces better history? Or is it because we simply like material objects so much that we want to lend them justification? Perhaps this is putting the question the wrong way round. For we could ask just as easily: what is the point of producing a global history in the first place? One good answer is that it helps academics and the public to understand cultural relations, both in the past and the present. The charisma of the object is a tremendous asset in this regard. Rather like relics in a religious context, historic artefacts exert a strong pull on the imagination, and are easily made into focal points for narrative. Museums—the world's greatest delivery system for popular history—are necessarily object-led enterprises. They reverse the historian's usual procedure, which is to pose an intelligent question and seek out the best available evidence to answer it. Object-based research begins with a piece of evidence (the thing itself), and slowly but surely teases questions out of it. The result of this exercise may, at times, offer a useful corrective to received histories based on textual sources. For example, objects can be of inestimable use in studying illiterate populations, everyday activities deemed so unimportant that they attracted little comment, or the lives of those whose voices were not considered worth recording, such as slaves, women, and the poor. But these are exceptional cases. Most surviving material culture does not yield dramatic correctives, but it can definitely be used to compress histories into a digestible and compelling form.

A case in point is the recent radio programme 'A History of the World in 100 Objects', produced by the British Museum in conjunction with the BBC.[1] In each episode the museum's director, Neil MacGregor, discusses one item in the collection, using it to address various themes within cultural history. Sometimes the emphasis is on intercultural exchange, as in the discussion of a group of shards from disparate sources found at a single site in East Africa. But all is not peace and harmony. Conflict and its attendant horrors also make frequent appearances, and to the credit of the show's creators, there is a regular emphasis on the things an object *cannot* tell us about the past. There is also an implicitly comparative approach in the programme's structure; a certain theme (like godly worship) may be pursued across geographies in a series of episodes. This museum initiative not only exemplifies the use of objects as nodal points within historical narratives. It also reflects recent methodologies in studies of the global. A professional academic's eyebrows might well be sent aloft by the very premise of the undertaking—the whole history of the world, in *objects*? Yet it might well be that this project, with its wide public reach and ability to excite the imagination through visual as well as historical description, may be doing more to proliferate recent thinking in global history than a library's worth of peer-reviewed monographs.

An important corollary of this rhetorical potential that resides within objects is that they are inherently contentious. It may even be that the very quality that makes artefacts seem unpromising as historical evidence—their relative poverty of encoded information—is what makes them so attractive as historical 'props'. Much more than a text, or even a representational image, one can project on to an object what one wants to see. For this reason, it is perhaps in the interpretation of things that global history is put to its toughest tests. This chapter will pursue that argument through three examples, each of which suggests one way that an artefact

---

[1] <http://www.bbc.co.uk/ahistoryoftheworld/> (accessed 12 June 2012).

can fit into a narrative of global history: objects that demonstrate cultural connection; objects that synthesize global difference within themselves; and objects that image the global. Each of these is an apparent virtue, but appearances, as they say, can be deceiving.

From Japan with love?

Tourists flock to the Tower of London, one of the most loved attractions in the British capital, to see the Crown jewels. Among the various artefacts that one encounters at the Tower is a suit of Japanese armour (Figure 12.1).

How did it arrive at the Tower of London? The label says that this suit of armour was made by Iwai Yozaemon of Nambu as part of a series of presentation armour in fifteenth-century Dō-maru style. This artefact encapsulates the story of the first contact between Japan and England as it was given by the Emperor of Japan as a diplomatic gift to King James I in 1613. It was taken to England by John Saris, the captain of the *Clove*, the first English East India Company ship to reach Japan in 1613.[2] As the East India Company acted as a representative of the Crown in Asia, Saris was effectively both an ambassador and an employee of a mercantile company. We know that he carried a letter for 'the Highe and mighties Prince the Emperour of Japan' from James I and several presents, among which were '1 verye faire Turkey carpet, 1 shash, 1 pes tapseele & 1 pes white byramme'.[3] Saris was able to gain an audience with the shogun thanks to the mediation of William Adams, an Englishman who had served on a Dutch vessel that was shipwrecked in Japan in 1600. In the following years, Adams gained the trust of Emperor Ieyasu and of his son Hideata, acting shogun in 1613 when Saris and Adams reached Edo. The shogun sent several gifts in return to James I, including '2 varnished Armours', a 'tatch' (tachi, a sword), and a 'wagadash' (a large sword).[4] We are led to believe that the armour at the Tower of London is one of the two mentioned by Saris.[5]

---

[2] The East India Company was a commercial body chartered by the British Crown in 1600 with a monopoly on trade with Asia.
[3] Anthony Farrington (ed.), *The English Factory in Japan 1613–1623* (London, 1991), vol. 2, p. 1018. *Tapseele* and *byramme* are types of textile.
[4] Ibid., vol. 2, p. 1019.
[5] Cited in Derek Massarella, 'James I and Japan', *Monumenta Nipponica*, 38/4 (1983), 378.

Figure 12.1 Japanese armour gifted by the Emperor of Japan to King James I of England and Scotland in 1613. (Royal Collection Trust / © HM Queen Elizabeth II 2012. Photograph: The Royal Armouries)

Ambassadorial presents were not uncommon and were used as symbols for the acceptance or rejection of commercial and political ties between different states. Because of the unexpected time of the arrival of the English delegation, we might safely assume that this armour was already complete and ready to be given as a 'pre-made' gift.[6] The British were not in any sense exceptional in receiving a suit of armour. This was considered by Japanese diplomatic etiquette the most appropriate type of gift among rulers (it is probable that Ieyasu and Hideata might have found the English present of a carpet rather less fitting for the occasion). The Japanese armour at the Tower of London is not even unique, as other examples had reached Europe as diplomatic gifts over the previous half a century. The first of its kind probably reached Europe in 1562 and was a present from the Daimyo of Bungo to Dom Sebastiao, the King of Portugal. Similar objects were presented in 1585 to the King of Spain (during a Japanese Imperial embassy to Europe), in 1611 to the representative of the Dutch East India Company in Japan, and in other embassies; similar examples survive in royal armouries in Denmark, Italy, Austria, and France.[7] If the first reaction is one of amazement in finding an object sent four centuries ago by the Emperor of Japan to the king of a small island at the other side of the world, it turns out to be just the kind of thing one would expect to find in royal armouries in Europe: a standardized 'corporate' present.

Needless to say, this single artefact represents an important episode in the relationship between England and Japan, and should be read in conjunction with the documentary evidence that survives from the first English voyage to Japan and the ten-year commercial settlement of the English there. But one should also ask what this object might hide or erase from view. Clearly it was a token of friendship, but one should not fall into the misleading impression that it signalled the start of a process, that of the diplomatic relationship between England and Japan. An artefact like the Japanese armour is connected to a certain point in time, but it should not be used to narrate things to follow. Notwithstanding the courtesy between James I and the Emperor of Japan in 1613, trading privileges granted to the English were curtailed just three years later.[8] Even more catastrophic was

---

[6] Ian Bottomley, 'Diplomatic Gifts of Arms and Armour between Japan and Europe during the 16th and 17th Centuries', *Arms & Armour*, 1/1 (2004), 13.

[7] Ibid., 6, 10, 15.

[8] Derek Massarella, 'Anglo-Japanese Relations, 1600–1858', in *The History of Anglo-Japanese Relations, 1600–2000: The Political-Diplomatic Dimension*, ed. Ian Hill Nish, and Yoichi Kibata (Basingstoke, 2000), vol. 1, p. 7.

the fate of a Spanish embassy to Japan. Richard Cocks, the head of the English factory in Japan between 1613 and 1623, recorded the fate of three Jesuit friars sent as ambassadors to the Emperor of Japan from Spain—England's enemy. Initially the emperor accepted their embassy and presents, but half a year later and much to Cocks's satisfaction, 'the Emperour retourned back the p'sent ... and Commanded the padres to avoid out of his Cvntry & never presume more to sue for entrance into Japon'.[9] In this case the return of the present, even after some time, symbolized the end of a cordial relationship.

The case of armour is also revealing of how objects that once were potent symbols of cultural, political, or economic encounter, could be reread and often misinterpreted with the passing of time. A 1793 catalogue of the armoury in the Real Armeria in Madrid referred to the Japanese armour there as 'very ridiculous' and added in a very casual manner that they were 'presented to Philip II by the Emperor of China or the King of Japan'. Another seventeenth-century suit of Japanese armour was bought by the British Royal Armouries in 1841 in the mistaken belief that it was the armour of a 'Moor of Granada', while a further set given to the Habsburg emperor was exhibited in Brussels until the nineteenth century as the armour of Montezuma and his son.[10] Even more surprising is the fact that one suit of armour given to James I (though it is not clear if it is the extant one) was described in 1662 as given by the 'Emperor of Mougul'.[11]

The risk is that we might see this armour as only 'different', an expression of 'otherness' that is often seen to characterize the phase of encounter. Derek Massarella, in discussing the first embassy to Japan that led to the armour being sent back to England, says that 'This particular encounter did not occur in the sort of no man's land which cultural anthropologists describe.' This was not 'a contested space across which "self" and "other" are supposed to have stared at one another with mutual incomprehension, possibly disdain'.[12] Though both parties might have been ignorant of each other, they did share a common purpose: commerce. The armour is therefore not symbolic of a surprising encounter, but is a token of 'understanding' between people willing for their own reasons to open their borders to each other's commodities. The armour is the first of

---

[9] Cited in Massarella, 'James I and Japan', 384.
[10] Bottomley, 'Diplomatic Gifts', 7, 17, 22.
[11] Ibid., 22.
[12] Massarella, 'Anglo-Japanese Relations', vol. 1, p. 5.

such commodities, a kind of 'free good' intended to smooth the trade that was going to follow.

An interpretation like this takes away the pathos that many of the objects in museum collections in Europe and elsewhere may acquire, when they are used to narrate stories of interaction taking place against all the odds. It takes us to a more mundane story of economic self-interest and appropriate etiquette. Yet, the very materiality of an artefact like the Japanese armour at the Tower of London encourages us to construct a narrative that is read mostly within the category of 'encounter' (be it diplomatic, commercial, or cultural). Is this correct? How different would the story of this first English voyage to Japan be if instead of a Japanese suit of armour, England had been left with the collection of erotic Japanese paintings (*shunga*) that John Saris had gathered during his stay in Japan?[13] This would have been a more fitting memento of the life of the Englishmen who travelled to Japan and stayed there, sometimes for years, marrying local women. Richard Cocks, William Adams, and William Eaton all lived in Japan for long periods and had offspring from Japanese spouses.[14] Their relationship with Japan and the Japanese was not diplomatic, not even an encounter; it was based instead on the negotiation of habits and manners that an object like the Japanese armour is not able to convey.

Has St Pancras Station moved to India?

Most of the artefacts used in constructing histories of connectivity between different parts of the world are 'portable' objects such as cloth and clothing, porcelain, lacquerware, ivory and mother-of-pearl knick-knacks, and larger furniture and screens that could be carried across long distances. Today they feature prominently in museums not just because of their meaningful historical worth or their high craftsmanship and qualitative value, but because—as in the case of the Japanese armour—they can be easily shown in display cases. Only in the nineteenth century did these tokens of global connection become larger in size. In the case of the Statue of Liberty, it is the technological sophistication and dimension of the artefact that makes

---

[13] On his return to Britain in 1615, Saris's collection was immediately confiscated, and 'in open presence, putt [. . .] into the fire' by Sir Thomas Smythe, the first Governor of the East India Company. Cited in Giles Milton, *Samurai Williams: The Adventurer who Unlocked Japan* (London, 2003), p. 158.

[14] Massarella, 'Anglo-Japanese Relations', vol. 1, p. 9.

it such a well-known symbol of national identity for Americans and of diplomatic courtesy between France and the United States.

The Statue of Liberty is however a very peculiar example of a connecting object of large dimension, physically transported across the Atlantic. Most large-scale objects are instead rather static, and none more so than the buildings of which our cities and built environment are made. Buildings are not museum objects (though sometimes they might be museums themselves) and are often seen as representative of a local idiom (architectural, stylistic, technological, and cultural), sometimes tempered by external influences. It is their size and stillness that make buildings quintessentially local or national. Yet an edifice like the Victoria Terminus in Mumbai is far from being your classic neighbourhood building (Figure 12.2). The Chhatrapati Shivaji Terminus (छत्रपति शिवाजी टर्मिनस), better known in the West as Victoria Terminus (VT), was one of the largest nineteenth-century railway stations. It was built between 1878 and 1887 at a cost of £300,000 by the English-born Frederick William Stevens (1847–1900), architect and engineer for the Public Works Department of India from 1867 until his death in 1900. As the name suggests, the VT was one of the many colonial buildings that came to be part of the infrastructure of British India and was

Figure 12.2 Victoria Terminus Station, Bombay (Mumbai), early twentieth century. (By permission of the author)

named after Queen Victoria, Empress of India, for her Diamond Jubilee. With its twenty-two platforms, it was one of the largest buildings in India and the headquarters of the Great Indian Peninsular Railway.

In what way is VT a global object? Many have interpreted it as one of the best—and perhaps most flamboyant—manifestations of empire, a key political process that had in the nineteenth century a truly global span. It is correct to say that VT encapsulates the British Empire at its pinnacle, but it is also a reminder that Bombay from the late 1860s onwards became one of the major ports in the world following the opening of the Suez Canal in 1869. The boom in cotton production, in particular with the American Civil War, made Bombay the most important city in the Empire after London. Connections with the rest of India were as important as those by sea. This is an 'artefact' that connected inner India with the rest of the Empire and in particular its metropolitan core: London. This was done not just functionally, by using VT as a terminus for the British commodities to be sold in the subcontinent and raw materials to be taken back to Britain, but also visually. VT is a 'Gothic revival' building similar in style to many of the civic buildings in Britain constructed in the second half of the nineteenth century.

Figure 12.3 St Pancras Station, London, *c*.1900. (By permission of the author)

Many have called VT the 'St Pancras of the East' because of its apparent similarity with London St Pancras Station built a couple of decades earlier (Figure 12.3). It has been argued that Stevens completed VT following the metropolitan Gothic idiom of St Pancras by George Gilbert Scott (built between 1865 and 1868, with the addition of a hotel between 1868 and 1873). The connection between the two architects cannot be denied. Scott designed the University Convocation Hall and Library in Mumbai, although he never visited India.[15] It is evident that Stevens was influenced by him, although there is no proof that he saw St Pancras.[16] Stevens in fact spent most of his life in Bombay, building the Municipal Corporation Building, the Royal Alfred Sailor's Home, the Post Office Mews at Apollo Bunder, the head offices of the BB&CI (The Bombay, Baroda, and Central India) Railway at Churchgate, and the Oriental Life Insurance Offices at the Flora Fountain (which resembled even more Scott's St Pancras Station in London). But is it really correct to see VT as the 'St Pancras of the East', a colonial transposition or architectural imposition?

VT is actually quite different from St Pancras. It is not just larger, but is also symmetrical and develops itself horizontally rather than vertically as in the case of St Pancras. Unlike its London counterpart, it is domed by a large stone cupola, something alien to the nineteenth-century Gothic revival.[17] It is also vividly polychrome, and integrates a variety of sculptures produced by the Bombay School of Art and combining European (Venetian Gothic and Italianate influences) and Oriental styles (Indo-Saracenic). John MacDonald Mackenzie has defined it as 'an epic hybrid, sucking in and re-processing a range of styles, an analogue of imperial power'.[18] He underlines the fact that VT is not a manifestation of unilateral metropolitan power over the colonial periphery. Instead, it represents the very hybrid nature of the British Empire. Rather than VT being seen as an 'Asian' St Pancras, this building belongs to the style of architectural eclecticism, a 'flexible style of architecture' that was adaptable and therefore suitable to be used in different parts of the British Empire. This includes not just Bombay (VT, and the nearby Municipal Buildings by Stevens (1888–93, Figure 12.4)) but also the British Columbia Legislative Buildings

---

[15] John MacDonald Mackenzie, 'Victoria Terminus, Bombay', *History Today*, 39 (January 1989), 60.
[16] Simon Bradley, *St Pancras Station* (London, 2007), pp. 47–8.
[17] 'Chhatrapati Shivaji Terminus (India)', UNESCO World Heritage document, no. 945rev <http://whc.unesco.org/pg.cfm?cid=31&id_site=945> (accessed 3 May 2010).
[18] MacDonald Mackenzie, 'Victoria Terminus, Bombay', p. 60.

Global objects: contention and entanglement

Figure 12.4 Bombay (Mumbai), the Municipal Buildings by Stevens, 2005. (By permission of the author)

in Victoria, Canada (1893–97), Prince's Building in Hong Kong (1904), or the Royal Exhibition Building in Melbourne (1880).[19]

A building that at first sight might appear alien to its own topographical and stylistic context, VT should not necessarily be read as an 'object of colonial power' or a derivation of a metropolitan model. Rather, VT belongs to a category of buildings whose style was deemed as suitable for the late nineteenth-century project of a global empire. However, as in the case of the Japanese armour, the meaning of VT today is different from what it stood for in the late nineteenth century. VT was renamed Chhatrapati Shivaji Terminus (after the seventeenth Maratha ruler) in 1996 in response to the policy of renaming locations with Indian names, and India successfully lobbied UNESCO to have the station included as a UNESCO World Heritage site in 2004. Today, VT is a symbol of modern India: this is probably why in recent years this building has featured on television and in film. (It was, for example, the location for one of the key scenes of the 2008 hit film *Slumdog Millionaire*.) In November of the same year images of VT were televised to households around the world when it became one of the centres of a terrorist attack.

Eye on the ball

If one had to choose a single activity that emblematizes globalism today, the game of football might be a good choice. Called 'soccer' in America and Australia, *fútbol* in Spanish, *calcio* in Italian, *zuqiu* in Chinese, and *sakka* (an approximation of the American term) in Japan, football is played worldwide and commands the highest television audience of any sport. It has also, inadvertently, given rise to widespread alarm about global labour. In 1996 the journalist Sydney Schamberg travelled to Pakistan to see how footballs were made. His article, entitled 'Six Cents an Hour', showed that the workforce of manufacturers like Nike and Adidas was composed largely of children, living in conditions that were tantamount to slavery. It was a textbook case of displacing labour in order to hide it. 'The words

---

[19] G. Alex Bremner, '"Some Imperial Institute": Architecture, Symbolism, and the Ideal of Empire in Late Victorian Britain, 1887–93', *Journal of the Society of Architectural Historians*, 62/1 (2003), 67–8.

Hand Made are printed clearly on every ball,' Schamberg noted, 'not printed is any explanation of whose hands made them.'[20]

Following Schamberg's exposé, the image of children sewing footballs for starvation wages became a kind of shorthand for exploitative labour conditions. Activists and NGO officials heaped scorn on sporting goods companies. Free-market proponents rushed to argue that 'sweatshops' were an unfortunate but necessary by-product of developing economies. Economic theorists posited a breakdown in the established relations between national and private interests, so that labour became 'a naked commodity, no longer embedded in relations of reciprocity rooted in social and political communities'.[21] There was only one point of agreement. Everyone concurred that globalism had radically changed the reality of production.

Amidst the debate, people kept making footballs. And while arguments continue over the plight of labourers in Pakistan, another thing has become clear. Manufacturers are highly aware of the politicized nature of their products, and they have gone to considerable lengths to change the narrative. Nike, by many accounts the worst offender in the industry, signed up to a 'Global Compact' to protect human rights, and Adidas promised to exert pressure on its Indonesian suppliers.[22] More surprisingly perhaps, footballs themselves have been activated as actors in the debate. The most explicit example of this is Puma's 'Peace One Day' ball, designed by the Japanese consultancy Nendo. Made as part of a public relations campaign in conjunction with the 2008 African Cup of Nations, the ball is quite literally a global image, with the world's continents rendered in various traditional fabric patterns (Figure 12.5). Though it may seem improbable to claim, as Puma's CEO Jochen Zeitz did, that a football design could 'make a contribution to the generation of global peace',[23] the very fact that the design

---

[20] Sydney Schamberg, 'Six Cents an Hour', *Life* (June 1996). See also Bob Herbert, 'Brutality in Vietnam', *New York Times* (28 March 1997); Bill Bigelow, 'The Human Lives Behind the Labels: The Global Sweatshop, Nike, and the Race to the Bottom', *Phi Delta Kappan*, 79/2 (1997), 112–19.

[21] William I. Robinson, 'Social Theory and Globalization: The Rise of a Transnational State', *Theory and Society*, 30/2 (2001), 170–1.

[22] Gary Gereffi, Ronie Garcia-Johnson, and Erika Sasser, 'The NGO-Industrial Complex', *Foreign Policy*, 125 (2001), 56–65; Jason Burke, 'Child Labour Scandal Hits Adidas', *Observer* (19 November 2000).

[23] See <http://peace.puma.com/us/en/page/2/> (accessed 8 June 2012).

Writing the History of the Global

Figure 12.5 Puma's 'Peace One Day' ball, designed by the Japanese consultancy Nendo, 2008. (© Nendo)

was fashioned around this rhetoric suggests how sensitive the antennae of corporations have become to the issue of globalism.

More recently, a football has made the news for rather different reasons. The 'Jabulani' (a word meaning 'to celebrate' in the Zulu language) was developed by Adidas specifically for use in the 2010 World Cup. Assembled using a minimum of seams achieved through a novel design of interlocking curved panels, covered in slick polyurethane, and light in weight, the ball was meant to be a technical marvel. Instead it was a public relations disaster. The Jabulani's flight proved unpredictable, and players dismissed it as a 'beachball', 'appalling', a 'supermarket ball', a 'disaster'. Coaches called it 'impossible'. Goalkeepers suspected a conspiracy; as Claudio Bravo from Chile put it, 'they created it to make life difficult for keepers, so they make more mistakes and there are more goals'.[24]

[24] 'World Cup's Jabulani is a Rotten Ball, Says Casillas', *Agence France-Presse* (31 May 2010).

Inevitably, the furore over the Jabulani's playability drew attention to the details of its production. Where was this strange thing from? Certainly not South Africa, where the World Cup was being played.[25] Like so many other global commodities, it was manufactured in China, partly from components made elsewhere.[26] As a short promotional film released by Adidas reveals, it was made in the manner that has led to Chinese domination of many industries: a combination of repetitive handwork and full automation.[27] Much of the labour of making the Jabulani goes into its assembly, as might be expected, but a great deal of the work involves applying decals to the surface: logos, trademarking, and a pattern of multicoloured rings that evoke both African decorative patterning and the Olympic insignia. Compared with the roadside sheds that Schamberg saw in Pakistan, crowded with underage pieceworkers, the factory where the Jabulanis were fabricated is quite high-tech, clean, and impressive. But one still wonders about the experience of working there. It may be significant that not a single operative's face is included in the Adidas footage—only adept hands, going about their tasks at incredible speed.

The real story of the Jabulani, then, is not that it is difficult to kick or catch. Rather, it is the way that the ball marks a typical displacement within globalism: from one site of outsourcing to another—which is perhaps less exploitative, but more likely, just more efficient. As Jane Collins has noted, 'skill' itself has been redefined by multinational corporations; it now signifies not knowledge, but rather raw speed.[28] Pakistan has seen its share in the global football market slip from a high of 85 per cent to something below 40 per cent in the past few years, thanks to inroads made by their Far Eastern competitors. The loss of the World Cup contract must have hurt (though workers in the Punjab were still kept busy making low-quality Jabulani knock-offs).[29] Part of the reason for this shift is the sensitivity

---

[25] On Africa's inability to participate in global commodity production, see Y. Z. Ya'u, 'The New Imperialism and Africa in the Global Electronic Village', *Review of African Political Economy*, 31/99 (2004), 11–29.

[26] The glue, ink, and fabric in the ball were all produced in China, but the polyurethane coating is from Taiwan and the inner latex bladder is from India.

[27] <http://www.youtube.com/watch?v=zbLjk4OTRdI> (accessed 8 June 2012). On contemporary Chinese manufacturing, see also Edward Burtynsky's film *Manufactured Landscapes* (Zeitgeist Films, 2006).

[28] Jane L. Collins, 'Mapping a Global Labor Market: Gender and Skill in the Globalizing Garment Industry', *Gender and Society*, 16/6 (2002), 921–40.

[29] Zofeen Ebrahim, 'The Other Side of World Cup Footballs', *Asia Times* (9 July 2010).

mentioned above; companies like Adidas have a financial stake in keeping their name clean, and once established, the image of the Pakistani sweatshop is hard to dispel. But it also has to do with the ongoing cycle of global production, in which different patterns of work, most of them exploitative in one way or another, displace one another at a bewildering pace. How can we adequately formulate a politics of production, when our understanding of labouring conditions changes more slowly than the conditions themselves do? This is exacerbated by the fact that the (perhaps deceptive) image projected by an object has become much more important; after all, the Jabulani was seen in action by nearly thirty billion people in the summer of 2010. Paradoxically this means that investigating the means of production, at the most basic and physical level, has never been more important.

Conclusion

By using three rather different artefacts, we have attempted to provide different ways in which material objects can help to address problems and issues that are part of the agenda of global history. Our choices might appear random, but they have in fact been based on some of the ways of conceptualizing and writing about 'the global'. We considered an object, the Japanese armour, that is often in a curatorial museum environment as a tool to convey narratives of global connections, a theme that has received particular attention for the early modern period. We have then considered a building such as VT in Mumbai that can instead be read as the result of different influences and of a 'global project' of empire based on hybridism. And finally, a soccer ball has taken us to the present to consider instead the meaning of a 'global condition' or globalism as the fruit of a process that we call globalization.

The three objects considered come from very different contexts, and their own natures have changed over time. This is particularly true of the Japanese armour, once a diplomatic gift and today an artefact displayed in one of the most visited museums in the world. VT is instead a 'public' object, a building still in operation whose function and meaning has changed substantially over time. And finally the soccer ball, though much more recent, is an object that belongs to popular culture, but whose enjoyment and political dispute is instantly mediated. None of these three objects is a transparent carrier of meaning, especially in their capacity to

Table 12.1 Global objects: a matrix

	Object 1. Japanese Armour	*Object 2. Victoria Terminus in Mumbai*	*Object 3. A Soccer Ball*
Nature of object	Curatorial	Public	Popular
Type of global history	Connection	Hybridism	Globalism
Type of object	An Asian object that is in Europe	An object in India that is not Indian	An object that is everywhere

encapsulate notions of global history. Partially this is a matter of their histories: the fact that they have travelled over long distances, or that they were perceived as 'foreign' in a local context, or that they are dislocated in any specific space. They are at once anomalous and revealing.

Our hands-on approach has tried to show how objects can be used to critically engage with global history; but we also have a further intent of prompting historians to think of the spaces of global history beyond the traditional territorial, topographical, and geographical classification. We have also attempted to show how the object itself can produce its own global history or can be used as a way to challenge, revise, or relativize established narratives. Objects might appear at first sight passive remnants of something past, but are often the debris with which histories small and large can be constructed.

Part V
Round Table

13
Panel discussion: ways forward and major challenges

Globe and empire

John Darwin

Is 'global' history a distinct kind of history with its own subject matter, or simply an approach to be used in all kinds of history? Perhaps the answer is both.

There is no shortage of competing approaches to global history. Perhaps the best developed of these, with the most sophisticated literature, addresses the 'great divergence' in economic performance between Western Europe and Asia after 1800. Indeed, the concepts and methods devised to test the Europe–Asia comparison are now being extended to rethink the economic histories of other continents as well. In theory at least, exploring divergence serves as a platform for examining a vast range of other similarities and differences in political and legal institutions, cultural values, demographic trends, and religious beliefs in various parts of the world. One by-product of this is often to highlight the existence of long-distance trading connections and the cultural exchanges implied in the consumption of remotely produced trade goods. A second approach, also much favoured, has been to insist more explicitly on the study of intercontinental connections by stressing the role of oceanic spaces as vectors of migration, goods, and ideas. Braudel's 'Mediterranean' (a zone extending as far north as Poland) was the first great model of how this could be done. The 'Indian Ocean World', the 'Atlantic World', the 'Black Atlantic', and numerous other examples of 'thalassic' history, have shown how attractive this kind of global history can be. But if the 'great divergence' risks an overemphasis on the importance of material progress, thalassic history's stress on oceanic community can occlude allegiance and identity in dangerously presentist ways. Dismissing much Atlantic World history as merely American exceptionalism writ large, the Canadian historian Ian Steele remarked sardonically: 'No-one ever fought, prayed or died for the Atlantic World.'[1]

However, these and other approaches (such as histories of diasporas, migrations, missionary enterprise, or modern 'globalization') can be seen as subsets of something more fundamental. The particular concern of the global historian is, or should be, with the history of 'connectedness'—and especially with those forms of connectedness that are oceanic and trans- or intercontinental (since Eurasia may be thought of as a 'supercontinent'). Connectedness is a part of the human condition, at least as far back as we can trace human activity. It arises from the instinct that Adam Smith famously noted, to 'truck, barter and exchange'.[2] Smith was thinking of trade, and pressing the case that the commercial urge was both irrepressible and necessary. But his insight can be widened. A no less irrepressible urge, on a large scale or small, has been the urge to migrate—as a means of escape or in search of opportunity, pacific or predatory. The third form of connectedness arises from the demand for ideas and the eagerness to supply, or spread, or impose them. The diffusion of religious belief, technical know-how, cultural values, and political ideology might even be thought of as the most dynamic of all forms of connectedness—although a moment's thought will remind us how often their impact was closely bound up with (or even dependent upon) movements of people and trade.

The methodological difficulty that confronts the global historian is how to track and measure such connectedness, let alone how to explain it. The very 'informality' that typically characterized it (the activities of nameless merchants, migrants, missionaries, and mercenaries) means that it rarely leaves (or so we must assume) an archival footprint. Too often, then, the global historian is thrown back upon the most fragmentary evidence: the exploits of one individual whose records have survived by a historical 'accident'. Large claims must be made which, to the sceptical eye of more conventional historians, look like balancing a house on the top of a needle. Even where the record is less parsimonious, it is often hard to reconstruct the institutional or cultural context: the brutal fact is that (despite the enormous progress of recent years in finding and opening new archival deposits) there is an extreme variation in the survival of archives in different parts of the world.

---

[1] I. K. Steele, 'Bernard Bailyn's American Atlantic', *History and Theory*, 46/1 (2007), 48.
[2] Adam Smith, *The Wealth of Nations* (Everyman edn., London, 1910), Book 1, Ch.2, p. 12.

One way (but only a partial way) out of this methodological cul-de-sac is to rethink the value of imperial histories. The starting point here is to acknowledge the near-universality of empires in world history as the 'default mode' of political organization as far back as we can see. Empires arose from the maldistribution of state-building resources. But the precondition of expansion beyond their 'core' zone was the existence of connectedness, regional, continental, and global. Empires grew by encouraging and exploiting the effects of connectedness which supplied the critical means to penetrate, destabilize, and reorder neighbouring or even faraway societies. Empires of all kinds (not just European empires) had a vested interest in connectedness but also a prime motive to interpret its meanings and regulate its impacts. For connectedness of the 'wrong' kind could do them more harm than good, or promote the expansion of rivals whose success might be fatal. All empires, therefore, with the capacity to do so, might be expected to engage in the constant surveillance of those forms of connectedness that affected them most—or were thought to do so. The records of this ceaseless watch and ward, whether of predatory or defensive intent, will form part (and perhaps a large part) of their imperial archives.

Perhaps the logic is obvious. If the myriad actors who created connectedness remain in most cases beyond the historian's reach, those whose business it was to surveille their activity should be much more accessible to systematic enquiry. However flawed in reality (by no information, misinformation, or disinformation), this would offer at least some approximation to the contemporary understanding of the phenomena of connectedness, and an escape from the inevitable solipsism of the one-actor archive. But it is no easy answer. Since few historians can have the linguistic equipment (let alone the time) to study more than a small range of archives and master their protocols, this approach will depend upon cooperative ventures. There will still be many cases (perhaps a huge number) where no imperial archive existed or has been allowed to survive. There will be much else to explain that never reached the eyes or ears of the agents of empire. But 'imperial' histories of connectedness—and as many as possible for comparative purposes—would be nonetheless a formidable addition to our knowledge of world history.

Africa and global history

Megan Vaughan

Historical scholarship on Africa is not well represented in the literature in global history. My comments here are aimed at trying to understand why that is the case. Certainly historians of Africa have long been concerned to counter the impression that Africa as the 'dark continent' was isolated from the major currents of world history. In particular, the study of the slave trade and the growth of Atlantic history (and, more recently, of Indian Ocean studies) have been important developments. Scholars of African history have been central to these fields, contributing to our understanding of the nature of slavery in the Atlantic and Indian Ocean worlds, and also reflecting on the impact of the slave trade (and, crucially, its abolition) on societies and economies on the African continent. However, it is important to be aware of the limits of framing the history of an entire continent in terms of its external relations and incorporation into global trading and political systems. The African continent is vast and varied. Though parts of precolonial Africa were very significantly affected by the development of external trading links and particularly the Atlantic slave trade, this is not true of whole regions. The study of global history tends to privilege movements that cross oceans and continents, and contacts between peoples of distinctly different origins. But some of the major developments in the *longue durée* history of Africa have been internally generated within this vast continent. A truly global history would have to incorporate these intra-continental processes.

The second issue is a rather different one. Scholars of African economic history have also contributed very significantly to our understanding of the variable and sometimes highly specific ways in which international trading systems interacted with local economies, producing new cultures of commoditization and new value systems. They have also produced very important insights into the relationship between environment, population, economic change, and political systems. This work, however, is relatively neglected by those working in the field of global economic and comparative history. This seems to be due to the perception that there is very little reliable historical data for Africa, in part because of the lingering sense that Africa is 'different' and therefore should be left to the specialists. This is unfortunate. There is great scope for comparative work. By this I do not mean comparisons between 'Africa' and the rest of the world, but between specific regions of Africa and other regions of the world.

Finally, we must recognize that some of the neglect of African studies within the field of global history is due to the very difficult circumstances in which African academics carry out their work. For as long as African universities remain chronically underfunded, and African scholars find difficulty in publishing their work in international journals, the marginalization of African historical scholarship is likely to continue.

Writing the history of the global and the state[3]

Peer Vries

I will focus on what might be done in future and confine myself to a couple of remarks on things that, to my taste, might have been discussed more extensively during the conference. The first thing that struck me was that more could have been said about the actual writing of the global; the focus clearly was on research and argumentation rather than on how to write a synthesis or present one's findings. Writing historical texts in general and, probably a fortiori writing global histories, presents quite peculiar challenges to the historian. These require ample discussion. In that respect more attention to what has already been done and how, that is, some historiographical reflection, would have been welcome. Global history is not something unprecedented and completely novel: there have been precursors and there are traditions that might provide us with inspiration and lessons.

A sensible discussion on how to write histories of the global, presupposes a certain consensus on why one would want to write such histories in the first place. Patrick O'Brien would claim that is because one ought to know about 'the others': it would be morally wrong to be historically self-centred. That view in the end entails that one has to be (also) interested in the histories of other inhabitants of the globe in order to know something about their past and not just in function of understanding the present, let alone our present.[4] More pragmatic, and quite probably the

---

[3] These comments were made during the Conference 'Writing the History of the Global', held at the British Academy, London, 21–22 May 2009, where the authors of this volume and several other scholars referred to in my comments were present and delivered papers or comments.

[4] See e.g. his 'Historiographical Traditions and Modern Imperatives for the Restoration of Global History', *Journal of Global History* 1, (2006), 3–39.

most popular reason for doing global history, would be that globalization is turning the world into such a small place that one needs some knowledge about 'the others'. We all are in the same boat now. This easily leads to a kind of global history that shows us, in the words of Professor Hobsbawm, how we got to where we are now.[5] These are sensible positions. My main argument in support of global history would be a plain, scholarly argument: what reasons could there be for a discipline that claims to study the past, to actually ignore enormous parts of it in terms of time and space, and not to be interested in global communalities, comparisons, and connections?

Global history to me is the study of the human condition in all its varieties. These of course are only answers at the highest level of generality. As such they do not tell us how to write a specific text dealing with the global. But the 'why' question ought to be seriously addressed, if only because answering it may help in the process of selection that is so fundamental in global history. No historian can escape it, least of all the global historian. The question then is—and I think this question could have been addressed more during the conference—selection on what grounds? Various speakers and participants pointed at the fact that in current global history certain periods—in particular the early modern one—and certain places—to wit Eurasia—would be strongly over-represented, whereas other periods and other parts of the world would get short shrift. But on what grounds can one make such claims? What are the criteria of relevance? Is every era, every region, every historical person, equally important?

If one is interested in global history that shows us how we got where we are now, different things might be of relevance than if one is interested in what it was like to live then, or in the general question of what we can learn about the human condition by studying part(s) of the past . In tackling such questions, and in particular in writing down one's answers, one will not be able to—and I doubt whether one should want to—erase one's assumptions about the nature of men and history. In writing, in particular in writing a synthesis, the global historian will have to structure the material he or she wants to use. Assumptions as to what drives history, what is relevant in it, or where it is heading, will impinge on his or her work. Explicit reflections on this meta-level should not be avoided as they are unavoidable at an implicit level anyhow.

---

[5] Professor Hobsbawm made this comment during one of the discussions at the conference.

As history, global history cannot only be abstract. The majority of our potential 'public' will not be fond of a macrohistory full of logic but bereft of concrete people, full of structure but lacking agency, and full of large issues but with no small facts. Global historians therefore will have to engage the question of how to 'represent' their history and how to communicate it to their audience. Here I found the reflections on the role of narratives in global history and on the presenting of global history in museums quite stimulating and relevant.

Such communication does not happen in a void. We are not on Olympus—and we definitely are not neutral gods. We all have a certain background, live in a certain culture, and write for a certain audience in a certain language with certain specific goals. That can only mean that global history will not and cannot be the same to all people. The people gathered at this conference communicate in English; overall, they refer to literature written in English, and come from specific parts of the world.

Hardly anyone, or even no one at all present here, is from for example East, Central or Southern Europe, Africa, Latin America, or the Middle East. What does this mean?

Another topic that needs more discussion is how to turn global history from a serious endeavour into a serious discipline. Global historians are known for 'the bold stroke' and for crossing disciplinary borders. But might not their boldness actually be the superficiality of the non-expert who does not know any better and bases him- or herself on the often even quite random reading of pieces of secondary literature? Might not their 'interdisciplinarity' be a euphemism for amateurishly dabbling in someone else's specialism? Sanjay Subrahmanyam apparently thinks it is. I do not.[6]

Or rather, I think that it does not have to be that way. Superficiality and sloppiness can be combated by involving specialists in what one is doing, by exchanging one's texts and discussing them in panels before they are published, and by efforts to develop a kind of source criticism for secondary sources. If the global historian is not allowed to, of course as critically and prudently as possible, use the work by specialists, but has to basically go to the primary sources himself, then what is the use of specialists? When it comes to 'interdisciplinarity', no one will deny that

---

[6] Sanjay Subrahmanyam is Professor, the Navin and Pratima Doshi Endowed Chair in Premodern Indian History at the University of California Los Angeles and made some comments on the problems of being interdisciplinary at the conference.

this is an often misused buzzword. Practising it is indeed far from easy. But it can be done and has been done, and efforts to implement it in any case have often led to enriching and stimulating experiences. Many topics in global history can only be dealt with satisfactorily in an interdisciplinary way. So one simply has to try and find a way to get the maximum of synergy out of working with people from other disciplines. I personally think that institutionalizing contacts in networks like the Global Economic History Network or the kind of 'collaboratories' that Jan Luiten van Zanden was referring to in his chapter, can go a long way in at least substantially reducing Subrahmanyam's problems.

Global history could do with more institutionalization. There are many people who 'do' global history, but very few who are global historians by profession, card-carrying global historians so to speak, whose job it is to be global historians. As compared with other, older fields in the discipline of history, it is still not well-embedded in teaching, especially at the masters and graduate levels where the future generations of scholars are selected and educated. The position of global history when it comes to organized research, let us say research projects, and structural research funding is even weaker. I think we have to show the outside world how one does global historical research. We need Ph.D. students in global history, who can show that global history also is a field of research in which one can qualify. That is very important for professionalization. It is quite a challenge to implement this intellectually. It is even more of a challenge, and of a necessity, to find structural funding for such research. Who feels responsible enough for the history of the world to pay someone to research it?

When it comes to actual research and writing, there is only one comment I would want to make. It has almost become a truism to claim that global history is about global comparisons and global connections, and I would personally add 'communalities', that is, challenges that every society in history has had to face. If I am not mistaken, studying connections at the moment is the most popular approach. What is striking, not just at this conference but more in general amongst global historians, is the tendency to increasingly talk about such connections in terms of 'networks', 'exchanges', 'transfers', or, something that already is becoming more unusual, 'misunderstandings'. These are all quite 'cosy' terms. Wars, violence, conflicts, clashes, 'asymmetric' relations of whatever kind, appear to be less in vogue. This will not be unrelated to a clear tendency amongst global historians to increasingly ignore the source of much, if not most, of the violence in history, that is, the state. This is not by accident: the main reason for most global historians to promote their approach was their dissatisfaction with mainstream historiography for being so preoccupied with state and nation as the obvious 'bearers' of history and its main actors. There were and are excellent reasons to criticize that state- and nation-centred approach. But I think that should not lead to an often somewhat forced removal of the state from the global scene to focus on all sorts of 'regions'—that mostly do not have armies and police forces and do not levy taxes! One should instead try to allot state and nation their share, which would mean their highly important place in global history, and try to incorporate them in more encompassing global stories.

States and nations and their formation have been enormously important, in particular in modern history. That history is simply incomprehensible without them. And they still are enormously important: their much proclaimed 'withering away' is very premature. My guess would be that never in world history have there been more state laws and state taxes than at this very moment, and with the current global economic crisis the role of the state will increase rather than decrease. Going beyond state-centred history should not mean throwing away the huge state baby with the bathwater. Traditional history may have been one-sided, but it definitely looked at an important and big aspect of history.

Identity in global history: a reflection

Sufumi So and Billy Kee-Long So

This comment reflects upon the identity of the individual—or *personal identity*—in the discourse of global history. The study of global history emerged as a challenge to such long-existing areas of historical study as world history, national history, regional history, and local history. As shown in this volume, it deals with convergence, divergence, connection, and comparison. Units of analysis in examining these themes may be such broad concepts as culture, civilization, nation, state, and society; or more specifically, city, community, locality, economy, gender, class, and so on. Further, enquiries in global history can accommodate the realities of diversity and are not entrenched in any particular form of political–cultural hegemony like Eurocentrism.

But how about individuals? Is there a new role for individual human beings in the study of history in a global perspective? Individual human beings have always been an essential part of historiography. For instance, biographies and autobiographies of heroes and heroines, as well as of ordinary and socially marginalized people, are familiar examples. Most writings on global history, however, have tended to treat individuals as members of different groupings or categories such as nation and gender, or as agents connecting between cultures and between societies. In these instances the individual is not a focus and certainly not a unit of analysis. Individuals are subsumed under some other units of analysis, which are each broader than individual human beings. For instance, a biography of a certain woman that illustrates her gender role in a specific cultural setting in a global context may belong to global gender history. If the emphasis is on her national sentiment, however, the same book becomes a study of global history with a national or transnational theme. In both cases, however, the woman's personal identity is not a central theme.

Personal identity constitutes the very basic unit of human existence and experience. Would it not be useful to take the individual as a unit of analysis in their own right? To facilitate discussion further, we should first distinguish various *specific identities* (SIs) of the individual from the individual's *manifest identity* (MI). SIs such as nationality, gender, and profession lead to a sense of belonging to a specific social grouping that defines *we–they* relations and together they form a bundle of multiple SIs available to a single individual. The individual's MI is a result of the person's conscious or subconscious choosing from his or her SIs and it becomes a dominant characteristic of the person under certain circumstances. The same MI can become a latent SI at any time under other circumstances.

Historically speaking, SIs were seldom associated with global implications. Examples of global SIs may have been limited to cases where people spread from a national group to other parts of the world and interacted with local people through cultural, economic, and political activities. Traders, missionaries, and soldiers operating in foreign lands are good examples. The rapidly accelerated pace of globalization in the last couple of decades, however, has transformed the nature of SIs. A great majority of SIs have caught global tendencies. Some common SIs have embraced global connotations and moved beyond specific communities. For instance, political identity (conservative, liberal, etc.), geographically determined identity (European, Asian, etc.), gender identity (female, male, etc.), professional identity (doctor, lawyer, etc.), religious identity (Christian, Muslim, etc.), ethnic identity (Chinese, Hispanics, etc.), economic identity (capitalist, socialist, etc.), social class identity (working class, upper class, etc.), and educational identity (alma mater, MBA, etc.) can cross borders and exist beyond the official or unofficial lines surrounding the individual.

There is yet another SI or what we call *personal global identity* (PGI). PGI is the very product of globalization; it is not the kind that has transformed itself due to globalization. We believe that PGI can make a useful theoretical construct in studying the global history of our times and reconstructing a new narrative of it. Before embarking on such projects, however, we should spend some time considering definitional features of PGI as listed below.

- It is derived from perceived commonalities but not necessarily from the desire for the sameness, hence it is more useful in focusing on the individual rather than any groups.
- It is transnational, transregional, and translocal; thus, it defies any intent to create a new political or geographical divide on the globe.
- It can be nurtured, aroused, and reinforced through global narratives just as the way national or community narratives have done so for national or community identity.
- It is transcultural and culturally transformative; thus, it is not bound by or entrenched in any particular culture.
- It is sensitive to differences but not difference-oriented; thus, it differs from such collective identities as national and cultural identities. It is, therefore, more accommodating and difference-bridging by nature.
- It is heterogeneous but inclusive and diversity-embracing as opposed to being homogeneous, exclusive, and conformist.
- It is not an outcome of ignorance of others but it is derived from and maintained through access to information about others in different parts of the world. Such process continues accelerating due to ever-advancing information and communication technologies and globalizing educational endeavours.
- It is not independent of national, regional, local, communal, or any other culturally or geographically bound identities. It is built upon the individual's subjective and objective meanings of these categories. Further, it exists within the bundle of the individual's SIs and thus, it is among the many identities one may choose from as MI under particular circumstances.

- It should not conflict with or suppress the meanings of national, regional, local, communal, and other culturally and geographically embedded identities; rather, it enhances them.

One way to operationalize PGI in the study of global history is to identify traits of PGI in an individual and weave them together into a unified whole in the form of oral history, biography, or autobiography. PGI could put the individual at the forefront in writing global history that counts on both individuality and diversity.

Index

Abe, Stanley 175
Adams, William 179, 183
Africa and global history 200–1
Allen, Robert 113
Amerindian societies 54
Anderson, Perry 4
art, history of
　Chinese art 169, 171–5
　Chinese painting *vs* European painting 165–6
　connection between Sienese and Oriental painting 171
　contemporary arts 167
　European visual art 169
　Flemish paintings 175–6
　Gandharan art 166
　Italian Renaissance art 168
　Japanese art 167
　Oriental painting 170–1
　Siena art 170
asymmetry (ies)
　defined 51
　use of framework of 52
Atlantic economy 131, 136
Atlantic regional world 85, 197–8
ATLAS Project 111n16
Aztec Empire system 53

Bal, Mieke 16–17, 171, 175
Baxandall, Michael 171
Bayly, Christopher 3, 5, 30, 45
Berenson, Bernard 168, 174
'big science', concept of large-scale projects 112
biosphere-derived energy sources 142
Bloch, Marc 38, 69–73, 75, 120
Boston Museum of Fine Arts 169
Braudel, Fernand 10, 35–6, 72, 85–7, 197
Brenner, Robert 75
BRICs (Brazil, Russia, India, and China) 28
'British' industrial revolution 14, 23
British printing industry 79
Brook, Timothy 41
Burbank, Jane 5, 49

caballero cristiano 64
Cameron, Rondo 107
Cao, Zhao 161
capital-intensive industrialization 143
Chakrabarty, Dipesh 25–6, 30, 41, 48
Chandavarkar, Rajnarayan 76
Charlemagne, empire under 35
Chaudhuri, K. N. 86
Chinese agricultural workers, living standards of 134n14
Chinese craft production 103
Chinese culture 150–1
　jade ornaments, use of 152–3
　marking objects, history of 156–8
　silk and porcelain as a means of power 151, 153–4
Christian conquerors 56
Christian, David 121
Church doctrine and institutions, role in reformations 88
civil service, concept of 26
CLIO INFRA project 114
coal economy 104, 140

209

Index

Britain–China 80–81
Cobb, Richard 25
Cocks, Richard 182–3
collaboratories 110–14
  development of 112
  objectives 111–12
Colley, Linda 3, 12, 17
Collins, Jane 191
colonial Anglo-Hindu law 31
colonialism, history of 26
commercial laws, development of
  in China 89–90
  in Europe 88–89
  in facilitating economic change 89
comparative history
  comparison and connection 10–11
  divergence and comparison 6–10
  features of 38–9
  global approaches 129–32
    allocation of resources 134–5
    early modern comparisons 131
    economy developments 133–4
    England *vs* France 130–1
    recurring growth, idea of 130
    in terms of path dependency 131–2
    two paths thesis 132–7
    United States *vs* Soviet Union 129
    Western Europe *vs* Asian empires 130
connectedness, concept of 3
Cooper, Frederick 5, 49
Cortés, Hernán 53
cosmopolitanism, concept of 3
cotton industries, study of 73, 79–80
  Britain–Ottoman Empire comparison 79
  cotton–linen mixture product 79
  mechanization, impact of 80
Crosby, Alfred 16, 122–3, 125

Dapper, Olfert 166
Darwin, John 3, 5, 17, 43, 71, 197
Davis, William Morris 173

De Las Casas, Bartholomew 56
De Montaigne, Michel 55
dependency theory 28–9
divergences in global history
  among human groups 121–3
  and convergences 120
  events and outcomes 124–5
  French economic history 119
  frontier expansion 124–5
  issue of 'origins' 120–1
  Japanese economic history 119
  of life expectancies 125
  of literacy rates 125
  as a matter of perspective 119–20
  nineteenth century expansions 120
  in terms of
    comparisons 117–18
    time 118–19
Dürer, Albrecht 169–71
Dutch East India Company 37, 181

East Asian development path, concept of 13, 16
East Asian rice farming 138, 140
ecosystem conservation 142
Edgerton, David 148
Eichmann, Adolf 53
energy-intensive industrialization 143–4
English, as a global language 39
English East India Company 179
environmental sustainability 132, 141–4
ethnocentric narratives 48–51
Eurasia 22
  eighteenth-century 76–7
  history of 42–3
  revolution 43
Eurocentric narratives 49
Eurocentrism 5, 30, 42, 48–9, 91, 106, 205
European capitalism 24
European historians, characteristics of 49–50

210

Index

European maritime movements 86
European miracle 137–41
Europe-centred world history 47n40

footballs, 189–92
fossil fuel-based economy 133, 142–3
French Revolution 125, 126
Friedman, Tom 39, 45, 47
Fukuyama, Francis 62

general purpose technologies (GPT) 102
George III, King 99
geosphere-derived energy sources 142
Gerritsen, Anne 158
global economic history
   collaboratories 110–14
   economic success and failure of different regions 107
   global datasets, significance of 109, 112–13
   human capital formation 107–9
   prices and wages variations 112–13
Global Economic History Network 73, 204
global history
   as an academic enterprise 37–9
   and archives 37–8
   centres 2, 161
   comparisons in 10–11
      as an aid in historical enquiry 73–4
      Bloch's mode 69–70
      Britain–China, coal economy 80–1
      Britain–Ottoman Empire 79
      cotton industries, study of 73, 79–80
      impact on historian 72–3
      India–Europe, industrial development 81–2
      Indian–British comparisons 77–8
      mutual influences, study of 70, 73–4
      parallel study of societies 70
      problem of divergence in eighteenth and early nineteenth centuries 77
      reciprocal comparison, method of 75–6
      in terms of space and time 69–70
   of connections 10–11, 41, 199
   consciousness approach to 33
   contagion (or contact) 34
   contemporary history 40
   convergence 34–35
   divergence and comparison of 6–10
   in era of globalization 39–42
   as flat history 39–42
   identity of the individual 205–8
   influential exercises on Eurocentrism and modernization 42–4
   levels of 32
   and manifest identity (MI) 206
   methods of investigation 12–14
   microhistories and 11–12
   as an 'organized complexity' 46–7
   as a path-dependent process 47
   periodization and narratives 46–7
   and personal global identity (PGI) 207–8
   promise of 45
   regions *see* regions and global history
   and specific identities (SIs) 206
   technology and innovation, role in. *see* technology and innovation, role in global history
   trading networks 35–6
globalization 39–40, 106, 108
   changes in human contact 44
   Flynn and Giraldez's definition 45
   modern 47
   nineteenth-century 47
   as a path-dependent process 47
   Steger–Giddens–Scholte definition 45
   in terms of modernization 44–5
   trade-based definition 45

Index

globalizing entities 45, 46
global language 39
Global Price and Income History Group 110, 113
global Westernization 57
'glocal', notion of 84
Goldstone, Jack 3, 16, 124, 125
Gramsci, Antonio 56
Great War of 1914–18 107
Guizot, François 58
Gulliver's Travels 55

Hamashita, Takeshi 86
Held, David 40
Hicks, John 140n29
historical narratives
  anthropological discussions 49–50
  of asymmetrical experiences 51–5
  and dynamics of compensation 56–9
  of European consciousness 61–4
  European historians and ethnocentric narratives 48–51
  experiences of contact 53–4
  implementation of colonial regimes abroad 53
  Jewish culture and destruction of European Jewry 53
  model for asymmetrical relations 59–61
  of modernization 50–1
Historical Prices and Wages database 110, 112–13
Huizong, Emperor 152
Human Development Index (HDI) 119
Human Genome Project 111n16
Huntington, Ellsworth 173
Huntington, Samuel 62

Ieyasu, Emperor 179, 181
imperial history 1, 3, 17, 21, 27, 46, 199
industrialization in Britain, emergence of 22
industrious revolution 11, 14, 16, 135, 139

information commons 110
international network of cities, development of 33
Islamization, issue of 59

Japan 134n16, 135
  Meiji 137
Jones, Eric 2, 71, 75, 130

Kang, Youwei 171–3
Kircher, Athanasius 166
knowledge networks 25
Kracauer, David 125
Kugler, Franz 167
Kuznets, Simon 129

labour-intensive industrialization 136, 143
Landes, David 2, 24, 71, 75, 107
Lévi-Strauss, Claude 49, 54
Lieberman, Victor 92–4
Lombard, Denys 49, 85–86
Long, Pamela O. 149

McCloskey, Donald N. 127
MacGregor, Neil 2, 178
Mackenzie, John MacDonald 186
Madison, Angus 108–9
maritime Asia 86
market exchange dynamics 99–105
marking objects, history of 156–8
  individual marking system 160
Marxism 4, 30, 173
Marx, Karl 77, 131, 173
Massarella, Derek 182
Mauss, Marcel 49
Mediterranean world 85–7, 197
mestizo societies 52–4, 58
Mexicanization, issue of 59
Milevska, Suzanna 174
Ming dynasty, China 97–98, 149, 151–5, 159
mixed farming 138–40
modernity, universal path to 49

212

Index

modernization paradigm 50–1
Moore, Barrington 75
Mughalization, issue of 59
multiculturalism, concept of 31
museums 17, 177–8, 183–4, 192, 203

narrative approaches, to modern history 43–4
Needham, Joseph 102, 154n13
nomads 64, 92–93
North, Douglass C. 90

object-based global history, 181–8
  ambassadorial presents 181
  British Columbia Legislative Buildings, Canada 186
  buildings 184–8
  Flora Fountain, Mumbai 186
  football 188–92
  Japanese armour 179–82
  Municipal Corporation Building, Mumbai 186–7
  Oriental Life Insurance Offices, Mumbai 186
  Post Office Mews, Mumbai 186
  Prince's Building, Hong Kong 188
  Royal Alfred Sailor's Home, Mumbai 186
  Royal Exhibition Building, Melbourne 188
  Statue of Liberty 183–4
  St Pancras Station, London 185–6
  Tower of London 179
  Victoria Terminus (VT) station, Mumbai (Chhatrapati Shivaji Terminus) 184–6, 188
O'Brien, Patrick 71, 119, 201
Olstein, Diego 38n17, 46
Orient oder Rom? (Strzygowski) 172–3
O'Rourke, Kevin 106, 121

personal global identity (PGI) 207–8
Pirenne, Henri 35, 36
political economy, of spring wheat district 33
political shifts, in Europe 5
Pollard, Sydney 141
Pomeranz, Kenneth 2, 38, 43, 72, 74, 76, 101, 133
Portugal revolution (1974) 5
professional history 37
Protestant missionaries, records of 37–8

Qianlong, Emperor 99–100, 152, 158
Qing dynasty 97–8, 151–5
  granary system 81

regions and global history, 90–9
Reid, Anthony 86
'resourcegobbling' type of economic development 133
Riegl, Alois 172
rimlands 92–4
Roberts, John 24
Romanization, of the Mediterranean 59
Rosenthal, Jean-Laurent 103
Rostow, W. W. 129

Said, Edward 167
Sandrart, Joachim von 165–6, 168, 171, 175
Saris, John 179, 183
scientific racism 23, 26
Scott, George Gilbert 186
Sewell, William 71
Sinicization 59–60
slave trades 5, 25, 80, 200
Smithian growth 107, 133, 139–40
Song, Yingxing 162
South East Asian mainland polities 92, 98
South-to-South trade routes 25
space world history 83–87
state formation, regional approach to 94–99
Staudenmaier, John 162

213

Index

stele inscriptions 155
Stevens, Frederick William 184, 186
Strzygowski, Josef 172–3
Subrahmanyam, Sanjay 3, 49, 203–4
Sullivan, Michael 165
Swedish East India Company 5

technology and innovation, 151–7
Thompson, E. P. 56
Tilly, Charles 36, 71
trade networks 35–6
transnational history centres 2
two paths thesis 132–7
Tymans, Luc 175

Vasari, Giorgio 172

Wachtel, Nathan 54
Wallerstein, Immanuel 4, 36, 86
Wang, Zuo 161
Weber, Max 36, 75, 131

Western academic narrative 56
Western domination 60–1
Westernization, issue of 57, 60
Western science and technology, development of 102–3
Westphalian Model, of social sciences 40
Westphalia, Treaty of (1648) 96, 98
Wickhoff, Franz 167–68, 171
Williamson, Jeffrey 106, 121
Winckelmann, Johann Joachim 166
world history groups 2
Wrigley, E. A. 139–41
writing of historical texts 201–5

Yozaemon, Iwai 179

Zeitz, Jochen 189
Zhang, Cheng 161
Zhao, Guanzhi 161
Zheng, He 96–7
Zhu, Yuanzhang (Ming emperor) 153

Printed and bound by CPI Group (UK) Ltd, Croydon, CR0 4YY